FROM

Emeril's

KITCHENS

Other books by Emeril Lagasse

Emeril's There's A Chef in My Soup

Prime Time Emeril

Every Day's A Party
with Marcelle Bienvenu and Felicia Willett

Emeril's TV Dinners
with Marcelle Bienvenu and Felicia Willett

Emeril's Creole Christmas
with Marcelle Bienvenu

Louisiana Real & Rustic
with Marcelle Bienvenu

Emeril's New New Orleans Cooking
with Jessie Tirsch

FROM Emeril's KITCHENS

Favorite Recipes from Emeril's Restaurants

EMERIL LAGASSE

WM
WILLIAM MORROW
An Imprint of HarperCollins*Publishers*

HarperCollins books may be purchased for educational, business, or sales promotional use. For information please write: Special Markets Department, HarperCollins Publishers Inc., 10 East 53rd Street, New York, NY 10022.

FIRST EDITION

Book design by Jill Armus

Photo insert design by William Ruoto

Photographs by Quentin Bacon, except page 149 by Chris Granger

Printed on acid-free paper

Library of Congress Cataloging-in-Publication Data

Lagasse, Emeril.
From Emeril's kitchens : favorite recipes from Emeril's restaurants /
Emeril Lagasse.— 1st ed.
p.   cm.
Includes bibliographical references and index.
ISBN 0-06-018535-X
1. Cookery.   I. Title.

TX714 .L335224   2003
641.5—dc21
2002027568

03 04 05 06 07 WBC/RRD 10 9 8 7 6 5 4 3 2 1

In memory—

I dedicate this book in memory of my dear friend and pal Louis "Mr. Lou" Lynch. Loving husband, father, grandfather, and a rock to all who knew him.

One of the greatest pastry chefs in America, he started with me in the beginning at Emeril's New Orleans, and created many of the signature dishes that so many people still enjoy today. He will be greatly missed but always remembered.

With love from Emeril and Alden Lagasse, Emeril's restaurants, and Emeril's Homebase family

Chef Emeril Lagasse's portrait by artist Rise Delmar Ochsner, Emeril's New Orleans

INTRODUCTION

A new cookbook always gives me the opportunity to communicate with my fellow foodies and fans. And you know who you are! You're the folks who watch *Emeril Live* and *The Essence of Emeril*, the visitors who enjoy eating at my restaurants, and the home cooks who love to prepare recipes from my cookbooks.

From Emeril's Kitchens is my eighth cookbook and soon we will open our ninth restaurant. Can you believe it? Writing each cookbook and opening each restaurant has represented a particular creative phase in my life, and it's gratifying to look back and trace this culinary evolution.

Born and raised in Fall River, Massachusetts, I had a love of food instilled in me by my parents at a very early age. Not only is my mom, Miss Hilda, a terrific cook—and particularly when she makes the traditional Portuguese dishes of her heritage—but my dad, Mr. John, always did a fair amount of weekend cooking that reflected his French-Canadian background. Wow! Talk about a food-of-love flavor explosion! In high school, I worked in a local Portuguese bakery, and then graduated from the prestigious culinary school, Johnson & Wales University in Providence, Rhode Island.

The university inspired me to be creative and gave me an understanding of how important discipline is for the practical challenges that a cook faces. I then worked as an apprentice in Paris and Lyon, France, where I refined my knowledge of classic French cooking. Time in New York, Boston, and Philadelphia restaurants gave me perspective on current American food trends and spurred my love of farm-fresh ingredients.

The Brennan family hired me as executive chef of Commander's Palace Restaurant in 1983. When I started, I was awed by the great tradition of haute New Orleans Creole cuisine for which the restaurant and the city were known. The bountiful fresh regional produce, game, and seafood equally stunned me. The Brennans were eagerly marrying the nouvelle cuisine that had emerged from France the decade before with a New Orleans sensibility and local culinary traditions. While taking Commander's to the next stage was a tall order, I was ready to learn and create, and I was passionate to succeed. I accepted the challenge and never looked back. What evolved was a dynamic new era, and my "new New Orleans" cuisine began to take root.

Eric Linquest and I worked together at Commander's Palace; he in the front of the house, me in the kitchen. We became fast friends. When I was ready to strike out on my own and open Emeril's, I knew Eric was the only person I wanted to manage my restaurant. Over many meals and many glasses of wine, we discussed what was important to us. Although we had big dreams, we also had a limited budget. Everything had to be considered very carefully—from the number of menu items, food costs, and kitchen equipment to the wine list, linens, and storage facilities.

When we opened Emeril's on March 26, 1990, my goal was to take contemporary Creole cuisine to the next level and make the menu a reflection of my culinary thinking. For instance, barbecued shrimp had long been served in New Orleans restaurants, but instead of baking the shrimp in their shells with butter, garlic, and seasonings, I intensified the flavors by making a robust stock and sauce base first, and then, after sautéing, cooking the shrimp in a rich cream reduction for a concentrated flavor.

I've given new twists to other classic dishes and made them my own. When Emeril's opened, we developed a savory appetizer cheesecake to take the place of the usual dessert one: the Home-Smoked Salmon Cheesecake is on the menu to this day. Same thing with my ultra-rich Banana Cream Pie, which continues to be one of our most-ordered desserts.

My goal at Emeril's was to serve flavorful, unique food that was creative and exciting. I wanted all of our ingredients—herbs and lettuces, rabbits and pigs, quail and seafood—to be fresh from the gardens, farms, and waterways of Louisiana and Mississippi, or wherever the best sources might be. (Dan Crutchfield of Crickhollow Farms still provides fresh rabbits and hogs.) To this end, we made our own breads, pastries, ice creams, andouilles, tassos, sausages, spice blends, and more in-house (just as they are made today at each of the restaurants). In addition to borrowing from local cuisines, I introduced techniques and ingredients from Asia, Europe, and the Southwestern United States. From the day we opened, our customers were enthused and ate everything up!

My first cookbook, *Emeril's New New Orleans Cooking*, introduced my style of cuisine to home cooks everywhere, with recipes from the Emeril's menu and favorites reflecting my Portuguese and French-Canadian heritages. Some favorites from that book included the Kale and Andouille Soup, Portuguese Chorizo Clam Stew with Garlic Aioli, Crawfish Rellenos with Red Bean Sauce, and Tamarind-Glazed Pork Chops with Mole Cream and Roasted Sweet Potatoes.

Two years later we opened a restaurant in the French Quarter—NOLA. NOLA, an acronym for New Orleans, Louisiana, reflects my passion for food, but in a more informal setting than Emeril's. NOLA's logo is a blue swirl, symbolic of a powerful hurricane churning with relentless energy, and the multistoried restaurant churns up its own excitement every evening. The food at NOLA is a heartier, more rustic version of the fare served at Emeril's. In no time the word spread, and NOLA soon had its own identity, with eager diners lined up halfway down our block of St. Louis Street every evening for the 6:00 P.M. opening.

Our opening chefs, Dave McCelvey, now director of culinary operations for all of our restaurants, and Michael Jordan developed a menu bursting with Louisiana products. NOLA, though constantly busy, has very high standards. Many chefs in my company cut their teeth at NOLA, starting as eager, passionate line cooks and earning their stripes as they moved through the ranks. Christian Czerwonka, Neal Swidler, Joel Morgan, and Sean Roe—who are represented as chefs de cuisine in this book—all started at NOLA.

The food bar at NOLA offers a front-row view of the wood-burning oven, and guests can watch as our chefs cook Cedar-Planked Fish with Horseradish Crust and Lemon Butter Sauce, Garlic-Smeared Wood Oven–Baked Pocket Bread, and NOLA pizzas. In the open kitchen, signature dishes such as Cornmeal-Crusted Oysters, Louisiana Crab Cakes, and Grilled Double-Cut Pork Chops with Bourbon-Mashed Sweet Potatoes are prepared. The menu, wine list, and ambience cater to more casual diners, both visitors and local New Orleanians. The result is a resounding success.

As a result of this success and to give others a sample of NOLA's local flavor, I wrote my second cookbook, *Louisiana Real & Rustic* in 1996. Though I'm not a Louisiana native, I strongly felt that authentic Acadian—"Cajun"—recipes needed recognition and a new audience. I wanted the whole country to taste what I was tasting and to enjoy the rich, full-bodied flavors of my adopted state. I stayed as true to the traditional recipes as possible, including all the techniques, customs, and ingredients of this classic American regional cuisine.

With my next book, *Emeril's Creole Christmas,* it was time to celebrate and have some fun. Once again, I used indigenous ingredients, but this time in over-the-top holiday menus. Simple corn cakes were garnished with caviar to kick them up a notch, and smoked salmon went into an elegant terrine. Beef tenderloin was smeared with fresh horseradish and black pepper. And where is it written that bread pudding has to be sweet? Not when you try my exotic mushroom bread pudding!

Two years after opening NOLA, I was introduced to Lou Silvestri, who, in turn, initiated a meeting with Danny Wade, then president of the MGM Grand Hotel and Casino in Las Vegas. At that time, Las Vegas had just three well-known restaurateurs (Charlie Trotter, Wolfgang Puck, and Mark Miller) with established places. The MGM folks were looking to bring more fine-dining restaurants to Las Vegas.

Emeril's New Orleans Fish House at the MGM Grand Hotel and Casino was our first restaurant outside of New Orleans, and Las Vegas was ready for my version of dining and hospitality. Although offering many of the signature recipes from Emeril's and NOLA, the Fish House is a New Orleans–style seafood restaurant and oyster bar, with fresh Louisiana seafood flown in daily. As a bonus, our proximity to the West Coast enables us to source a wealth of produce and seafood from California, the Pacific Northwest, South America, and the Far East, giving the menu a global feel.

New Orleans–style dishes include awesome seafood gumbos, Fried Oyster Po'-Boys, Fried Creole–Marinated Calamari with New Orleans–Style Olive Salad, and Panfried Louisiana Crab Cakes. International dishes given the Emeril twist include Spicy Salmon Roll and Cucumber-Wrapped Tuna Tartare with Wasabi Tobikko Salad, Atlantic Salmon with Louisiana Crawfish, and Maine Lobster boiled like crawfish in spicy Creole seasoning and served with andouille. One of the biggest hits at the Fish House is the Shellfish over Fettuccine with a spicy piri piri sauce, a tribute to my Portuguese heritage. The Seared Yellowfin Tuna with Tomato-Fennel Confit is now a house classic.

With three successful restaurants up and running, my career with the Television Food Network took off. Although I'd been hosting shows on the network since 1993, *The Essence of Emeril* really captured the public's attention in 1996, when *Time* magazine named it one of the "Top Ten TV Shows." Production began for *Emeril Live* in January 1997, and I then started appearing as food correspondent for ABC-TV's *Good Morning America* in January 1998.

In 1998, *Emeril's TV Dinners* cookbook was published. This book is a compilation of favorite television-show recipes, including many recipes that viewers had requested through the years. It was an enormous undertaking because we included everything, and I mean everything—from stocks to desserts.

The next year saw the publication of *Every Day's A Party*. Everyone knows about Mardi Gras, but unless you're from Louisiana, you probably have never heard about the Shrimp Festival, the St. Joseph's Day Festival, or the Gumbo Cook-Off. We included recipes and menus for those events as well as local twists on national holidays and celebrations such as Easter, the Fourth of July, Halloween, and, of course, Thanksgiving and Christmas.

As a result of television exposure, combined with the restaurants' successes, other opportunities started to roll in. Tom Williams, CEO of Universal Studios in Orlando, approached us regarding the Citywalk project that he and his team were undertaking. He wanted us to consider opening a fine-dining restaurant in the prime location of the project. When Tom and his development team showed us a scale model of the restaurant they had in mind, we were impressed, to say the least. They wanted to replicate the Emeril's New Orleans experience in Orlando, and we decided it was indeed the perfect place for us to go. There was no better person to send to Orlando as executive chef than Bernard Carmouche, whose recipes are represented in this book. (Bernard and I have worked together for almost twenty years, since our Commander's Palace days!)

With Bernard at the helm of Emeril's in Orlando, it was as though I was cooking there myself. The menu Bernard put in place remains true to my New Orleans vision and to my dedication to fresh produce, and everything is made from scratch whenever possible. We make the same great homemade sausages and sauces, and serve the same familiar dishes, such as Smoked Mushrooms and Tasso over Angel Hair, Andouille-Crusted Redfish, and Rack of Lamb with Creole Mustard Crust. At Emeril's in Orlando we also feature the best of Florida's local products on the menu—Hearts of Palm Salad, and Grilled Florida Pompano with Lemon-Poached Leeks and Shrimp–Lemon Butter Sauce.

What a time it was! Shortly after agreeing to develop Emeril's Orlando, two amazing restaurant offers came our way. First, the LaFranca family, owners of Delmonico Restaurant in New Orleans for more than seventy-five years, approached us about taking over the reins and keeping the restaurant's 110-year tradition alive. What an honor! And Rob Goldstein and Lou Silvestri were courting us to become part of The Venetian, an exciting new resort hotel and casino in Las Vegas. Given the success of Emeril's New Orleans Fish House, we were soon convinced that this was an ideal opportunity.

So, we had three operating restaurants, and within an eighteen-month period, we staggered another three restaurant openings. Luckily, we had such a strong team on board and the structure in place that we knew we could make this a reality. It was a terrific opportunity to grow and we had a lot of dedicated employees who were excited about the possibilities of moving forward.

When we opened Emeril's Delmonico Restaurant and Bar in June 1998, I was apprehensive. Delmonico had long been a grande dame of the New Orleans food scene, and my goal was to take it to the next level of splendor it deserved. I wanted to pay homage to classic New Orleans Creole food and yet give the menu a distinct Emerilized identity. We elegantly restored the St.

Charles Avenue building and, among other special treatments, reinstated tableside preparation, befitting the restaurant's history. We offer timeless New Orleans classics such as Turtle Soup with Sherry, Redfish Amandine, Shrimp Remoulade, and Bananas Foster. And in true local fashion, Sunday jazz brunch features a wide variety of traditional and original eye openers and favorites, including Poached Eggs Erato, and Souffléd Spinach and Brie Crêpes, among others.

These favorites are paired with stylish Creole variations, such as Garlic Escargot with Goat Cheese, Fennel, and Bacon-Stuffed Mushrooms; Pecan-Crusted Oysters with Brie, Bacon-Barbecue Glaze, and Green Apple Slaw; and Creole Seafood Courtbouillon.

Delmonico Steakhouse in Las Vegas opened in 1999. I had always wanted a real American steakhouse featuring the best beef, aged in-house to our specifications, and more, with a dynamic, contemporary menu. We have a kicked-up charcuterie program with homemade salamis and pastramis as well as the usual andouille, boudin, and tasso made especially for our daily antipasto plate. The Delmonico name had great collateral for us, not only because of our New Orleans restaurant but also because of the great tradition established by the country's first full-service restaurant, the grand Delmonico in New York City. We knew that the elegance the name conferred ideally summed up what we wanted to represent in Las Vegas—sophistication, great food, and serious steak.

The menu, of course, predominantly features the most popular cuts of meat—from filets mignons and New York strip steaks to veal chops and Châteaubriand carved tableside—carefully cooked to order. Popular steakhouse starters such as sliced tomato salad, Caesar salad, and shrimp cocktail are served along with traditional sides and sauces, like scalloped potatoes, creamed spinach, béarnaise sauce, and marchands de vin sauce. At the same time, the very meaty Tchoupitoulas Gumbo can knock your socks off!

The year 2001 saw the release of two new cookbooks. The first, *Prime Time Emeril,* is a collection of all new recipes from my television shows—*Emeril Live, The Essence of Emeril,* and *Good Morning America.* The second, *Emeril's There's A Chef in My Soup,* is a tribute to my younger fans. This step-by-step book includes kitchen how-to's and simple recipes for starter cooks, including 1-2-3 Lasagna, Baby Bam Burgers, Cinnamon Toast of Love, Emerilized Tuna Casserole, Junior's Jambalaya, Mile-High Blueberry Muffins, and Pokey Brownies.

This brings us to the book you now hold in your hands—*From Emeril's Kitchens*—with many of the most requested and most frequently ordered recipes from all of our restaurants! *From Emeril's Kitchens* traces the evolution of how one New Orleans restaurant spun off into nine across the country, each with a distinct personality and culinary twist. It's a look at the evolution of flavor in my cooking. Most of all, it's a story of passionate chefs with dreams that dovetail with mine, and of sharing the food of love with others. It's a story of how I landed in New Orleans to create what is known as "new New Orleans" cuisine.

So what's the best way to use this book? Sit down, read it through, and flag the recipes you want to try. *From Emeril's Kitchens* is by no means a "basic" cookbook. The recipes come directly from our chefs and their kitchens, and each one may have several components—but don't let that stop you from trying a dish. If an entire recipe seems too complicated, then make just the accompanying vegetable or sauce to serve with another item. Having a dinner party? Mix up the restaurants' recipes and try one dish from each. Planning a Sunday brunch? Go straight to the brunch dishes.

So, what's next? Well, it's constant change; we're continually evolving, taking everything to the next level. For instance, we undertook a massive renovation of the original Emeril's restaurant just after its tenth anniversary, in July 2000, to bring it into the next decade and nurture a new generation of passionate diners.

Since opening that first Emeril's Restaurant on Tchoupitoulas Street in New Orleans over ten years ago, I'd wanted to open a Polynesian and Asian-themed restaurant nearby. I even knew what I'd call it—Emeril's Tchoup Chop ("chop chop"), a play not only on the Tchoupitoulas name and the chopping involved in Asian cooking but the constant, rapid pace of a busy restaurant kitchen. My vision was realized in January 2003 at Universal Orlando's Royal Pacific Resort. Emeril's Tchoup Chop is everything I'd ever hoped for, and the climate, backdrop, and energy of Orlando and Universal are a perfect fit for the restaurant.

Emeril's Tchoup Chop is a complete departure from my past restaurants. The décor of the resort and the restaurant is lush and tropical, and simulates the natural beauty found throughout the Pacific Islands. The menu focuses on the foods of the Pacific, and is a perfect extension of the hotel's South Pacific–inspired paradise, with muted natural woods accented by bright tropical flowers and lush plants, batik fabrics and canopies, carved wood reliefs, and waterfalls.

New York City architect David Rockwell, whose acclaimed Rockwell Group is best known for themed restaurant interiors, designed Emeril's Tchoup Chop. The focal points of the restaurant's water theme are the zero edge pool in the center of the room and the water wall above the ten-seat food bar, adjacent to the open kitchen. The serene water theme is underscored by warm colors and lighting.

Instead of the usual bread on the table, guests enjoy prawn chips and crispy wontons served in a folded take-out box. An open exhibition kitchen features rows of woks turning out delicious stir-fry and noodle dishes, like Duck and Vegetable Chow Mein, Kalúa Pork (slow roasted), and Noodle Sauté with Tchoup Chop Spices and Seasonal Vegetables. And some of my favorite restaurant dishes featured in this book include Mussels in Lemongrass Broth, Shrimp Toast, Kimchee, and Vegetable and Egg Fried Rice.

The Atlanta Emeril's Restaurant is due to open in 2003. The opportunity to be part of such a thriving and dynamic market is, by far, our most exciting project to date. The two hundred-plus-seat restaurant is located in the bustling Buckhead district and is designed by David Rockwell.

In the style of the original Emeril's in New Orleans and Emeril's Orlando, the Atlanta spot features many of the favorites found in this book, such as Barbecued Shrimp on Rosemary Biscuits, Smoked Mushrooms and Tasso over Angel Hair, and Home-Smoked Salmon Cheesecake. The menu also will represent classic gumbos, Andouille-Crusted Redfish, and the Tamarind-Glazed Pork Chops with Green Mole Cream that our friends have enjoyed through the years, as well as items created especially for Atlanta diners.

Taking the Florida toehold a step farther, Emeril's Miami Beach opens in November 2003—my ninth restaurant! We'll be right on South Beach in the Loews Miami Beach Hotel. David Rockwell will be designing the restaurant in keeping with the colorful palette found in the Art Deco South Beach neighborhood. Again, the menu will feature Emeril's favorites, with a dash of Nuevo Latino flair.

That's the great thing about being in this business: having ideas and bringing them to fruition. Each restaurant has evolved into its own, with a distinct identity and flavor palate, and a passionate staff creating menus with the best possible ingredients. And just as this book traces my evolution up to this point, it too is a snapshot in time of our organization. The very nature of the restaurant business is change. Just as locales, techniques, and ingredients inspire menus, by the same token people are inspired and move on.

I'm thankful to the chefs who worked with me to create this fabulous book, whether they're at the same restaurant as they were when we started or whether they're with me now. What matters most is that we're inspiring a passion among our friends and spreading the food of love! BAM!

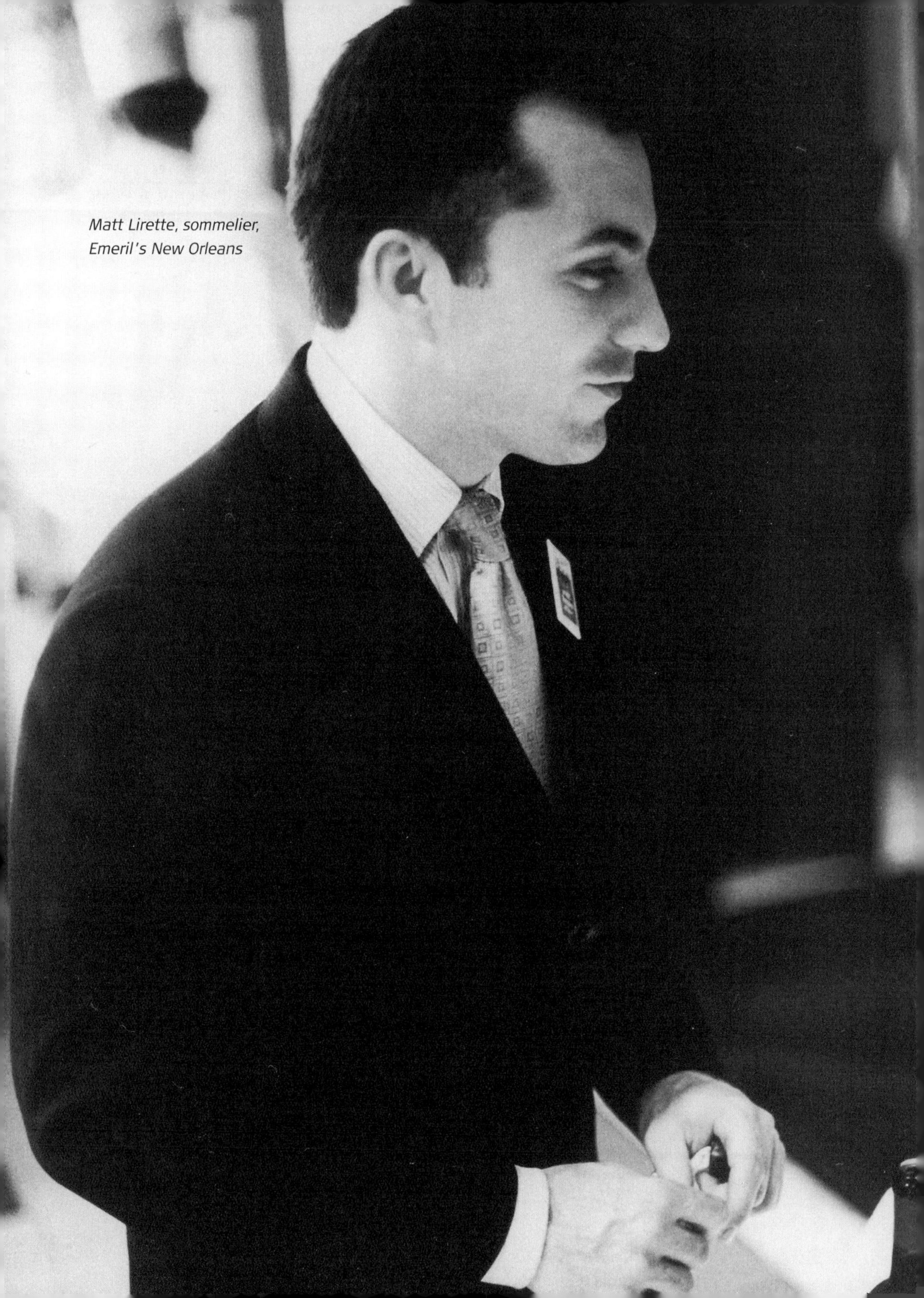

Matt Lirette, sommelier, Emeril's New Orleans

ENJOYING WINE AND FOOD

I'm passionate about wine. I drink it everyday and feel that wine turns every meal into a special occasion. So, when you dine at my restaurants, enjoying wine is an essential part of the complete dining experience, no less important than the ambience or service. Before opening the restaurant, Eric Linquest and I spent the better part of a year discussing, over many glasses of wine, all the elements that we believed were integral to running a successful restaurant. A strong wine program was essential to our concept and we outlined what we wanted to achieve. We wanted wines of quality, so we searched for the best ones from around the world. We shared a passion for food and a dedication to pairing our food with great wines, so we picked wines to complement our menu. When Emeril's opened in 1990, the wine list offered just seventy-five hand-selected varieties.

To accompany a menu of about thirty items, we started with a small selection of wines—white and sparkling wines were on one page and reds on another. Being a new American restaurant, our wine list was dominated by California bottlings. (Keep in mind that in 1990, California vintners were in the midst of releasing the 1985 Cabernet Sauvignons and had a string of great vintages from 1984 on for all varietals, so many excellent wines were available to us.)

Our wine program has grown tremendously. Each restaurant has an in-house sommelier and a wine list that averages one thousand selections. Today the wine list at Emeril's New Orleans features fourteen hundred selections and fifteen thousand bottles!

So, what's the big deal, you might ask; every good restaurant sells wine, right? True. But few have devoted the resources—from manpower and proper storage facilities to dollars invested in inventory—necessary to create the great wine lists that we have. Our wine lists are limited only by the imaginations of our sommeliers and their enthusiasm for pairing each chef's dishes with the appropriate wines. The goals of our wine program remain the same as the ones Eric and I established in 1990.

When we created our first wine list, Eric and I established a system that is still followed at every restaurant. Every bottle is tasted with potential food pairings in mind. Creative food calls for creative pairings, and the wines on each list are chosen to complement my vision as translated by each chef. Each restaurant list is well rounded, featuring wines that range from crisp white wines to accompany shellfish to tangy, fruit-driven red wines for piquant dishes and ripe, rich, Bordeaux-style reds to pair with meats and game.

Each list contains what other restaurants might call reserve list wines, with a variety of acclaimed, difficult-to-find wines and allocated artisan releases. You'll find big collectable Bordeaux on each list, like Château Lafite Rothschild, Château Cheval Blanc, and Château Margaux, as well as premier cru from Burgundy, Italian Montepulciano, Crozes-Hermitage of the Rhône, Shiraz from Australia, and vintage Ports and Champagnes. We also offer wines from less well-known regions and producers. Emeril's Delmonico Restaurant currently offers fifty-one different Pinot Noirs from the cult Sonoma County winery Williams-Selyem, as well as a vertical selection of 1988 to 1997 Bonneau du Martray Corton Charlemagne. NOLA lists sixteen Zinfandels from the boutique Turley Wine Cellars.

When we opened Emeril's, our wine slogan was, "We're in the business of selling wine, not storing wine." Each selection is very carefully chosen and not only priced to sell but paired with the menu to sell.

At the Fish House, the mostly seafood menu offers a wine list rich in bright, floral-toned Riesling, Pinot Gris, and Gewürztraminer from Alsace, Austria, and Germany. So it follows that Delmonico Steakhouse's predominantly meat menu is well complemented by a wide selection of Napa Valley Cabernet Sauvignons and Merlots, as well as Sonoma and Oregon Pinot Noirs and Central Coast Syrahs.

When NOLA opened, Emeril's was only two years old with a 250 to 300 selection wine list. We were still a young organization with only a meager budget to open the new restaurant. At the same time, we wanted NOLA to be a more casual, friendly restaurant, so the wines were grouped by price. Most people have a comfort level about what they'll pay for a bottle of wine, and to make it easy for customers, we developed a list with five different price levels, and three or four white and three or four red wines at each level. We hoped that by making the wines accessible, diners readily would come to enjoy wine with their meals as much as we did. Within a year, the list had grown to nearly 150 selections.

At the same time, the Emeril's list took off and climbed to nearly 450 selections. We also hired our first sommelier at Emeril's, Erin White, who was followed by Greg Harrington. Greg brought a level of cutting-edge expertise to Emeril's, and within three years, the list featured one thousand selections.

When Emeril's New Orleans Fish House opened two years later, we opened the restaurant with three hundred selections, carefully chosen for balance and depth, and we tasted the wines as we developed the menu in order to assure compatibility. This mammoth undertaking enabled us to start with a list that could compete with the very best in Las Vegas and elsewhere.

What an exciting time this was for us! Not only was the Fish House an immediate success but all three wine programs were recognized by the *Wine Spectator*—the Fish House and NOLA received the "Award of Excellence" and Emeril's received the "Best Award of Excellence."

In quick succession, we opened three new restaurants—Emeril's Restaurant at Universal Studios in Orlando, Emeril's Delmonico Restaurant in New Orleans, and Delmonico Steakhouse at The Venetian in Las Vegas. Emeril's Orlando was the first restaurant planned to house a ten thousand-bottle inventory in a temperature- and humidity-controlled environment, and the same was done at Emeril's Delmonico and Delmonico Steakhouse.

Each restaurant, except Delmonico Steakhouse, features a nightly degustation, or multi-course tasting menu, as a means of pairing wine and food. These special meals are "ingredient driven," and each chef designs his menu based on the best, most flavorful seasonal ingredients available. The dinners range from five to seven courses, with four to six wines chosen to complement the flavors in each dish. Each sommelier works carefully with his respective chef, discussing and tasting the degustation menu to determine which wines to serve. Hugely popular, these menus offer our guests the opportunity to enjoy the evening without having to make specific wine choices.

The by-the-glass program works in a similar fashion, with each sommelier offering a variety of hand-selected wines, giving guests the chance to broaden their horizons. By-the-glass selections average twenty wines at each restaurant, along with thirty to fifty-six half bottles.

Since opening Emeril's, I'd wanted to craft a house wine to pair with my particular style of cooking. So, it was good fortune when in 1994 I met proprietor and winemaker Jim Clendenen of Au Bon Climat, a highly respected Santa Barbara County winery. Jim had a reputation as a ground-breaking winemaker, handcrafting great Burgundian-style wines. We agreed to collaborate and develop a red and white private label wine program for my then two—and later six and nine—restaurants to pour by the glass. Despite low yields at harvest that first year (1995), Jim crafted rich, concentrated, yet low in alcohol wines that complemented my style of new Creole cuisine. We're proud to feature Emeril's Chardonnay and Emeril's Red from Au Bon Climat by the glass and bottle at each restaurant.

The awards the restaurants have received also reflect our ongoing commitment. Today, Emeril's Restaurant in New Orleans continues to maintain the top *Wine Spectator* "Grand Award" that it's held since 1999. NOLA, the Fish House, Emeril's Delmonico Restaurant, and the Delmonico Steakhouse each have the *Spectator*'s "Best Award of Excellence," while Emeril's Orlando holds the "Award of Excellence."

Of our new restaurants, the Polynesian-themed Tchoup Chop's focus is somewhat away from wine. Instead, premium sakes, special tropical drinks, and a variety of quality loose teas are paired with the full-flavored menu. Emeril's Atlanta and Emeril's Miami Beach restaurants, however, feature extensive wine programs along the lines set by our New Orleans flagship.

When you think about it, the "wine of love" is as important as the "food of love." Our wine program comes down to a love of food and wine, and, above all, sharing and making people happy. And you know what? Our customers are right there with us. Many pick their wines first and ask me to cook to match them. Now that's a real thrill and what it's all about at the end of the day. And just as the dishes found in this book are served with wine at the restaurants, I hope you will pair them with wine at home to share with your family and friends.

1|BASICS

French bread baguettes from
Emeril's Delmonico pastry shop

Boiled Artichokes

MAKES 4 ARTICHOKES

4 quarts water
4 bay leaves
3 tablespoons salt
2 teaspoons black
   peppercorns
4 large globe artichokes
   (about 10 ounces each)
1 lemon, cut in half

1. Combine the water, bay leaves, salt, and peppercorns in a large pot and bring to a boil.

2. With a small sharp knife, trim the tough outer skin from the artichoke stems and remove the bottom row of leaves. Add the artichokes and lemon to the pot and return to a boil. Place a heavy plate on top of the artichokes to keep them submerged, lower the heat, and cook at a low boil until the artichokes are tender, about 20 minutes. Drain in a colander.

Blanched Asparagus

MAKES 1 POUND

1 pound asparagus

1. With a sharp knife, remove the tough woody ends from the asparagus. Align the asparagus tips and trim the spears to the same length.

2. Bring a large saucepan of salted water to a boil. Add the asparagus and cook until just tender, 1 to 2 minutes, depending upon their thickness. Drain and transfer to an ice bath to stop the cooking; drain.

Asparagus being prepared for dinner at Emeril's Orlando

Clarified Butter

MAKES ABOUT ¾ CUP

**½ pound (2 sticks)
unsalted butter, cut
into pieces**

What makes clarified butter so great is its higher smoke point. That means you can cook meats and fish at a higher temperature than you could with regular butter, making it ideal for panfrying. Chef Dave uses clarified butter to make his Panéed Veal Medallions (page 239) and it's the butter of choice in classic Hollandaise Sauce (page 29). You'll see that the clarified butter imparts a rich flavor to the veal and gives the meat a light, puffy crust.

By clarifying butter during a slow cooking process, you're able to remove the milk solids that burn quickly, as well as the water; you'll lose about one-quarter of your original butter amount during the process.

1. Place the butter in a heavy saucepan and melt very slowly over low heat. Remove the pan from the heat and let stand for 5 minutes.

2. Skim and discard the foam from the top of the butter, and slowly pour it into a container; discard the milky solids in the bottom of the pan.

3. The butter will keep, refrigerated in an airtight container, for about 1 month.

*Chef's table in
Delmonico Steakhouse
kitchen*

BASICS

Duck Confit

1½ cups kosher salt

2 tablespoons coarsely
   ground black pepper

1 tablespoon chopped fresh
   thyme, plus 1 sprig

2 bay leaves

2 sprigs fresh rosemary,
   1 sprig coarsely chopped,
   the other left whole

6 garlic cloves, peeled and
   smashed

4 duck leg quarters, rinsed
   and patted dry

5 cups duck fat (see Source
   Guide, page 333) or
   vegetable oil

Salting and slow-cooking meat in its own fat is an old-fashioned French method of preserving meat. At Emeril's restaurants we use the process not to preserve meat, but to obtain optimum flavor and a surprisingly moist texture. Duck confit is used in several of the recipes in this book, including Chef Chris's Duck Confit Salad with Dried Berries, Stilton Cheese, and Arugula (page 114). You also could substitute duck confit for the roasted duck in Chef Dave's Duck and Mushroom Risotto (page 156). Be sure to keep the duck fat for other dishes—simply strain and use to roast potatoes or other vegetables for an unbelievably rich flavor.

1. Combine the salt, pepper, chopped thyme, bay leaves, chopped rosemary, and 4 of the garlic cloves in a medium bowl; stir to mix well. One at a time, add the duck legs, turning to coat and firmly packing the seasoning mixture onto both sides.

2. Place the duck legs skin side down on a rack set over a baking sheet, and top with any remaining seasoning mixture.

3. Refrigerate, uncovered, for at least 24 and up to 48 hours.

4. Preheat the oven to 225°F.

5. Rinse the ducks under cold running water to remove the seasoning mixture, and pat dry. Place in a medium roasting pan, without overlapping, and cover with the duck fat. Place the remaining 2 garlic cloves, the sprig of rosemary, and the sprig of thyme on top. Cover tightly with aluminum foil and roast until the meat is falling off the bone, 6 to 7 hours. Remove from the oven and let cool to room temperature.

6. Transfer the duck to an airtight container, cover with the fat, and refrigerate for up to 2 weeks.

Roast Duck

MAKES 1 DUCK (2 TO 3 CUPS
SHREDDED MEAT)

One 5-pound duck
1 teaspoon salt
**½ teaspoon freshly
   ground black pepper**

1. Preheat the oven to 500°F.

2. Remove all visible fat from the duck. With a sharp fork, prick the skin all over, without piercing the meat.

3. Sprinkle the duck with the salt and pepper. Place on a rack in a roasting pan and roast for 40 minutes.

4. Reduce the oven temperature to 400°F and roast until the thigh juices run clear when pierced, about 30 minutes more. Remove from the oven and let cool.

5. Remove the duck skin and discard. Remove the meat from the bones and discard the bones. Shred the meat. The meat can be stored, tightly covered, in the refrigerator for up to 3 days.

Hard-Boiled Eggs

MAKES 6 EGGS

6 eggs

It's important to peel the eggs as soon as they are cool enough to handle, since once the eggs cool, the shells tend to stick more.

1. Put the eggs in a small saucepan that can hold them in one layer. Add enough water to cover by ½ inch and bring to a boil over high heat. Reduce the heat to a gentle boil and cook for 10 minutes. Remove from the heat and drain.

2. Put the eggs in a colander under cold running water just until cool enough to handle, then peel.

Brabant Potatoes

MAKES 4 SERVINGS

**4 pounds Idaho potatoes,
   peeled**
**4 cups vegetable oil, for
   deep-frying**
1 teaspoon salt

Brabant potatoes are fried potato cubes that are partially cooked in boiling water before frying, which gives them a light, crunchy texture. Brabants are a traditional accompaniment to a variety of classic New Orleans Creole dishes and so are often found on the plates at Emeril's Delmonico. They serve them with Redfish Amandine (page 162), among other favorites. You'll find they're also terrific with chicken and other fish.

1. Cut each potato into an even rectangular shape by slicing off the ends and four sides, then cut into ½-inch cubes. Put in a medium heavy saucepan and add enough water to cover. Bring to a boil and cook until the potatoes are slightly tender, about 10 minutes. Drain, spread on paper towels, and blot dry.

2. Heat the oil in a large, deep heavy pot or deep-fryer to 360°F. Add the potatoes, in batches, and deep-fry, turning to brown evenly, for 3 to 4 minutes.

3. Remove and drain on paper towels. Season with the salt, and serve hot.

*Chef Joel Morgan working
the line at NOLA*

White Rice

MAKES 7 CUPS

2 cups long-grain white rice
4 cups water, Rich Chicken Stock (page 21), or canned low-sodium chicken broth
1½ teaspoons salt
2 bay leaves

We use rice as a component in a lot of different restaurant dishes— from gumbo to red beans and rice. Here's a quick refresher recipe for basic rice that's great every time. Just don't stir it until it's had a chance to rest after cooking! Try this with the amazing Tchoupi- toulas Gumbo (page 88), or my Kick-Butt Gumbo (page 86).

1. In a 2-quart saucepan, combine the rice, water, salt, and bay leaves and bring to a boil over high heat. Reduce the heat to low, cover, and simmer until all the liquid is absorbed, about 20 minutes. Remove the pan from the heat and let sit, covered, for 10 minutes.

2. Fluff the rice with a fork, and remove the bay leaves before serving.

Home-Smoked Salmon

MAKES 1 POUND

1 pound salmon fillet, skin on
1 tablespoon Emeril's Original Essence or Creole Seasoning (page 28)

Home-smoked salmon has been a feature on all the menus since we opened Emeril's New Orleans in 1990. While the restaurants use professional smokers to make smoked salmon, for this recipe we used a stovetop hot-smoke method. Home smokers are readily available and easy to use; cooking times may vary by manufac- turer. Chef Chris uses home-smoked salmon in the smoked salmon cheesecake (page 60). It's also delicious in terrines, spreads, and salads. It will keep in an airtight container in the refrigerator for up to 3 days.

1. Prepare a stovetop smoker according to the manufacturer's directions.

2. Season the salmon on all sides with the Essence. Place the salmon skin side down on the rack in the smoker. Place over medium heat (or as directed by the manufacturer), cover, and cook until the salmon is firm and flakes easily, 20 to 30 minutes. Remove the salmon from the smoker and let cool.

Candied Pecans

MAKES 2 CUPS

2 cups water
2 cups plus 1 teaspoon sugar
³/₈ teaspoon cayenne
2 cups pecans
4 cups vegetable oil, for
   deep-frying
¹/₂ teaspoon salt
¹/₄ teaspoon ground
   cinnamon

Chef Dave uses these decadent pecans to spice up his Kentucky Limestone Bibb Lettuce Salad (page 105). You'll quickly see they make ideal cocktail fare, too.

1. Combine the water, 2 cups of the sugar, and ¼ teaspoon of the cayenne in a medium heavy saucepan over medium-high heat and cook, stirring occasionally with a wooden spoon, until the mixture comes to a boil and thickens slightly, about 5 minutes.

2. Add the pecans and cook for 5 minutes, stirring often. Drain the pecans in a colander set over a bowl, and shake off the excess liquid.

3. Line a baking sheet with parchment or wax paper.

4. Heat the oil to 360°F in a large deep skillet, or a pot or deep-fryer. Add the pecans, and deep-fry in batches until a deep mahogany color, 4 to 5 minutes, stirring often. Remove with a slotted spoon and spread on the prepared baking sheet. Stir the pecans with a fork to prevent them from sticking together.

5. Combine the salt, the remaining ⅛ teaspoon cayenne, the cinnamon, and the remaining 1 teaspoon sugar in a bowl. Sprinkle over the pecans, tossing to coat. Let cool before serving.

6. The pecans can be stored in an airtight container at room temperature for up to 1 week.

Rich Chicken Stock

MAKES 2 QUARTS

4 pounds chicken bones (backs, necks, wings, etc.)
1 cup coarsely chopped yellow onions
½ cup coarsely chopped carrots
½ cup coarsely chopped celery
5 garlic cloves, peeled and smashed
One 6-ounce can tomato paste
1 cup dry red wine
5 sprigs fresh parsley
5 sprigs fresh thyme
2 bay leaves
1 teaspoon black peppercorns

This is the way to go when you need a more intense flavor than regular chicken stock can give you. While making this is an all-day project, the extra effort is definitely worth the end result. This stock is used as the base for the Natural Jus accompanying the Mushroom Stuffed Quail (page 219), and Chef Dave uses it in his Caribbean-Style Chicken (page 202), and Chicken Baked in Aromatic Salt Crust (page 194).

1. Preheat the oven to 375°F.

2. Spread the chicken bones evenly in a large roasting pan. Roast for 2 hours, stirring after 1 hour.

3. Remove from the oven and add the onions, carrots, celery, garlic, and tomato paste, stirring to mix. Roast for 45 minutes longer.

4. Transfer the hot vegetables and bones to a large heavy stockpot. Place the roasting pan over two burners on medium-high heat, add the wine, and stir with a wooden spoon to deglaze and dislodge any browned bits from the bottom of the pan. Pour the hot wine mixture into the stockpot. Add the parsley, thyme, bay leaves, peppercorns, and enough water to cover by 1 inch.

5. Bring to a boil over medium-high heat. Reduce the heat to medium-low and simmer, uncovered, for 4 hours, skimming frequently to remove the foam that forms on the surface.

6. Remove from the heat and strain through a fine-mesh strainer into a clean container, and let cool completely. The stock can be stored in the refrigerator for up to 3 days, or frozen in airtight containers for up to 2 months.

Duck Stock

*2 duck carcasses (about
4 pounds)*
10 sprigs fresh thyme
8 sprigs fresh parsley
5 sprigs fresh tarragon
1 tablespoon vegetable oil
2 teaspoons salt
*1/8 teaspoon freshly ground
black pepper*
*3 cups chopped yellow
onions*
1 cup chopped carrots
1 cup chopped celery
*1 head garlic, split
horizontally in half*
4 bay leaves
1 cup dry red wine
1/4 cup tomato paste
3 quarts water
*1 teaspoon black
peppercorns*

1. Break up and crack the bones of the duck carcasses. Wrap the thyme, parsley sprigs, and tarragon in a piece of cheesecloth and tie it together with kitchen twine.

2. Heat the vegetable oil in a 6-quart stockpot over medium-high heat. Season the bones with 1 teaspoon of the salt and the pepper, add to the pot, and brown for about 10 minutes, stirring often. Add the onions, carrots, celery, garlic, bay leaves, and the remaining 1 teaspoon salt. Cook until the vegetables are soft, about 5 minutes, stirring often. Add the wine and tomato paste, stir to mix, and cook for 5 minutes, stirring occasionally. Add the water, the cheesecloth packet, and the peppercorns and bring to a boil. Skim off any cloudy scum that rises to the surface. Reduce the heat to medium and simmer, uncovered, for 3 hours, skimming occasionally.

3. Remove from the heat and strain through a fine-mesh strainer into a clean container. Let cool, then cover and refrigerate overnight.

4. Remove any congealed fat from the surface of the stock. The stock can be stored in the refrigerator for up to 3 days, or frozen in airtight containers for up to 2 months.

Fish Stock

2½ pounds bones and heads from any white-fleshed fish, such as cod, pollock, grouper, snapper, or flounder (do not use bones from oily fish such as pompano, redfish, mackerel, or bluefish)
1 cup dry white wine
1 cup coarsely chopped yellow onions
½ cup coarsely chopped celery
½ cup coarsely chopped carrots
3 garlic cloves, peeled and smashed
3 bay leaves
1 lemon, quartered
3 tablespoons fresh lemon juice
2 teaspoons salt
1 teaspoon black peppercorns
1 teaspoon dried thyme

1. Rinse the fish bones and heads well in a large colander under cold running water.

2. Put all of the ingredients in a stockpot, add enough cold water to cover by 1 inch, and bring to a boil over high heat. Lower the heat to medium-low and simmer, uncovered, for 1 hour, skimming occasionally to remove any foam that rises to the surface.

3. Ladle the stock through a fine-mesh strainer into a clean container, and let cool completely. Cover and refrigerate. The stock can be stored in the refrigerator for up to 3 days, or frozen in airtight containers for up to 2 months.

Chef Jean Paul Labadie in Emeril's New Orleans Fish House kitchen

BASICS

Shrimp Stock

*1 pound (about 8 cups)
    shrimp shells and heads*
*1 cup coarsely chopped
    yellow onions*
*½ cup coarsely chopped
    celery*
*½ cup coarsely chopped
    carrots*
*3 garlic cloves, peeled and
    smashed*
3 bay leaves
*1 teaspoon black
    peppercorns*
1 teaspoon dried thyme
2 teaspoons salt
4 quarts water

Shrimp stock imparts a depth of flavor to soups such as Chef Dave's Creole Bouillabaisse (page 186) and other dishes, like Barbecued Shrimp (page 42). When you peel shrimp, store the shells in a plastic bag in the freezer until you have enough to make this stock.

1. Place the shrimp shells and heads in a large colander and rinse under cold running water.

2. Place all the ingredients in a heavy 6-quart stockpot and bring to a boil over high heat, skimming to remove any foam that rises to the surface. Reduce the heat to medium-low and simmer, uncovered, for 45 minutes, skimming occasionally.

3. Remove the stock from the heat and strain through a fine-mesh strainer into a clean container, and let cool completely. The stock can be stored in the refrigerator for up to 3 days, or frozen in airtight containers for up to 2 months.

*Fresh oysters at Emeril's
New Orleans Fish House*

Reduced Veal Stock

MAKES 1½ QUARTS

4 pounds veal bones
with some meat
attached, sawed into
2-inch pieces (have
the butcher do this)
2 tablespoons olive oil
2 cups coarsely chopped
yellow onions
1 cup coarsely chopped
carrots
1 cup coarsely chopped
celery
5 garlic cloves, peeled
and smashed
¼ cup tomato paste
6 quarts water
4 bay leaves
1 teaspoon dried thyme
1 teaspoon salt
1 teaspoon black
peppercorns
2 cups dry red wine

1. Preheat the oven to 375°F.

2. Place the bones in a large roasting pan and toss with the oil. Roast, turning occasionally, until golden brown, about 1 hour.

3. Spread the onions, carrots, celery, and garlic over the bones. Smear the tomato paste over the vegetables and return the pan to the oven. Roast for another 45 minutes. Remove from the oven and discard the fat from the pan.

4. Remove the roasting pan from the oven and transfer the bones and vegetables to a large stockpot. Do not discard the juices in the roasting pan. Add the water, bay leaves, thyme, salt, and peppercorns to the stockpot and bring to a boil.

5. Meanwhile, place the roasting pan over two burners on medium-high heat. Add the wine and stir with a heavy wooden spoon to deglaze and dislodge any browned bits clinging to the bottom of the pan. Add the contents of the pan to the stockpot. When the liquid returns to a boil, reduce the heat to low and simmer, uncovered, for 8 hours, skimming occasionally to remove any foam that rises to the surface.

6. Ladle the stock through a fine-mesh strainer into a large clean pot. Bring to a boil, reduce to a gentle boil, and cook, uncovered, until reduced to 6 cups, about 1 hour. Let cool, then cover and refrigerate overnight.

7. Remove any congealed fat from the surface of the stock. The stock can be stored, covered, in the refrigerator for up to 3 days, or frozen in airtight containers for up to 2 months.

Lamb Stock

6 to 8 pounds lamb bones,
sawed into 2- to 3-inch
pieces (have the butcher
do this)

2 tablespoons olive oil

1 cup tomato paste

8 tomatoes, coarsely
chopped

2 large onions, peeled,
halved, and sliced

2 carrots, peeled and
chopped

2 ribs celery, chopped

2 heads garlic, cut
horizontally in half

2 quarts water

4 bay leaves

2 teaspoons dried basil

2 teaspoons dried thyme

2 teaspoons dried tarragon

2 teaspoons dried oregano

$\frac{1}{2}$ cup chopped fresh
parsley, including stems

1 tablespoon plus
1 teaspoon salt

$1\frac{1}{2}$ teaspoons black
peppercorns

2 cups dry red wine

1. Preheat the oven to 425°F.

2. Place the bones in a roasting pan and toss with the oil. Roast until brown, about 15 minutes. Turn the bones and spread with the tomato paste. Roast for 10 minutes. Add the tomatoes, onions, carrots, celery, and garlic and stir to combine. Roast until the bones are a deep brown color and the vegetables are tender, about 25 minutes.

3. Remove the roasting pan from the oven and transfer the bones and vegetables to a large stockpot. Do not discard the juices in the roasting pan. Add the water, bay leaves, basil, thyme, tarragon, oregano, parsley, salt, and peppercorns to the stockpot and bring to a boil.

4. Meanwhile, place the roasting pan over two burners on medium-high heat. Add the wine and stir with a heavy wooden spoon to deglaze and dislodge any browned bits clinging to the bottom of the pan. Add the contents of the pan to the stockpot. When the liquid returns to a boil, reduce the heat to low and simmer, uncovered, for about $3\frac{1}{2}$ hours, skimming occasionally to remove any foam that rises to the surface.

5. Strain the stock through a fine-mesh strainer into a clean container. Skim the fat from the surface, and let cool thoroughly. Cover and refrigerate overnight.

6. Remove any congealed fat from the surface of the stock. The stock can be stored in the refrigerator for up to 3 days, or frozen in airtight containers for up to 2 months.

Vegetable Stock

1 tablespoon olive oil
1 large yellow onion, peeled, halved, and sliced
1 carrot, peeled and chopped
1 celery rib, chopped
3 heads garlic, cut horizontally in half
4 quarts water
1 green bell pepper, cored, seeded, and chopped
2 tomatoes, coarsely chopped
2 ears corn, kernels scraped off, kernels and cobs reserved
½ pound mushroom stems, rinsed
4 bay leaves
1 teaspoon chopped fresh basil
1 teaspoon chopped fresh thyme
1 teaspoon chopped fresh tarragon
1 teaspoon chopped fresh oregano
1 teaspoon chopped fresh parsley
1 teaspoon chopped fresh chives
½ teaspoon black peppercorns

1. Heat the oil in a large stockpot over high heat. Add the onions, carrot, celery, and garlic and cook, stirring occasionally, until the onions are soft, 3 to 4 minutes. Add the remaining ingredients and bring to a boil. Reduce the heat to low and simmer, uncovered, for 1¾ hours. Remove from the heat and strain through a fine-mesh strainer into a clean container. Let cool completely.

2. The stock can be stored, covered, in the refrigerator for up to 3 days, or frozen in airtight containers for up to 2 months.

Working the pantry station at Emeril's Orlando

Creole Meunière Base

MAKES 3 CUPS

2 tablespoons olive oil
2½ cups chopped yellow
  onions
¾ cup chopped carrots
¾ cup chopped celery
4 cups Reduced Veal Stock
  (page 25)
4 cups Worcestershire sauce
¼ cup Emeril's Kick It Up
  Red Pepper Sauce or
  other hot pepper sauce
2 bay leaves
1 teaspoon chopped garlic
1 teaspoon black
  peppercorns

Creole Meunière Sauce has become a signature ingredient in many of our recipes, and is used in various forms at all the restaurants, in dishes from Redfish Amandine (page 162) and Redfish Meunière to Panéed Veal (page 239). In order to make the sauce, you need to make this base. While the procedure is time-consuming—the reduction time is about 3 hours—it's a simple one, and it's essential for the intensely flavored sauce that's a great accompaniment to seafood, meat, and poultry.

Remember when using this that it is just a base—a little goes a long way.

1. Heat the olive oil in a medium heavy pot over medium heat. Add the onions, carrots, and celery and cook, stirring occasionally, until very soft, about 10 minutes. Add the remaining ingredients and bring to a boil. Reduce the heat to medium-low and simmer until reduced to 3 cups and thick enough to coat the back of a spoon, about 3 hours.

2. Strain through a fine-mesh strainer into a clean container, pressing on the solids with the back of a spoon.

3. The base will keep refrigerated in an airtight container for up to 1 month, and can be frozen for up to 3 months.

Creole Seasoning

MAKES ⅔ CUP

2½ tablespoons paprika
2 tablespoons salt
2 tablespoons garlic powder
1 tablespoon freshly ground
  black pepper
1 tablespoon onion powder
1 tablespoon cayenne
1 tablespoon dried oregano
1 tablespoon dried thyme

Combine all the ingredients in a bowl and mix thoroughly. Store in an airtight container for up to 3 months at room temperature.

Hollandaise Sauce

MAKES 1 CUP

3 large egg yolks
2 teaspoons water
½ cup melted Clarified
** Butter (page 15) or**
** 8 tablespoons**
** (1 stick) unsalted**
** butter, melted**
1½ teaspoons fresh
** lemon juice**
¼ teaspoon salt
⅛ teaspoon cayenne

The frequent appearance of hollandaise sauce on each of the restaurants' menus is testament to the amazing versatility of this classic French egg-based sauce. You'll find it paired with Delmonico's Veal Marcelle (page 243), and it's the basis for béarnaise sauce, which accompanies Eggs Erato (page 123) and is so often paired with the steaks at Delmonico Steakhouse. It's also a traditional accompaniment to Blanched Asparagus (page 14) and Boiled Artichokes (page 14).

1. In the top of a double boiler or in a large heatproof bowl set over a pot of simmering water, whisk the egg yolks with the water until thick and pale yellow, removing the pan or bowl from the heat as needed to prevent the eggs from overcooking. Gradually add the butter, whisking constantly until thickened. Add the remaining ingredients and whisk well to blend. Adjust the seasoning to taste.

2. Remove from the heat and cover to keep warm until ready to serve. (Or place in a bowl set over a pot of warm water and cover; stir occasionally.)

Emeril's Orlando exterior

Lemon Butter Sauce

MAKES 1½ CUPS

1 cup dry white wine
3 lemons, peeled and
    quartered
1 tablespoon minced
    shallots
1 tablespoon minced garlic
½ cup heavy cream
½ pound (2 sticks) cold
    unsalted butter, cut into
    pieces
1 teaspoon salt
⅛ teaspoon freshly ground
    black pepper

This sauce is a bit different from the standard French butter sauce, or **beurre blanc**. *We've added cream to ours as a stabilizer, so it won't break so easily if you want to hold it for a little while before serving. The cream also gives the sauce a slightly richer flavor. The garlic gives the sauce a definite kick; maybe you should call it New Orleans lemon butter sauce!*

1. Combine the wine, lemons, shallots, and garlic in a medium saucepan and bring to a boil. Reduce the heat to medium-low and simmer until reduced by half, about 20 minutes, stirring occasionally and mashing the lemons with the back of a spoon to break them up.

2. Add the cream and cook until reduced by half, about 3 minutes.

3. Whisk in the butter 1 tablespoon at a time, adding each new piece before the previous one has been completely incorporated and removing the pan from the heat periodically to prevent the sauce from getting too hot and breaking; it should be thick enough to coat the back of a spoon. Whisk in the salt and pepper.

4. Strain the sauce through a fine-mesh strainer into a saucepan or bowl, pressing against the solids with the back of a spoon. Cover to keep warm until ready to serve, stirring occasionally.

Mayonnaise

MAKES ABOUT 2 CUPS

1 large egg
1 large egg yolk
2 teaspoons fresh lemon juice
1 teaspoon Dijon mustard
2 tablespoons water
½ teaspoon salt
1½ cups vegetable oil or olive oil
⅛ teaspoon cayenne, optional

Chef Chris uses homemade mayonnaise in the coleslaw that accompanies his Braised Beef Short Ribs (page 233). You also could use this as a substitute for the various mayonnaises made by other chefs, such as the Green Onion Mayonnaise (page 127), or the White and Red Rémoulade Sauces that accompany the Fried Green Tomatoes (page 107). For a treat, make this basic mayonnaise as a dip for Boiled Artichokes on (page 14), or use as a spread on your favorite sandwich.

1. Place the egg, egg yolk, lemon juice, mustard, 1 tablespoon of the water, and the salt in a food processor or blender and process for 20 seconds. With the motor running, start to pour the oil in a thin stream through the feed tube, processing until the mixture begins to thicken. When half of the oil has been incorporated, add the remaining tablespoon of water. With the motor running, add the remaining oil in a thin stream, processing until incorporated. Adjust the seasoning to taste with salt and cayenne, if desired.

2. Cover and refrigerate. The mayonnaise will keep, stored in an airtight container, for up to 1 day.

Emeril's Worcestershire Sauce

MAKES 3 PINTS

2 tablespoons olive oil
6 cups coarsely chopped
　　yellow onions
4 jalapeños, chopped
　　(including stems and
　　seeds)
2 tablespoons minced garlic
Four 2-ounce cans anchovy
　　fillets
2 medium lemons, skin and
　　white pith removed
12 ounces fresh horseradish,
　　peeled and grated
2 quarts white distilled
　　vinegar
4 cups water
4 cups dark corn syrup
2 cups Steen's 100% Pure
　　Cane Syrup (see Source
　　Guide, page 333)
2 tablespoons salt
1/2 teaspoon whole cloves
2 teaspoons freshly ground
　　black pepper
Three 1-pint canning jars

Serve this very versatile sauce with all cuts of meat, particularly grilled meats. Try it on your hamburgers or add zing to your favorite Bloody Mary. Store this in an airtight container in the refrigerator for up to 2 months. (You'll find the sauce mellows a bit and develops more flavor as it stands.)

1. Combine the oil, onions, and jalapeños in a large stockpot over high heat and cook, stirring, until the onions are slightly soft, 2 to 3 minutes. Add the garlic, anchovy fillets, lemons, horseradish, vinegar, water, corn syrup, cane syrup, salt, cloves, and pepper and bring to a boil. Reduce the heat and simmer, uncovered, stirring occasionally, until the mixture is reduced to about 6 cups and just barely coats the back of a wooden spoon, about 6 hours. Strain through a fine-mesh strainer into a clean container.

2. Sterilize three 1-pint canning jars and their lids and rings according to the manufacturer's instructions. Spoon the hot mixture into the jars, filling them to within 1/2 inch of the rims. With a clean damp towel, wipe the rims, and fit with the hot lids. Tightly screw on the metal rings.

3. Place the jars, without touching one another, on a rack in a canning kettle or large stockpot filled with enough rapidly boiling water to cover by 1 inch. Process for 15 minutes.

4. Using tongs, transfer the jars to a towel and let cool completely. Test the seals, and tighten the rings as needed. Store in a cool, dark place for at least 2 weeks before using. After opening, store in the refrigerator.

Large Croutons

MAKES 12 TO 20 CROUTONS

One 12- to 15-inch-long loaf French or Italian bread, cut into ¼- to ½-inch slices
¼ cup olive oil
¼ teaspoon salt
⅛ teaspoon freshly ground black pepper

While it's easy just to pick up crackers at the store, there's nothing like having homemade croutons (or French bread toasts) to serve with your spreads, cheeses, and dips. They've got a fantastic crunch, and the freshness just can't be beat.

1. Preheat the oven to 400°F.

2. Place the bread on a baking sheet and brush one side of each slice with the olive oil, then lightly season with the salt and pepper. Bake for 8 minutes, or until light golden brown. Remove from the oven and let cool slightly.

3. Serve the croutons to accompany dips, or spread with toppings.

Small Croutons

MAKES 1 CUP

1 cup ½- to ¾-inch cubes French bread
¼ cup extra-virgin olive oil
2 teaspoon Emeril's Original Essence or Creole Seasoning (page 28)

Everybody loves crunchy, homemade croutons, and these are a key component of the Caesar Salad (page 98) that's a Delmonico Steakhouse signature dish. Try them on any salad of your own design. If you want garlicky croutons, rub the bread with a split garlic clove before cubing and toasting.

1. Preheat the oven to 400°F.

2. Place the bread in a medium bowl and toss with the oil and Essence. Place on a baking sheet and bake, stirring occasionally, until light golden brown, about 6 minutes. Remove from the oven and let cool slightly before using.

Brioche

MAKES 1 LOAF

½ cup whole milk, warmed
  to 110°F
1½ tablespoons active dry
  yeast
2½ cups bread flour
3 large eggs
1 tablespoon sugar
½ teaspoon salt
12 tablespoons (1½ sticks)
  unsalted butter, at room
  temperature
1 large egg yolk, beaten with
  2 tablespoons milk for
  egg wash

This rich egg bread makes frequent appearances on the menus at all of the restaurants—from croutons or toast to bread puddings. While the usual French version is baked in a special mold, we make ours in a regular loaf pan so that it can be cut easily and used in a variety of ways.

1. Combine the warm milk and yeast in the bowl of a stand mixer and stir to mix. Let sit until foamy, about 5 minutes.

2. Add ½ cup of the flour and stir to combine. Cover with plastic wrap and let rise in a warm, draft-free place until doubled in size, about 1 hour.

3. Using a dough hook, beat the eggs one at a time into the yeast mixture. Slowly add the remaining 2 cups flour, the sugar, and the salt and beat until well incorporated, about 5 minutes. Add the butter 2 tablespoons at a time, beating well after each addition. Cover with plastic wrap and let rise in a warm, draft-free place until doubled in size, about 1 hour.

4. Transfer the dough to a 9 × 5-inch loaf pan and press firmly with the palms of your hands to fill the pan evenly. Using a pastry brush, brush the egg wash on the top of the dough. Set aside until slightly risen, about 20 minutes.

5. Meanwhile, preheat the oven to 375°F.

6. Bake the bread until golden and cooked through, 30 to 35 minutes. Remove from the oven and let cool in the pan for 5 minutes. Turn out onto a wire rack and let cool before serving.

Cornbread

MAKES ONE 9-INCH ROUND;
ABOUT 6 SERVINGS, OR
4 CUPS CRUMBLED

¼ **cup plus 1 tablespoon**
   vegetable oil
1 cup yellow cornmeal
1 cup all-purpose flour
2 teaspoons baking
   powder
1 teaspoon salt
¼ **teaspoon cayenne**
1 cup buttermilk
1 large egg, beaten

At the restaurants, we use crumbled cornbread in a variety of bread puddings and stuffings, and I use it in my Tasso-and-Cornbread-Stuffed Quail (page 217). At NOLA, they also make jalapeño cornbread for the bread baskets that accompany every meal. You'll find that this basic cornbread is great with a variety of dishes—from fried chicken to grilled fish. If you're using it in a cornbread dressing, let it sit out overnight to get slightly stale.

1. Preheat the oven to 400°F. Pour 1 tablespoon of the vegetable oil into a 9-inch round baking pan or heavy cast-iron skillet. Place the pan in the oven to preheat for at least 10 minutes.

2. Combine the cornmeal, flour, baking powder, salt, and cayenne in a large mixing bowl and stir with a wooden spoon. Add the buttermilk, the remaining ¼ cup oil, and the egg and stir well to blend.

3. Pour the batter into the preheated pan. Bake until lightly golden brown, about 25 minutes. Remove from the oven and let cool for 10 minutes before serving.

*Attention to detail at
Emeril's Delmonico*

BASICS

Flaky Butter Crust

MAKES ONE 9-INCH TART
CRUST OR PIE

1¼ cups all-purpose flour
¼ teaspoon salt
7 tablespoons cold unsalted butter, cut into small pieces
¼ cup ice water, or more as needed

Chef Dave uses this crust for the Savory Leek and Prosciutto Tart (page 122) and the Savory Pies of Roasted Duck, Foie Gras, and Root Vegetables (page 66). It is also great for quiches, chicken and meat potpies, and empanadas (the recipe makes enough dough for six 4½-inch crusts). Another great thing is that the crust can be made quickly, either in the food processor or by hand. The recipe doubles easily and can be frozen, tightly wrapped, for up to 2 months.

1. To make the dough in a food processor, combine the flour, salt, and butter in the processor and pulse for 10 seconds. Add the ice water and pulse quickly 5 or 6 times, or until the dough comes together. Transfer the dough to a floured surface. Work the dough into a ball, flatten it into a disk, and wrap in plastic wrap. Refrigerate for at least 30 minutes.

2. To make the dough by hand, combine the flour, salt, and butter in a medium mixing bowl and mix with a pastry blender or your fingertips until the mixture resembles coarse crumbs. Add the water 1 tablespoon at a time, mixing until the dough comes together, being careful not to overmix. Form into a disk, wrap in plastic wrap, and refrigerate for at least 30 minutes.

3. Roll out the dough on a lightly floured surface according to the recipe, fit it into the pan, and allow to rest again in the refrigerator before baking.

Sweet Pie Dough

MAKES ONE 9- OR 10-INCH
PIECRUST

**1½ cups plus 2
   tablespoons
   all-purpose flour**
1 tablespoon sugar
½ teaspoon salt
**8 tablespoons (1 stick)
   cold butter, cut into
   ¼-inch pieces**
**2 tablespoons solid
   vegetable shortening**
**4 to 5 tablespoons ice
   water, or as needed**

Sift the flour, sugar, and salt into a large bowl. Using your finger-tips, work in the butter and shortening until the mixture resembles coarse crumbs. Add 2 tablespoons of the ice water and work with your fingers until the dough comes together, adding more water as needed to make a smooth dough; be careful not to overmix. Form the dough into a disk, wrap tightly in plastic wrap, and refrigerate for at least 30 minutes before using.

*Chef Chris Wilson inside
Emeril's New Orleans*

BASICS

APPETIZERS AND FIRST COURSES

Working the line at Emeril's New Orleans

Shrimp Cakes with Roasted Shrimp Sauce

1 pound large shrimp, peeled, deveined, and cut into ½-inch pieces

3 tablespoons Emeril's Original Essence or Creole Seasoning (page 28)

¼ cup plus 1 tablespoon vegetable oil

½ cup chopped yellow onions

¼ cup chopped celery

¼ cup chopped green bell peppers

1 teaspoon minced garlic

1 very cold large egg white

¼ cup very cold heavy cream

½ cup chopped green onions (green parts only)

1 tablespoon Dijon mustard

2 teaspoons fresh lemon juice

1 teaspoon Worcestershire sauce

1 teaspoon Emeril's Kick It Up Red Pepper Sauce or other hot pepper sauce

1 teaspoon finely chopped fresh basil

1 teaspoon finely chopped fresh parsley, plus ¼ cup chopped parsley for garnish

1 cup all-purpose flour

2 large eggs

1 tablespoon water

1 cup fine dry bread crumbs

1 recipe Roasted Shrimp Sauce

This is one of the first appetizers I created for the menu at Emeril's New Orleans, and we still occasionally run it as a special. The combination of shrimp and "the trinity" (chopped onions, bell peppers, and celery) and a delicious, delicate shrimp sauce make this one heck of a starter. The sauce also can be used for other shellfish or grilled fish. Over the years, we've sometimes smoked the shrimp for the cakes, which you can easily do at home in a stovetop smoker.

1. Toss the shrimp with 1 tablespoon of the Essence. Place half of the shrimp in the refrigerator until well chilled, about 20 minutes. Also place a food processor bowl and blade in the refrigerator to chill.

2. Heat 1 tablespoon of the oil in a large skillet over medium-high heat. Add the onions, celery, bell peppers, and garlic and cook, stirring, for 3 minutes. Add the remaining shrimp and cook until pink and cooked through, about 3 minutes. Remove from the heat and spread on a plate to cool completely.

3. Place the chilled shrimp in the bowl of the food processor and process for 10 seconds. Add the egg white and process for 5 seconds. With the machine running, add the heavy cream in a steady stream. Transfer to a large bowl. Add the cooked shrimp mixture, green onions, mustard, lemon juice, Worcestershire sauce, hot pepper sauce, basil, and the 1 teaspoon parsley and mix well. Form into 8 cakes.

4. In a shallow bowl, combine the flour with 1 tablespoon of the Essence. In another bowl, beat the eggs with the water. In a third bowl, combine the bread crumbs with the remaining tablespoon of Essence. One at a time, dredge the shrimp cakes first in the the seasoned flour, then the eggs, and then the bread crumbs, shaking to remove any excess breading.

5. Heat 2 tablespoons of the oil in a large skillet over medium-high heat. Add 4 of the cakes and cook until golden brown, about 2½ minutes per side. Remove and drain on paper towels. Heat the remaining 2 tablespoons oil and cook the remaining cakes.

6. To serve, spoon the shrimp sauce onto four plates and top with 2 shrimp cakes each. Garnish with the parsley and serve.

MAKES 2 CUPS

Roasted Shrimp Sauce

2 tablespoons olive oil
4 cups shrimp shells and heads
1/2 cup chopped yellow onions
1/4 cup chopped carrots
1/4 cup chopped celery
1 teaspoon chopped garlic
1 1/2 teaspoons paprika
1 teaspoon tomato paste
3/8 teaspoon salt
1/8 teaspoon cayenne
2 tablespoons brandy
1/2 cup water
3 cups heavy cream
4 tablespoons cold unsalted butter, cut into pieces
1/4 teaspoon fresh lemon juice

1. Heat the oil in a large heavy pot over high heat until smoking hot. Add the shrimp shells and cook, stirring, until bright orange and fragrant, 3 minutes. Add the onions, carrots, and celery and cook, stirring, for 3 minutes. Add the garlic, paprika, tomato paste, salt, cayenne and cook, stirring, until the tomato paste begins to color slightly, 2 to 3 minutes.

2. Add the brandy and cook for about 15 seconds. Add the water and cook until the pan is almost dry, stirring constantly with a wooden spoon to deglaze the pan. Add the cream and cook until reduced by half, about 7 minutes. Remove from the heat.

3. With a hand-held immersion blender, or in batches in a food processor, purée the sauce until smooth, about 1 minute. Strain through a fine-mesh strainer into a clean saucepan, pressing hard on the solids with the back of a spoon to extract as much liquid as possible. Place over medium heat and whisk in the cold butter one piece at a time. Whisk in the lemon juice and serve immediately.

Barbecued Shrimp with Rosemary Biscuits

MAKES 4 TO 6 SERVINGS

2 pounds medium shrimp in their shells

1 tablespoon Emeril's Original Essence or Creole Seasoning (page 28)

½ teaspoon freshly ground black pepper

1 tablespoon vegetable oil

1 cup heavy cream

¼ cup Barbecue Sauce Base

2 tablespoons unsalted butter, cut into pieces

1 recipe Rosemary Biscuits

These shrimp aren't really barbecued. Instead, this is my take on a classic New Orleans dish where whole shrimp are baked with butter, olive oil, and spices. When Emeril's opened, we took the dish up another notch and created this amazingly rich sauce for sautéed shrimp. Once you make the barbecue base, it will keep for a month, tightly covered in the refrigerator. Try the same sauce with oysters, adding the oysters to the sauce after it has reduced enough to coat the back of a spoon.

1. Peel and devein the shrimp, leaving their tails attached. (Reserve the shells, if desired, to make the shrimp stock.) Season the shrimp with the Essence and black pepper, tossing to coat evenly. Cover and refrigerate while you make the sauce base and biscuits.

2. Heat the oil in a large skillet over high heat. Add the seasoned shrimp and cook, stirring, until they begin to turn pink, about 2 minutes. Add the cream and barbecue sauce base, reduce the heat to medium-high, and simmer, stirring, until reduced by half, about 3 minutes. Transfer the shrimp to a platter with tongs. Over medium-low heat, gradually whisk the butter into the sauce. Remove from the heat.

3. Place 2 or 3 biscuits on each plate. Divide the shrimp among the biscuits, and top each serving with the sauce. Serve immediately.

Barbecue Sauce Base

1 tablespoon olive oil
½ cup finely chopped
   yellow onions
1 teaspoon salt
1 teaspoon coarsely
   ground black pepper
3 bay leaves
1 tablespoon minced
   garlic
3 lemons, peeled, white
   pith removed, and
   quartered
½ cup dry white wine
2 cups Shrimp Stock
   (page 24)
1 cup Worcestershire
   sauce

1. Heat the olive oil in a medium heavy saucepan over medium-high heat. Add the onions, salt, pepper, and bay leaves, and cook, stirring, until the onions are soft, about 2 minutes. Add the garlic, lemons, and white wine and cook for 2 minutes. Add the shrimp stock and Worcestershire sauce and bring to a boil over high heat. Reduce the heat to medium-low and simmer until the sauce is reduced to ½ cup, about 1 hour and 15 minutes.

2. Strain the sauce through a fine-mesh strainer into a clean container, pressing on the solids with the back of a spoon. Set aside until needed. (The sauce base can be refrigerated in an airtight container for up to 3 days, or frozen for up to 2 months.)

Rosemary Biscuits

1 cup all-purpose flour
1 teaspoon baking
   powder
½ teaspoon salt
⅛ teaspoon baking soda
3 tablespoons cold
   unsalted butter, cut
   into small pieces
½ to ¾ cup buttermilk
1 tablespoon minced
   fresh rosemary

1. Preheat the oven to 400°F.

2. Sift the dry ingredients into a large bowl. Work the butter into the flour with your fingertips or a fork until the mixture resembles coarse crumbs. Stir in the rosemary. Add ½ cup of the buttermilk a little at a time, using your hands to work it in just until incorporated and a smooth ball of dough forms. Add up to an additional ¼ cup buttermilk if necessary, being very careful not to overwork the dough, or the biscuits will be tough.

3. On a lightly floured surface, pat the dough into a circle about 7 inches in diameter and ½ inch thick. Using a 1-inch round cookie cutter, cut out 12 biscuits.

4. Place the biscuits on a medium baking sheet. Bake until golden on top and lightly browned on the bottom, 10 to 12 minutes. Serve warm.

APPETIZERS AND FIRST COURSES

MAKES 6 SERVINGS

**2 pounds medium shrimp,
peeled and deveined but
tails left on**

**¼ cup Emeril's Original
Essence or Creole
Seasoning (page 28)**

**One 3-ounce box Zatarain's
Crab and Shrimp Boil (see
Source Guide, page 333)**

¼ cup salt

2 lemons, halved

1 yellow onion, quartered

**3 stalks celery, coarsely
chopped**

**1 head garlic, cut
horizontally in half**

2 bay leaves

1 recipe Cocktail Sauce

1 lemon, cut into 6 wedges

Creole Boiled Shrimp Cocktail

A Steakhouse mainstay, this is a good, simple appetizer that never fails to please. And what better way to start a steakhouse dinner than with this tried-and-true classic? We feel that New Orleans cooks make the best boiled shrimp in the world. Why? Because we marinate the shrimp in Creole spices and then cook them just until they are done. Follow the method exactly as described, and you'll become a believer.

And for an extra kick, we add freshly grated horseradish as well as the usual prepared horseradish to the sauce. Fresh horseradish can usually be found in the produce section of supermarkets. Just take care when grating it that it doesn't burn your skin.

1. In a large bowl, toss the shrimp with 2 tablespoons of the Essence to coat evenly.

2. Combine 3 gallons water, the Zatarain's boil, the salt, the remaining 2 tablespoons Essence, the lemons, onion, celery, garlic, and bay leaves in a large heavy stockpot. Bring to a boil. Taste, and add more salt if needed; the salinity level should be that of seawater.

3. Add the shrimp and cook, stirring frequently, until pink and cooked through, 3 to 4 minutes. Drain in a colander, transfer to a bowl, cover with plastic wrap, and refrigerate until well chilled, about 1 hour.

4. Arrange the shrimp on each of 6 small plates, accompanied by the cocktail sauce in small decorative bowls or ramekins. Garnish with the lemon wedges and serve immediately.

Cocktail Sauce

1 cup ketchup
1 tablespoon Worcester-
    shire sauce
1 tablespoon fresh
    lemon juice
2 tablespoons drained
    prepared horseradish
1 tablespoon grated
    fresh horseradish
1 tablespoon V-8 juice
½ teaspoon Emeril's
    Kick It Up Red Pepper
    Sauce or other hot
    pepper sauce
⅛ teaspoon salt
⅛ teaspoon freshly
    ground black pepper

Combine all the ingredients in a bowl and whisk well to blend. Cover and chill for 2 hours before serving. (The sauce will keep refrigerated for 2 days.)

In Emeril's Delmonico kitchen

Jumbo Lump Crabmeat and Beluga Caviar Timbales in Clear Tomato Juice

MAKES 4 SERVINGS

1 pound jumbo lump
    crabmeat, picked over for
    shells and cartilage
1 teaspoon chopped fresh
    parsley
1 teaspoon chopped fresh
    tarragon
1 teaspoon minced fresh
    chives
2 tablespoons extra-virgin
    olive oil
1 teaspoon salt
½ teaspoon freshly ground
    white pepper
1 recipe Clear Tomato Juice
¼ cup finely diced zucchini
    (green skin only)
¼ cup finely diced yellow
    squash (yellow skin only)
¼ cup finely diced red bell
    peppers
1 tablespoon plus
    1 teaspoon thinly sliced
    fresh basil leaves
1 ounce Beluga caviar

We make this at the Fish House with heirloom tomatoes, because you just can't beat their rich, sweet flavor. Our particular favorite is the Creole tomato, a big, delicious red variety that we have flown in from Louisiana. Use whatever you're able to get in your area—just make sure they're at the peak of ripeness. If you can't get heirloom tomatoes in season, use very ripe Roma tomatoes instead.

1. Combine the crabmeat, parsley, tarragon, chives, olive oil, salt, and white pepper in a medium bowl and mix gently.

2. To assemble, place a 3-inch ring mold in the center of a shallow rimmed soup plate. Pack ½ cup of the crabmeat mixture into the mold and ladle ½ cup of the tomato juice into the bowl. Remove the ring mold, and repeat to make 3 more servings. Garnish the rim of each soup plate with 1 tablespoon each of the zucchini, squash, and red bell pepper. Sprinkle the basil over the broth, and top each timbale with about 1 teaspoon of the caviar. Serve immediately.

Clear Tomato Juice

MAKES 2 CUPS

3 pounds ripe tomatoes,
    seeded and quartered
½ teaspoon kosher salt
¼ teaspoon freshly ground
    white pepper
3 tablespoons vodka,
    optional

1. Place the tomatoes in a food processor and pulse to chop, not purée. Season with the salt and white pepper. Place in the center of a large piece of doubled cheesecloth, draw up the edges to form a tight bag, and secure with string. Hang over a bowl in the refrigerator and let drain overnight.

2. Discard the tomatoes. If the tomato juice is not perfectly clear, strain it through a coffee filter. Stir in the vodka if using and adjust the seasoning to taste. Cover tightly with plastic wrap and refrigerate until ready to use.

Steamed Manila Clams
with Fermented Black Beans
and Cilantro

MAKES 4 SERVINGS

2 pounds Manila clams, scrubbed

1 cup sake

2 tablespoons fermented black bean paste

½ cup chopped green onions (green parts only)

2 tablespoons chopped fresh cilantro

1 tablespoon unsalted butter, cut into pieces

Manila clams, also known as Japanese littlenecks or just steamers, have been farmed by the Japanese for centuries. They can be found on sand-gravel beaches, and also grow in the cool waters of the Pacific Northwest. Their sweet, tender meat lends an incredible flavor to this simple Asian-influenced dish, which makes a great appetizer or afternoon snack. Serve this with pasta for something more substantial.

1. Place the clams in a basin of lightly salted cold water to cover by 3 inches and let sit for 30 minutes. Transfer to a colander. If there is any sand on the bottom of the basin, repeat the process as necessary with fresh water until the water is clear.

2. Combine the sake and fermented black bean paste in an 8-quart stockpot. Bring to a boil and add the clams. Stir, cover tightly, and steam over medium-high heat until the clams just open, 5 to 8 minutes, depending upon their size. Remove from the heat.

3. Add the green onions, cilantro, and butter to the clams and stir to combine. Transfer the clams and their cooking liquid to a large serving bowl, discarding any unopened clams. Serve immediately.

Mussels in Lemon Grass Broth

MAKES 4 SERVINGS
AS AN APPETIZER, 2 SERVINGS
AS A MAIN COURSE

2 tablespoons olive oil
½ teaspoon sesame oil
1 tablespoon chopped green onions (green parts only)
1½ teaspoons minced garlic
1½ teaspoons grated ginger
½ teaspoon red pepper flakes
2 pounds mussels, well rinsed in several changes of water, scrubbed, and debearded
1 recipe Lemon Grass Broth
1 cup canned unsweetened coconut milk
½ cup coarsely chopped fresh cilantro

I've been a fanatic for mussels ever since I was a child growing up in New England. The lemon grass broth is exceptional with the mussels, but you can substitute crabmeat or shrimp if mussels are not available. Be sure to have plenty of crusty bread to dip in the excellent Asian-inspired broth.

Combine the olive oil and sesame oil in a medium heavy pot and heat over medium-high heat until smoking hot. Add the green onions, garlic, ginger, and red pepper flakes, stir, and cook for 5 seconds. Add the mussels and stir to coat. Cover and cook for 2 minutes. Add the lemon grass broth, cover, and cook for 1 minute. Add the coconut milk and cilantro, stir well to combine, and cook until the coconut milk is just warmed through, 15 seconds. Remove from the heat and serve immediately.

MAKES 1 CUP

3 cups Shrimp Stock (page 24)
2 kaffir lime leaves or 1 tablespoon finely grated lime zest
¼ cup chopped fresh lemon grass
1 tablespoon chopped shallots
1 tablespoon rice wine vinegar
1 tablespoon sugar
1 teaspoon black peppercorns
½ teaspoon salt

Lemon Grass Broth

1. Combine all the ingredients in a medium heavy pot and bring to a boil. Reduce the heat to medium-low and simmer until reduced to 1 cup, 20 to 25 minutes.

2. Strain the broth through a fine-mesh strainer into a clean container. Use immediately, or cover and refrigerate until ready to use. (The broth can be refrigerated for up to 3 days.)

*½ pound (2 sticks)
  unsalted butter, at
  room temperature*
*¼ cup chopped fresh
  parsley*
*2 tablespoons minced
  garlic*
1 teaspoon salt
*½ teaspoon freshly
  ground white pepper*
*1 cup fine dry bread
  crumbs*
*18 freshly shucked
  oysters, on the half-
  shell, drained*
*3 cups baby lettuces or
  mesclun, well rinsed
  and patted dry*
*1 recipe Lemon Butter
  Sauce (page 30),
  optional*
*1 recipe Fried Leek
  Strips, for garnish*

Garlic-Broiled Oysters on the Half-Shell with Fried Leek Strips

The topping on these oysters is my take on what in New Orleans is called a bordelaise sauce, although it differs substantially from the classic interpretation. The oysters are topped with a garlic-parsley butter made stiff with bread crumbs and then broiled in their half-shells. If you want to kick this up into the stratosphere, do as they do at Delmonico and drizzle the oysters with the Lemon Butter Sauce before serving!

1. Combine the butter, parsley, garlic, salt, pepper, and bread crumbs in a bowl and mix well. Chill slightly in the refrigerator so the butter can easily be molded.

2. Preheat the broiler.

3. Arrange the oysters on a baking sheet. Top each with a heaping tablespoon of the butter mixture. Broil until the oysters are bubbly and the crumbs are golden brown, 3 to 4 minutes. Remove from the broiler.

4. To serve, arrange ½ cup of the lettuce on each of six plates. Arrange 3 oysters on each plate, and, if desired, drizzle 1 heaping tablespoon of the Lemon Butter Sauce on each. Garnish with the fried leek strips. Serve immediately.

Fried Leek Strips

*3 medium leeks (white
  parts only)*
*4 cups vegetable oil, for
  deep-frying*
Salt

1. Cut the leeks into long strips about ⅛ inch wide. Rinse well in at least two changes of water; drain well and pat dry.

2. Heat the oil in a medium, deep heavy pot or deep-fryer to 360°F. Add the leeks, in batches, and fry until golden, about 45 seconds. Remove with a slotted spoon and drain on paper towels. Season with salt and serve.

APPETIZERS AND FIRST COURSES

Poached Oysters in Herbsaint Cream with Black Pepper Crème Fraîche, Beluga Caviar, and Deep-Fried Spinach

1 cup crème fraîche
  (or ½ cup sour cream and
  ½ cup heavy cream, well
  combined)
1¼ teaspoons salt, plus
  more to taste
1 teaspoon freshly ground
  black pepper
36 freshly shucked oysters,
  with their liquor
6 tablespoons unsalted
  butter
¼ cup minced shallots
3 cups heavy cream
1 cup Herbsaint or other
  anise-flavored liqueur,
  such as Pernod or Ricard
1 pound spinach, trimmed,
  rinsed, patted dry, and
  cut into thin strips
4 cups vegetable oil, for
  deep-frying
2 ounces Beluga or Sevruga
  caviar

The Fish House serves not only delicious Louisiana oysters, but, as the seasons change, a bountiful array of oysters from elsewhere. As they come into season, Olympia, Blue Point, Cotuit, Fanny Bay, and many others find their way to our tables.

A quick note about this dish—get ready to be awed. This was modeled on the classic Oysters Rockefeller, but instead of a purely vegetable sauce, ours is made from reduced heavy cream and oyster liquor. The Fish House has introduced many a Las Vegas customer to the intriguing flavor of Herbsaint, a licorice-flavored liqueur long popular in New Orleans.

1. Combine the crème fraîche, ¼ teaspoon of salt, and ½ teaspoon of the pepper in a small bowl and mix well. Transfer to a fine-mesh strainer set over a bowl, refrigerate, and let drain, for up to 2 hours. Transfer to a bowl, cover, and refrigerate until needed.

2. Drain the oysters in a fine-mesh strainer set over a bowl. Reserve 1½ cups of their liquor, and refrigerate the oysters.

3. Melt the butter in a medium pot over medium-high heat. Add the shallots and cook, stirring, for 2 minutes. Add the heavy cream, the 1½ cups oyster liquor, and the Herbsaint and bring to a boil. Add the remaining 1 teaspoon salt and ½ teaspoon black pepper, reduce the heat to medium, and simmer until the liquid is reduced by half, about 10 minutes. Remove from the heat.

4. Add half of the spinach to the pot and purée with an immersion blender, or purée in batches in a blender or food processor. Strain the mixture through a fine-mesh strainer into a large clean sauté pan, and cover to keep warm.

5. Heat the oil in a deep heavy pot or deep-fryer to 350°F. Fry the remaining spinach, in batches, in the hot oil until crispy, about 45 seconds. With a slotted spoon, remove the spinach and drain on paper towels. Season lightly with salt.

6. Add the oysters to the cream sauce, bring to a gentle simmer, and cook just until the edges of the oysters start to curl, about 3 minutes. Remove from the heat.

7. To serve, arrange 6 oysters around the edge of each of six shallow rimmed soup plates. Spoon ½ cup sauce around the oysters in each bowl, spoon a dollop of crème fraîche into the center of the bowl, and top with a teaspoonful of the caviar. Garnish with fried spinach and serve immediately.

Chef Neal Swidler working the line at dinner, Emeril's Delmonico

Fried Oysters with Chili-Corn Sauce and Tomatillo Salsa

MAKES 4 SERVINGS

1 cup masa harina
1 cup yellow cornmeal
3 tablespoons Emeril's Original Essence or Creole Seasoning (page 28)
24 freshly shucked oysters, drained
6 cups vegetable oil, for deep-frying
1 recipe Tomatillo Salsa
1 recipe Chili-Corn Sauce

Since the Tomatillo Salsa needs to rest for 30 minutes, make it first, then proceed with the rest of the recipe.

This was one of the first lunch dishes created at Emeril's New Orleans. In the late '80s and early '90s, I became a huge fan of the ingredients and techniques of Southwestern cuisine. This combination really worked wonderfully as a marriage of New Orleans' fried oysters with a Southwestern masa harina coating, along with the chili-corn sauce and brightly flavored tomatillo salsa.

1. Combine the masa harina, cornmeal, and 2 tablespoons of the Essence in a large bowl. Add the oysters, several at a time, and toss to coat; shake to remove any excess breading.

2. Heat the oil in a medium heavy pot or deep-fryer to 360°F. Add the oysters, in batches, and deep-fry until golden, stirring so they cook evenly, 2 to 3 minutes. Remove and drain on paper towels. Season with the remaining tablespoon of Essence.

3. To serve, spoon the salsa and sauce onto the center of four plates. Arrange the oysters around the sauces, and serve immediately.

Tomatillo Salsa

Combine all the ingredients in a small bowl. Cover and chill for 30 minutes before serving.

4 tomatillos (about
    8 ounces), husked,
    rinsed, and chopped
1 tablespoon plus
    ½ teaspoon fresh
    lime juice
2 tablespoons chopped
    red onions
1 tablespoon extra-virgin
    olive oil
1 teaspoon minced,
    seeded jalapeños
¼ teaspoon salt
¼ teaspoon freshly
    ground black pepper

Chili-Corn Sauce

1. Melt the butter in a large nonstick skillet over high heat. Add the corn and cook, stirring occasionally, until it is deep golden brown and beginning to pop, 4 to 5 minutes. Reduce the heat to medium-high, add the shallots and garlic, and cook, stirring, for 1 minute. Add the syrup, lime juice, and chili powder, and cook for 1 minute. Add the chicken stock, salt, and pepper and cook until most of the stock has evaporated, about 2 minutes.

2. Add the heavy cream and cook until thickened enough to coat the back of a spoon, about 5 minutes. Remove from the heat, add the cilantro, and stir well. Cover to keep warm until ready to serve.

1 tablespoon unsalted
    butter
1 cup corn kernels
2 teaspoons minced
    shallots
¾ teaspoon minced
    garlic
1 tablespoon Steen's
    100% Pure Cane Syrup
    (See Source Guide,
    page 333)
2¼ teaspoons fresh lime
    juice
½ teaspoon chili powder
¼ cup Rich Chicken
    Stock (page 21)
½ teaspoon salt
¼ teaspoon freshly
    ground white pepper
1 cup heavy cream
2 teaspoons chopped
    fresh cilantro

APPETIZERS AND FIRST COURSES

NOLA

1 large Idaho potato (about
     12 ounces), scrubbed
6 cups vegetable oil, for
     deep-frying
1 cup masa harina
1 cup yellow cornmeal
1 tablespoon plus
     1 teaspoon Emeril's
     Original Essence or Creole
     Seasoning (page 28)
1¼ teaspoons salt
1 pint freshly shucked
     oysters (about 20),
     drained
½ pound baby spinach,
     tough stems removed,
     rinsed and patted dry
¼ teaspoon freshly ground
     black pepper
1 recipe Warm Bacon
     Dressing
One 14-ounce can hearts of
     palm, drained and cut on
     the bias into ¼-inch-thick
     slices
2 hard-boiled eggs (page
     17), peeled and thinly
     sliced

Cornmeal-Crusted Oysters with Baby Spinach, Warm Bacon Dressing, and Homemade Potato Chips

Take your basic spinach salad wilted with hot bacon dressing, and then kick it up with crunchy, fried oysters. What else can I say?!

1. With a mandoline or sharp heavy knife, slice the potato into rounds as thinly as possible. Rinse in several changes of water until the water runs clear. Soak in cold water until ready to cook.

2. Heat the vegetable oil in a medium heavy pot or deep-fryer to 360°F. Drain the potatoes and pat dry. Add to the hot oil, in batches, and cook, turning once with a long-handled spoon, until golden and crisp, 45 seconds to 1 minute. Transfer to paper towels to drain. Keep the oil hot.

3. Combine the masa harina, cornmeal, 1 tablespoon of the Essence, and 1 teaspoon of the salt in a medium bowl and stir to mix. Add the oysters and toss to coat evenly, then shake to remove any excess breading. Add to the oil, in batches, and cook until golden brown, 2 to 3 minutes. Remove with a slotted spoon and drain on paper towels. Season with the remaining teaspoon of Essence.

4. Place the spinach in a large bowl and toss with the remaining ¼ teaspoon salt and the pepper. Add about ¼ cup of the warm dressing and toss well.

5. Divide the spinach among four large salad plates. Garnish each with the hearts of palm and hard-boiled eggs, and place the potato chips in the center of the salads. Arrange the oysters around the edges of the plates and drizzle with the remaining dressing. Serve immediately.

Warm Bacon Dressing

3 slices bacon, chopped
½ teaspoon chopped
*   garlic*
2 teaspoons Dijon
*   mustard*
1½ teaspoons tomato
*   paste*
¼ cup red wine vinegar
¼ cup sugar
½ cup canola oil
¼ teaspoon salt
¼ teaspoon freshly
*   ground black pepper*

1. Cook the bacon in a medium skillet over medium-high heat until it begins to brown, about 4 minutes. Add the garlic and cook, stirring, for 30 seconds. Add the mustard, tomato paste, vinegar, and sugar and cook, stirring, until the sugar is dissolved, about 1 minute.

2. Transfer to a food processor or blender and purée. With the machine running, slowly add the oil in a steady stream and process until thick. Add the salt and pepper, and pulse once or twice to blend. Serve warm.

Emeril's ORLANDO

Napa Cabbage Beggars' Purses Stuffed with Wild Mushroom– Celery Root Duxelles, Sun-Dried Tomato and Lentil Ragout, and Celery Root Threads

MAKES 4 SERVINGS

1 teaspoon salt
4 large Napa cabbage leaves
4 green onions
Salt and freshly ground black
    pepper
1 recipe Wild Mushroom–
    Celery Root Duxelles
4 cups vegetable oil, for
    deep-frying
½ pound celery root, thinly
    sliced
1 recipe Sun-Dried Tomato
    and Lentil Ragout

Beggars' purses are usually small crepes stuffed with an expensive item, such as caviar or lump crabmeat. This dish takes the idea another step by stuffing Napa cabbage leaves with a full-flavored wild mushroom and celery root mixture. When Chef Bernard conceived this dish, he put it on the menu as a hearty vegetarian main course, but I think it makes an excellent starter.

1. Preheat the oven to 350°F.

2. Combine 2 quarts water and the salt in a medium pot and bring to a boil. Blanch the cabbage leaves until soft, 3 to 4 minutes. Transfer to an ice bath to cool for 30 seconds, then drain on paper towels. Add the green onions to the water and blanch until softened, about 30 seconds. Transfer to an ice bath to cool for 30 seconds, then drain on paper towels. Trim the root ends from the onions.

3. Place 1 cabbage leaf on a work surface and sprinkle lightly with salt and pepper. Spoon ½ cup of the duxelles onto the center of the leaf. Fold the bottom of the leaf over, then fold over the sides, roll up, and tie with a blanched green onion. Place on a baking sheet. Repeat with the remaining leaves and duxelles and put in the oven to heat.

4. Heat the vegetable oil in a deep saucepan over high heat to 350°F. Add the celery root, in batches, and fry until crisp and golden. Transfer to paper towels to drain.

5. To serve, spoon about ⅓ cup of the ragout onto each of four serving plates. Place the cabbage purses in the center of the sauce and garnish with the fried celery root. Serve immediately.

Wild Mushroom–Celery Root Duxelles

*½ pound shiitake
mushrooms, stems
removed, wiped clean,
and coarsely chopped*

*½ pound oyster mushrooms,
stems trimmed, wiped
clean, and coarsely
chopped*

*½ pound button
mushrooms, stems
trimmed, wiped clean,
and coarsely chopped*

*¼ pound celery root,
coarsely chopped*

¼ cup chopped shallots

2 tablespoons chopped garlic

2 tablespoons unsalted butter

2 tablespoons olive oil

¼ cup dry sherry

½ teaspoon salt

*¼ teaspoon freshly ground
white pepper*

¼ cup chopped fresh parsley

1. Combine the mushrooms, celery root, shallots, and garlic in a food processor, in batches if necessary, and finely chop.

2. Melt the butter with the oil in a large skillet over medium-high heat. Add the mushroom mixture and cook, stirring, for 2 minutes. Reduce the heat to medium and cook, stirring occasionally, until the mixture becomes a thick paste, 25 to 30 minutes.

3. Add the sherry, salt, and pepper, stir well, and cook for 5 minutes, stirring occasionally. Remove from the heat, add the parsley, and stir well. Let cool. (The duxelles can be made 1 day in advance and refrigerated in an airtight container.)

Sun-Dried Tomato and Lentil Ragout

3 tablespoons olive oil

½ cup chopped yellow onions

½ cup chopped carrots

½ cup chopped celery

1 teaspoon minced garlic

*½ pound brown lentils,
rinsed and picked over*

*3½ cups Vegetable Stock
(page 27)*

½ teaspoon salt

*¼ teaspoon freshly ground
black pepper*

*¾ cup oil-packed sun-dried
tomatoes, drained and
coarsely chopped*

½ cup chopped fresh parsley

1. Heat the oil in a medium saucepan over medium-high heat. Add the onions, carrots, and celery and cook, stirring, until soft, about 3 minutes. Add the garlic and cook, stirring, for 1 minute. Add the lentils, vegetable stock, salt, and pepper and bring to a boil. Reduce the heat to low and simmer, uncovered, until the lentils are just tender, about 18 minutes. Remove from the heat.

2. Add the tomatoes, stir well, and let stand for 10 minutes. Stir in the parsley. Serve warm.

APPETIZERS AND FIRST COURSES

20 egg roll wrappers, about
    4 inches square
1 recipe Wonton Filling
½ cup Kimchee (page 113)
4 ounces mung bean sprouts
1 bunch fresh cilantro,
    stemmed
4 cups vegetable oil, for
    deep-frying
1 recipe Dipping Sauce

Firecracker-Roll Wontons with Dipping Sauce

As a big fan of Asian flavors, I put these on the menu at my restaurant Tchoup Chop (in Orlando). While kimchee normally is served as a side dish, I take a bit and roll it up right into the wontons to add a nice crunch and a bit of a kick.

1. Lay 1 wrapper on a work surface, with one of the points facing you. Place about 1½ tablespoons of the wonton filling in the center of the wrapper, top with a heaping teaspoon of kimchee and several bean sprouts, and arrange several cilantro leaves on the top corner of the wrapper. Moisten the edges with water, fold the bottom corner up over the filling to enclose, fold the left and right corners over, and roll up into a cylinder. Set aside, seam side down, and repeat with the remaining wrappers and filling ingredients.

2. Heat the oil to 350°F in a medium heavy pot or deep-fryer. Carefully add the wontons to the oil, in batches, and fry until golden brown, about 3 minutes; press down on the wontons with a flat spatula as they cook to ensure even browning. Remove and drain on paper towels. Serve hot, with the dipping sauce.

Working the line at Emeril's New Orleans

¼ *cup dried wood ear*
  mushrooms
½ *pound ground pork*
1 *teaspoon Emeril's*
  Original Essence or
  Creole Seasoning
  (page 28)
½ *pound shrimp, peeled,*
  deveined, and
  coarsely chopped
1 *teaspoon vegetable oil*
1 *teaspoon minced garlic*
1 *teaspoon minced*
  ginger
¼ *teaspoon red pepper*
  flakes
¼ *cup Rich Chicken*
  Stock (page 21)
1 *tablespoon oyster*
  sauce (see Note)
1 *tablespoon soy sauce*
2 *teaspoons sugar*
2 *teaspoons cornstarch*
2 *tablespoons water*
¼ *cup minced green*
  onions (green parts
  only)

Wonton Filling

1. Place the mushrooms in a bowl of warm water and soak until soft, about 20 minutes. Drain, pat dry, and thinly slice.

2. Combine the pork with ½ teaspoon of the Essence in a bowl. Combine the shrimp with the remaining ½ teaspoon Essence in another bowl.

3. Heat the oil in a large skillet until almost smoking hot. Add the garlic, ginger, and red pepper and cook for 5 seconds. Add the pork and shrimp and cook, stirring, until cooked through, about 4 minutes. Add the chicken stock, oyster sauce, soy sauce, sugar, and sliced mushrooms, bring to a boil, and cook for 5 minutes.

4. Dissolve the cornstarch in the water, stirring until smooth. Add to the pan, stir to combine, and simmer until the mixture thickens. Stir in the green onions and remove from the heat. Let cool.

Note: *Oyster sauce can be found in Asian markets and many supermarkets.*

½ *cup rice wine vinegar*
¼ *cup sugar*
1 *tablespoon soy sauce*
1 *tablespoon minced*
  green onions (green
  parts only)
1 *teaspoon minced garlic*
½ *teaspoon red pepper*
  flakes

Dipping Sauce

Combine all the ingredients in a small bowl and whisk to dissolve the sugar. Serve at room temperature.

APPETIZERS AND FIRST COURSES

Home-Smoked Salmon Cheesecake with Sweet Onion and Mirliton Slaw, Creamy Ravigote, and Marinated Black Beans

MAKES ONE 10-INCH CHEESECAKE;
ABOUT 12 SERVINGS

1 cup fine dry bread crumbs
¾ cup freshly grated
    Parmigiano-Reggiano
4 tablespoons unsalted
    butter, melted
1 tablespoon olive oil
1 cup finely chopped yellow
    onions
½ cup finely chopped red
    bell peppers
½ cup finely chopped yellow
    bell peppers
1 tablespoon salt
1¾ teaspoons freshly
    ground white pepper
2 tablespoons minced
    shallots
1 tablespoon minced garlic
2 pounds cream cheese, at
    room temperature
6 large eggs
1 cup heavy cream
¾ cup grated smoked
    Gouda
½ cup thinly sliced green
    onions (green
    parts only)
½ teaspoon Emeril's Kick It
    Up Red Pepper
    Sauce or other
    hot pepper sauce
1 tablespoon Worcestershire
    sauce
¼ teaspoon cayenne

This recipe requires home-smoked salmon, which is hot-smoked, rather than the salty cold-smoked salmon you normally see. Home-smoking salmon is very easy with a stovetop smoker, but hot-smoked salmon also can be found in some gourmet food stores and through the Internet.

1. Preheat the oven to 350°F.

2. Combine the bread crumbs, Parmesan, and melted butter in a medium bowl and mix well. Firmly press the mixture into the bottom and 1 inch up the sides of a 10-inch springform pan.

3. Heat the olive oil in a large skillet over medium-high heat. Add the onions, red and yellow bell peppers, ½ teaspoon of the salt, and ¾ teaspoon of the white pepper and cook, stirring, until soft, about 4 minutes. Add the shallots and garlic and cook, stirring, until fragrant, about 1 minute. Remove from the heat and let cool.

4. With an electric mixer, beat the cream cheese in a large bowl until smooth. Add the eggs one at a time, beating well after each addition. Add the cream, Gouda, green onions, pepper sauce, Worcestershire, the remaining 2½ teaspoons salt and 1 teaspoon white pepper, the cayenne, and parsley, and mix well. With a rubber spatula, fold in the cooled vegetable mixture and the salmon. Pour the mixture into the prepared springform pan. Bake until the cheesecake is golden brown on top and the center appears nearly set when shaken yet is still slightly loose, about 1½ hours. Remove from the oven and let cool for 15 minutes.

5. Run a small sharp knife around the cake and the sides of the pan, being careful not to cut into the crust, and release the

¼ cup minced fresh
  parsley
1 pound Home-Smoked
  Salmon (page 19),
  flaked
1 recipe Creamy Ravigote
1 recipe Marinated Black
  Beans
1 recipe Sweet Onion
  and Mirliton Slaw

sides of the pan (but do not remove). Let cool at room tempera-ture for 30 minutes, then cover tightly with aluminum foil and refrigerate until well chilled, at least 4 hours, or overnight.

6. Remove the sides of the pan and using a thin, sharp knife dipped in hot water, slice the cheesecake into 12 portions. Spoon a heaping 2 tablespoons of the ravigote into the center of each of twelve plates and place a slice of cheesecake on top. Garnish with the black beans and slaw, and serve.

*Scott Farber (left), Las Vegas
director of operations, at
Emeril's New Orleans
Fish House*

½ teaspoon Dijon mustard
1 large egg
1 tablespoon fresh lemon
    juice
1 cup vegetable oil
1 large hard-boiled egg
    (page 17), peeled
1 tablespoon minced red
    onions
1 tablespoon capers, drained
    and coarsely chopped
1½ teaspoons chopped
    fresh parsley
½ teaspoon chopped fresh
    tarragon
⅜ teaspoon salt
⅛ teaspoon freshly ground
    white pepper

Creamy Ravigote

Serving this rich sauce with the already-rich Home-Smoked Salmon Cheesecake may seem like gilding the lily. However, you'll find that it's an inspired combination that also nicely plays off the Sweet Onion and Mirliton Slaw and the Marinated Black Beans. Go ahead and indulge! This also makes a terrific dip or sauce for vegetables, such as steamed artichokes, and would pair beautifully with lump crabmeat or boiled shrimp in a cold seafood salad.

1. Combine the mustard, egg, and lemon juice in a food processor and process to blend. With the machine running, add the oil in a thin stream, processing until the mixture thickens. Transfer to a bowl.

2. Using a spoon, force the hard-boiled egg through a coarse sieve into the bowl. Fold in the remaining ingredients. Cover and refrigerate until ready to serve. (The sauce keeps refrigerated for up to 1 day.)

Seafood bar at Emeril's New Orleans Fish House

Marinated Black Beans

2 slices bacon, chopped
¼ cup finely chopped
yellow onions
2 teaspoons minced garlic
1 bay leaf
1 cup dried black beans,
rinsed, picked over,
and drained (or 2 cups
cooked beans, rinsed
if canned)
3 cups water
1½ cups finely chopped
seeded ripe tomatoes
1 cup finely chopped red
bell peppers
½ cup finely chopped
yellow bell peppers
½ cup fresh orange juice
¼ cup fresh lemon juice
¼ cup fresh lime juice
½ cup minced fresh
cilantro
¼ cup finely chopped red
onions
½ cup olive oil
¾ teaspoon salt
¼ teaspoon freshly
ground black pepper

1. Cook the bacon in a medium saucepan over medium-high heat, stirring, until golden brown, about 4 minutes. Add the yellow onions and cook, stirring, for 1 minute. Add the garlic and bay leaf and cook, stirring, for 30 seconds. Add the black beans and water and bring to a boil. Reduce the heat to medium-low and simmer, uncovered, stirring occasionally, until the beans are tender but still firm, about 50 minutes. Remove from the heat.

2. Combine the remaining ingredients in a large bowl. Add the cooked beans and stir well to mix. Cover and refrigerate for at least 3 hours before serving. (The beans can be prepared up to 1 day in advance. Remove the bay leaf before serving.)

Delmonico Steakhouse piano bar

Sweet Onion and Mirliton Slaw

1 mirliton (about 12 ounces)
*1 cup thinly sliced sweet
    onions, such as Maui,
    Walla Walla, or Vidalia*
*1 tablespoon plus 1
    teaspoon fresh lemon
    juice*
*1 tablespoon extra-virgin
    olive oil*
*2 teaspoons rice wine
    vinegar*
1 teaspoon sugar
½ teaspoon salt
*1 teaspoon chopped fresh
    parsley*
*½ teaspoon chopped fresh
    thyme leaves*

Make this slaw just before you're ready to serve it so that the mirliton and onions remain crisp. Mirlitons, also known as chayotes, vegetable pears, christophines, or cho-chos, grow on a vine and are very popular in the South, especially in Louisiana. They have a prickly outer skin and soft flesh surrounding a large flat seed. To get at the edible flesh and remove the tough skin and seed, they must be parboiled. But believe me, the little bit of effort required is definitely worth it.

1. Bring a medium saucepan of water to a boil over high heat. Add the mirliton, lower the heat, and simmer until tender, 30 to 40 minutes.

2. Drain, and let sit until cool enough to handle. Peel, seed, and thinly slice lengthwise.

3. Combine the mirliton and onions in a bowl.

4. Combine the lemon juice, oil, vinegar, sugar, and salt in a large bowl and whisk to dissolve the sugar and salt. Add the onion-mirliton mixture, the parsley, and thyme, and toss to coat evenly. Serve immediately.

Emeril's Hawaiian-Style Poke

½ cup crunchy peanut butter

½ cup canned unsweetened coconut milk

1 tablespoon soy sauce

2 teaspoons fresh lime juice

2 teaspoons Emeril's Kick It Up Red Pepper Sauce or other hot pepper sauce

1 teaspoon sesame oil

¼ cup minced red onions

¼ cup minced green onions (green parts only)

2 teaspoons minced garlic

1 pound sushi-grade yellowfin tuna, cut into large dice

¾ cup Ogo seaweed, rinsed and chopped (see Source Guide, page 333)

1 tablespoon plus 2 teaspoons chopped roasted peanuts

Poke ("POE-kay") is a traditional Hawaiian dish much like the seviche found in Central and South America. I learned to be a big fan of poke from my friend Sam Choy, who has several restaurants on the islands. Here's my take on the dish, which would make Sam proud!

1. Combine the peanut butter, coconut milk, soy sauce, lime juice, hot sauce, and sesame oil in a food processor and process until well blended. Add the red onions, green onions, and garlic and process until smooth.

2. Place the tuna in a large bowl and toss with the peanut butter dressing. Divide among small plates, top each portion with chopped seaweed and chopped peanuts, and serve immediately.

Fish carved tableside, Emeril's New Orleans Fish House

APPETIZERS AND FIRST COURSES

Savory Pies of Roasted Duck, Foie Gras, and Root Vegetables

MAKES 6 SERVINGS

¾ *pound Grade A duck foie gras (see Source Guide, page 333), veins removed*

2 *teaspoons salt*

1 *teaspoon freshly ground white pepper*

2 *tablespoons unsalted butter*

3 *tablespoons finely chopped shallots*

½ *cup plus 1 tablespoon all-purpose flour*

¼ *cup Cognac or brandy*

½ *cup ruby Port*

4 *cups Rich Chicken Stock (page 21)*

1 *cup shredded Roast Duck meat (page 17)*

½ *cup carrots cut into medium dice*

½ *cup parsnips cut into medium dice*

½ *cup turnips cut into medium dice*

½ *teaspoon dried thyme*

2 *bay leaves*

½ *teaspoon freshly ground black pepper*

1 *large egg, beaten with 1 tablespoon water for egg wash*

1 *recipe Flaky Butter Crust (page 36)*

½ *teaspoon sugar*

3 *tablespoons fig preserves*

Here's the ultimate winter first course. The elegant presentation and rich foie gras belie the comforting heartiness of this dish on a cold night. If you prefer, make a large pie instead, like the meat pies popular in England and bake 20 to 25 minutes, but be forewarned that serving it will be a little messy.

1. Cut half of the foie gras into ½-inch cubes. Place in a small bowl and season with ½ teaspoon of the salt and the white pepper. Cut the remaining foie gras into 6 slices about ¼ inch thick, and refrigerate until ready to use.

2. Heat a medium heavy saucepan over medium-high heat. Add the cubed foie gras and cook, stirring, until golden brown and the fat is rendered, about 3 minutes. Transfer with a slotted spoon to a plate.

3. Melt the butter in the fat remaining in the pan. Reduce the heat to medium-low, add the shallots, and cook, stirring, just until wilted, about 1 minute. Add the flour, whisking to blend it into the fat, and cook, stirring constantly with a wooden spoon, to make a thick golden-brown roux the texture of wet sand, about 5 minutes. Add the Cognac and cook, stirring, for 30 seconds. Add the Port and cook, stirring, for 1 minute. Add the stock, the duck meat, carrots, parsnips, turnips, thyme, bay leaves, 1 teaspoon salt, and the black pepper, stir well to mix, and bring to a boil. Reduce the heat to medium-low and simmer, uncovered, until the vegetables are tender, about 40 minutes.

4. Remove from the heat and remove the bay leaves. Let cool for 1 hour, stirring gently every 10 minutes to prevent a film from forming on the top.

5. Preheat the oven to 400°F.

6. Add the sautéed foie gras to the duck mixture and stir to mix. Divide the mixture among six 8-ounce ramekins.

7. Roll out the pastry on a lightly floured surface to about ⅛ inch thick. Using a small plate or ring mold as a guide, cut out six 4½-inch circles. Paint the egg wash around the rims of the ramekins and place the pastry rounds on top, pressing down to seal. With a fork, crimp the edges to seal the pastry. Brush the pastry with the egg wash and, with a small knife, cut 8 small slits in a circular pattern in the top of each. Place the ramekins on a baking sheet and bake until the pastry is golden brown, 15 to 20 minutes. Remove from the oven and let rest for 5 minutes.

8. Season both sides of the reserved foie gras with the remaining ½ teaspoon each salt and white pepper, and the sugar. Heat a large skillet over medium-high heat. Add the foie gras slices and sear until golden brown, about 1 minute per side. Remove with a spatula and lay one slice on top of each savory pie. Top each slice with 1½ teaspoons of the fig preserves. Place the ramekins on 6 serving plates and serve immediately.

Chef Bernard Carmouche (right) in Emeril's Orlando kitchen

Brandied Duck Liver Mousse with Creole Mustard Sauce and Red Onion Confiture

MAKES 5 CUPS;
ABOUT 12 SERVINGS

1½ pounds duck livers (see
    Source Guide, page 333),
    cleaned, rinsed, and
    patted dry
1 cup whole milk
1 tablespoon plus 1
    teaspoon vegetable oil
1 cup chopped yellow onions
1½ teaspoons dried thyme
4 bay leaves
1½ teaspoons salt
½ teaspoon freshly ground
    white pepper
¼ cup brandy
12 ounces cream cheese, at
    room temperature
¾ pound (3 sticks) unsalted
    butter, at room
    temperature
1 recipe Creole Mustard
    Sauce
1 recipe Red Onion Confiture
1 recipe Large Croutons
    (page 33)

Instead of molding it into a terrine, the mousse can be served in individual small ramekins, or in a large bowl as a spread for croutons or crackers. Beware of making the servings too large, however; this is very rich!

1. Put the livers in a bowl and add the milk, to cover. Cover and refrigerate for at least 8 hours, or overnight. Drain well; pat dry.

2. Heat the oil in a large heavy skillet over medium-high heat. Add the livers, onions, thyme, bay leaves, 1 teaspoon of the salt, and the white pepper. Cook, stirring occasionally, until the livers are just slightly pink and the onions are soft, about 5 minutes. Carefully add the brandy and cook until the liquid has evaporated and the livers are cooked through but still tender, 2 to 3 minutes. Remove from the heat and spread on a large plate to cool. Discard the bay leaves.

3. Transfer the liver mixture to a food processor, add the cream cheese and butter, and process until smooth. Add the remaining ½ teaspoon salt and pulse to blend.

4. Line an 8½ × 4½ × 3-inch loaf pan with plastic wrap, leaving an overhang of several inches on each side. Spoon the mixture into the terrine, smoothing the top with a rubber spatula. Wrap with the overhanging wrap and chill until firm, at least 8 hours.

5. To serve, peel back the plastic wrap and lift the mousse from the mold. Invert onto a cutting board and remove the wrap. With a sharp knife dipped in hot water, cut into slices about ½ inch thick. Place 1 slice on each plate and garnish with a tablespoonful each of the mustard sauce and confiture. Serve with the croutons.

1 large egg yolk
1½ teaspoons soy sauce
1½ teaspoons Creole
    mustard or other
    whole-grain mustard
1½ teaspoons
    Worcestershire sauce
⅛ teaspoon salt
¼ teaspoon freshly
    ground black pepper
¾ cup vegetable oil

Creole Mustard Sauce

1. Combine the egg yolk, soy sauce, mustard, Worcestershire, salt, and pepper in a food processor or blender and process for 20 seconds. With the machine running, add the oil in a steady stream, and process until the sauce is smooth and thick. Adjust the seasoning to taste.

2. Place in an airtight container and refrigerate until ready to serve, or for up to 1 day.

2½ cups rice wine
    vinegar
½ cup sugar
1 tablespoon kosher salt
1 tablespoon coarsely
    ground black pepper
2 cups thinly sliced red
    onions

Red Onion Confiture

The confiture also would be good served with a charcuterie dish or roast pork. Or use this and a little blue cheese to kick up your next hamburger!

1. Combine the vinegar, sugar, salt, and pepper in a medium saucepan. Bring to a boil, and add the onions. Cook, stirring, until the onions turn a bright purple pink color and begin to become translucent, 2½ to 3 minutes. Remove from the heat and drain in a fine-mesh strainer set over a bowl. Reserve ¼ cup of the cooking liquid.

2. Combine the onions and reserved liquid in a bowl and toss to mix. Refrigerate until chilled, at least 3 hours. (The confiture can be refrigerated in an airtight container for up to 1 week.)

APPETIZERS AND FIRST COURSES

Garlic Escargot with Goat Cheese, Fennel, and Bacon-Stuffed Mushrooms

MAKES 6 SERVINGS

18 large button or cremini mushroom caps, about 2 inches in diameter, wiped clean

4 slices bacon, chopped

¼ cup finely chopped fennel

¼ cup finely chopped yellow onions

4 ounces goat cheese, crumbled

1 tablespoon fine dry bread crumbs

½ teaspoon minced garlic

½ teaspoon minced fresh thyme

¼ teaspoon salt

⅛ teaspoon freshly ground black pepper

Three 7-ounce cans snails, rinsed well under cold running water and drained

1 recipe Garlic Butter

1 loaf French bread, sliced

Don't be afraid to prepare snails at home. They are readily available, precooked and canned, at supermarkets and gourmet food stores. Simply rinse and drain them well before using. This impressive, full-flavored first course never fails to generate oohs and aahs at Delmonico!

Make extra garlic butter to use with other dishes. Place a dollop on steaks, other meats, or chicken before serving, or use it to kick up boiled or roasted potatoes or vegetables. It keeps well in the freezer, tightly wrapped, for up to 1 month.

1. Preheat the oven to 400°F.

2. Arrange the mushrooms stem side up on a baking sheet and roast for 5 minutes. Turn and continue roasting until tender, about 5 minutes longer. Remove from the oven and let cool. Leave the oven on.

3. Cook the bacon in a medium skillet over medium-high heat until golden brown and crisp, about 6 minutes. Remove and drain on paper towels. Discard all but 1 tablespoon of fat from the pan. Add the fennel and onions and cook, stirring, until soft, about 4 minutes. Remove from the heat and spread on a plate to cool.

4. Combine the goat cheese, bread crumbs, garlic, thyme, salt, and pepper in a bowl. Add the fennel-onion mixture and bacon and mix well.

5. Place six medium round baking dishes on a baking sheet. Place 3 mushroom caps, stem side up, in each baking dish. Place 1 snail inside each mushroom and 3 snails in each dish between the mushrooms. Top each mushroom cap with about 2 teaspoons of the goat cheese mixture. Cut the garlic butter log into thin slices, about 1½ teaspoons each, and lay the slices over the snails and mushrooms to cover.

6. Bake the snails until bubbly, 8 to 10 minutes. Turn the oven to broil and cook until the goat cheese begins to turn golden brown around the edges, 1 to 2 minutes.

7. Serve immediately, with hot French bread for dipping.

Garlic Butter

*½ pound (2 sticks)
   unsalted butter, at
   room temperature
1 tablespoon plus
   1 teaspoon minced
   garlic
1 teaspoon fresh lemon
   juice
¼ teaspoon salt
¼ teaspoon freshly
   ground black pepper
⅛ teaspoon cayenne
2 tablespoons chopped
   fresh parsley*

1. Combine the butter, garlic, lemon juice, salt, pepper, and cayenne in a food processor and process for 30 seconds. Transfer to a bowl and fold in the parsley. (Alternately, place the butter in a medium bowl and cream with a wooden spoon or rubber spatula. Add the remaining ingredients and mix well.)

2. Spoon the butter mixture into the center of a large sheet of plastic wrap or wax paper, forming a log about 1 inch in diameter. Fold the wrap over the butter and gently push in and under to form a smooth cylinder. Twist the ends to seal. Refrigerate until firm, about 1 hour. (Refrigerate for up to 1 week or freeze for up to 1 month.)

*Chef Christian Czerwonka
in the meat-aging room at
Delmonico Steakhouse*

Emeril's

NEW ORLEANS FISH HOUSE

Gumbo of the day
Beef Chicken & Sausage

Soup of the day
Three Bean & Vegetable
Lobster Bisque
Clam Chowder

Grilled Fish of the day - Mahi Mah
Chilled Maine Lobster $49.00

3 | SOUPS, GUMBOS, AND CHOWDERS

Specials board, Emeril's New Orleans Fish House

French Onion Soup with Homemade English Muffins and Swiss Cheese

MAKES 2 QUARTS; 8 SERVINGS

1 tablespoon olive or vegetable oil

3 pounds yellow onions, julienned

1/3 cup Early Times or other bourbon

2 quarts Reduced Veal Stock (page 25) or canned low-sodium beef broth

4 cups Rich Chicken Stock (page 21) or canned low-sodium chicken broth

1 tablespoon plus 1 teaspoon fresh lemon juice

1 1/2 teaspoons salt

1 teaspoon freshly ground white pepper

1 teaspoon Emeril's Kick It Up Red Pepper Sauce or other hot pepper sauce

1/2 teaspoon Worcestershire sauce

1 recipe Homemade English Muffins

2 cups grated Swiss cheese

What could be more filling than French onion soup on a chilly day? This one certainly fills the bill. The homemade English muffins are our personal touch with this kicked-up classic. Bon appétit!

1. Heat the oil in a Dutch oven or other large heavy pot over medium-high heat. Add half the onions, reduce the heat to medium, and cook, stirring, until dark golden brown and caramelized, about 15 minutes. Add the remaining onions and cook, stirring frequently with a heavy wooden spoon, until a deep caramel color, about 1 hour. Add the bourbon and cook, stirring occasionally, until it has evaporated, about 5 minutes. Add the remaining ingredients except the muffins and cheese and stir well. Reduce the heat to medium-low and simmer uncovered, stirring occasionally, until thick and fragrant, about 1 hour. Remove from the heat and cover to keep warm.

2. Preheat the broiler. Split the English muffins and lightly toast. Place on a baking sheet and top each with 2 tablespoons of the cheese. Broil until the cheese is melted and bubbly, about 1 minute. Remove from the broiler. Arrange the muffin halves in soup bowls and ladle the soup into the bowls. Serve hot.

1 teaspoon vegetable oil
1¼ cups water, at room temperature
One ¼-ounce envelope (2¼ teaspoons) active dry yeast
½ teaspoon sugar
3½ cups bread flour, or more if needed
2 teaspoons salt
3 tablespoons nonfat dry milk
2 teaspoons solid vegetable shortening
¼ cup yellow cornmeal

Homemade English Muffins

You're not going to believe how easy these muffins are to make! Or how delicious! Once you make them, you'll never want to eat store-bought again. Believe it or not, these are cooked in a skillet on top of the stove—just 5 minutes per side—pressing down on them as you cook the second side to flatten them into that familiar shape. Making the dough is a cinch too. At the Steakhouse, they serve these with the French Onion Soup, but they'd also be terrific toasted for breakfast or as a snack.

1. Lightly grease a large bowl with the oil, and set aside.

2. Combine the water, yeast, and sugar in a large bowl, stir well, and let sit until foamy, about 5 minutes. Add the remaining ingredients except the cornmeal and mix with a large wooden spoon until well blended, about 3 minutes. Turn the dough out onto a lightly floured surface, and knead for 15 minutes, or until smooth, adding more flour 1 teaspoon at a time if the dough is too sticky. Place in the prepared bowl, cover with plastic wrap, and set aside in a warm, draft-free place until doubled in size, 1½ to 2 hours.

3. Dust a baking sheet with the cornmeal.

4. Turn the dough out onto a lightly floured surface and divide into 8 equal portions. Roll into smooth balls and place evenly spaced on the prepared baking sheet. Cover with a slightly damp kitchen cloth and let rise until doubled in size, about 30 minutes.

5. Heat a large skillet over medium heat. Add the dough balls, non-cornmeal-coated side first, in batches, and cook until golden brown on the bottom, about 5 minutes. Turn the muffins over, press down on them with a large spatula to flatten slightly, and cook until golden brown on the second side, about 5 minutes longer.

SOUPS, GUMBOS, AND CHOWDERS

NOLA

1 cup vegetable oil
1½ cups all-purpose flour
2 cups chopped yellow
    onions
1 cup chopped green bell
    peppers
1 cup chopped celery
3 tablespoons Emeril's
    Original Essence or Creole
    Seasoning (page 28)
2 tablespoons
    Worcestershire sauce
2 tablespoons Emeril's Kick
    It Up Red Pepper Sauce or
    other hot pepper sauce
¾ cup dry sherry, plus more
    for serving
1 pound ground turtle meat
2 quarts Rich Chicken Stock
    (page 21)
4 cups Reduced Veal Stock
    (page 25)
1½ cups chopped green
    onions (green parts only)
1 tablespoon minced garlic
1 tablespoon tomato paste
3 bay leaves
1 cup peeled, seeded, and
    chopped tomatoes
6 large hard-boiled eggs
    (page 17), peeled and
    coarsely grated
2 teaspoons salt
1 teaspoon freshly ground
    black pepper
1 tablespoon fresh lemon
    juice
½ cup chopped spinach

Turtle Soup with Sherry

A lot of people out there say you can substitute other types of meat for turtle, but we don't agree. In order to get the complex, rich, smoky flavor, you really have to use ground turtle meat to make this soup. See the Source Guide (page 333) for ordering information.

At NOLA, we also use the traditional sherry and grated hard-boiled egg garnishes, which contribute great flavors to the dish. This soup will be even better if made a day in advance; refrigerate it and allow the flavors to marry overnight. Simply reheat to serve.

1. Heat ¾ cup of the oil in a Dutch oven or other large heavy pot over medium-high heat until very hot but not smoking. Reduce the heat to medium-low and add the flour ½ cup at a time, whisking constantly until thoroughly blended. Cook, stirring constantly with a large wooden spoon, until the mixture becomes a thick dark roux the color of dark chocolate, 1 hour to 1 hour and 15 minutes.

2. Add ½ cup of the onions, ¼ cup of the bell peppers, ¼ cup of the celery, 2 tablespoons of the Essence, 1 tablespoon of the Worcestershire, 1 tablespoon of the hot sauce, and ½ cup of the sherry, stir well, and cook for 5 minutes. Remove the roux from the heat and let cool to room temperature.

3. Place the turtle meat in a small bowl and season with the remaining tablespoon of Essence.

4. Combine the chicken stock and veal stock in a large pot and bring to a simmer. Remove from the heat.

5. Heat the remaining ¼ cup vegetable oil in a large heavy pot over medium-high heat until hot. Add the remaining 1½ cups onions, ¾ cup bell peppers, ¾ cup celery, 1 cup of the green onions, and the garlic and cook, stirring, until soft, about 5 minutes. Add the turtle meat and cook, stirring, until browned, about 5 minutes. Add the tomato paste and bay leaves and cook for 1 minute. Add the remaining ¼ cup sherry and cook, stirring to loosen any browned bits on the bottom of the pot, for 1 minute. Add the tomatoes and cook, stirring, for 2 minutes.

6. Add the hot stock, stir well, and bring to a boil. Add the roux about 2 tablespoons at a time, whisking constantly until smooth. When all the roux is added, return to a boil, then reduce the heat to medium-low and simmer, uncovered, skimming occasionally to remove any foam that forms on the surface, until thick enough to coat the back of a spoon, about 1 hour.

7. Add the remaining ½ cup green onions, 1 tablespoon Worcestershire, 1 tablespoon hot sauce, 4 of the grated hard-boiled eggs, the salt, pepper, lemon juice, and spinach, stir well, and simmer for 15 minutes. Remove from the heat and remove the bay leaves.

8. Ladle the soup into large soup bowls. Garnish with the remaining eggs, add 2 teaspoons sherry to each serving, if desired, and serve immediately.

Chef Bernard Carmouche in Emeril's Orlando kitchen

Black Bean Soup with Ham Hock Dumplings

MAKES ABOUT 3 QUARTS;
10 SERVINGS

4 ham hocks (10 to 12
   ounces each)
1 cup chopped yellow onions
½ cup chopped carrots
½ cup chopped celery
6 quarts water
1 pound dried black beans,
   rinsed and picked over
1½ tablespoons chopped
   canned chiles in adobo
   sauce
1 teaspoon ground cumin
1 teaspoon chili powder
1 teaspoon salt
½ cup all-purpose flour
1 large egg, beaten
¼ cup beer
½ teaspoon baking powder

When I moved to New Orleans, I was introduced to and imme-diately fell in love with those things called ham hocks. I think you could put them in the laundry and they still would taste good! Being a huge fan of black beans and Latin American cooking, I decided to combine them for a unique flavor.

1. Combine the ham hocks, onions, carrots, celery, and water in a large pot and bring to a boil. Reduce the heat to medium-low and simmer until the meat starts to fall from the bones, about 1½ hours. Strain the stock through a colander into a clean pot. Set the ham hocks aside.

2. Add the black beans, chiles, cumin, and chili powder to the stock and bring to a boil. Reduce the heat to medium and cook at a brisk simmer until the beans are tender, about 1½ hours. Add ½ teaspoon of the salt during the last 5 minutes of cooking.

3. While the beans are cooking, remove the meat from the ham hocks and coarsely chop. Reserve ½ cup of the meat and add the rest to the black beans.

4. When the beans are nearly done, combine the ½ cup reserved meat with the flour, egg, beer, baking powder, and the remaining ½ teaspoon salt in a bowl. Mix to make a dough. To form the dumplings, drop the dough by the tablespoonful on top of the soup. You should have 10 dumplings. Cover and cook until the dumplings are set, 2 to 3 minutes.

5. To serve, spoon 1 dumpling into each soup bowl and ladle about 1 cup of soup over it.

Emeril's Favorite Tortilla Soup

MAKES ABOUT 6 CUPS;
4 TO 6 SERVINGS

2 tablespoons olive oil
1 cup chopped onions
2 teaspoons chopped
  garlic
1 poblano chile pepper,
  plus 1 jalapeño,
  seeded and chopped
1½ teaspoons salt
1½ teaspoons ground
  cumin
½ teaspoon ground
  coriander
1 tablespoon tomato paste
6 cups Rich Chicken Stock
  (page 21)
1 pound boneless,
  skinless chicken
  breasts, trimmed and
  cut into ½-inch cubes
¼ cup chopped cilantro
2 teaspoons fresh lime
  juice
6 stale corn tortillas, cut
  into ¼-inch-thick strips
2 cups vegetable oil
1 teaspoon Emeril's Original Essence or Creole
  Seasoning (page 28)
1 avocado, peeled,
  seeded, and chopped
1 recipe Chipotle Crema,
  optional

Through the years, I've been very intrigued by the different tortilla soups, with their many flavors, served in the Southwest. I started experimenting about ten years ago, and finally perfected this one. It's pretty darn good, and it pops up on the menus at Emeril's and Delmonico Steakhouse. The Chipotle Crema is optional.

1. Heat the oil in a Dutch oven or other large heavy pot over medium-high heat. Add the onions, garlic, chile pepper, salt, cumin, and coriander and cook, stirring, for 5 minutes. Add the tomato paste and cook, stirring, for 1 minute. Add the chicken stock, bring to a simmer, and simmer for 20 minutes.

2. Add the chicken to the soup and simmer for 5 minutes. Add the cilantro and lime juice and stir well. Remove from the heat and cover to keep warm.

3. Heat the oil in a small heavy pot to 350°F. Add the tortilla strips, in batches, and fry until golden and crisp, 1½ to 2 minutes. Remove with a slotted spoon and drain on paper towels. Season with the Essence.

4. Ladle the soup into four or six serving bowls. Garnish with the diced avocado, fried tortilla strips, and chipotle crema, if using. Serve immediately.

MAKES ½ CUP

½ cup sour cream
1 teaspoon chopped
  canned chipotle
  peppers in adobo sauce
⅛ teaspoon salt

Chipotle Crema

Combine all the ingredients in a food processor or blender and process until smooth. Cover and refrigerate until ready to serve. (The crema will keep in an airtight container refrigerated for up to 3 days.)

SOUPS, GUMBOS, AND CHOWDERS

Emeril's
NEW ORLEANS

Fresh Tomato Gazpacho with Mashed Avocado and Poached Seafood

This cold soup makes a refreshing first course on hot summer days, and it's always a favorite on the menu at Emeril's New Orleans. If you can't find Creole tomatoes, use whatever vine-ripened tomatoes are available in your area. The addition of mashed avocado and seafood turns this into a main course. Be sure to chill the gazpacho before serving.

MAKES 11 CUPS; 12 SERVINGS

1½ pounds ripe Creole tomatoes, finely chopped
2 cups peeled, seeded, and finely chopped cucumbers
1 cup finely chopped yellow onions
¾ cup each finely chopped red and yellow bell peppers
½ cup finely chopped green bell peppers
One 14-ounce can peeled Roma (plum) tomatoes, with their juice
One 16-ounce can V-8 juice
2 tablespoons balsamic vinegar
2 tablespoons sherry vinegar
½ cup extra-virgin olive oil
2 tablespoons kosher salt
1 teaspoon freshly ground black pepper
1½ teaspoons chili powder
2 teaspoons minced garlic
1 tablespoon plus 1 teaspoon minced, seeded jalapeño peppers
⅓ cup plus 2 tablespoons fresh lime juice
2 tablespoons each chopped fresh cilantro, parsley, basil, and oregano
1 recipe Mashed Avocado
1 recipe Poached Seafood

1. Combine half of the chopped tomatoes with half of the cucumbers, onions, and bell peppers in a food processor. Add the canned tomatoes and their liquid, and purée.

2. Combine the remaining chopped vegetables in a very large bowl. Add the puréed vegetables and all of the remaining ingredients except the avocado and seafood, and stir well to blend. Cover and refrigerate until chilled.

3. To serve, ladle the soup into twelve small bowls or large cups. Top each with about 2 tablespoons of the mashed avocado, and garnish with the poached seafood.

1 pound ripe Hass
    avocados, peeled,
    seeded, and chopped
1 tablespoon fresh lime
    juice
1 tablespoon fresh
    lemon juice
1½ teaspoons sour
    cream
¾ teaspoon chopped
    fresh parsley
¾ teaspoon chopped
    fresh cilantro
½ teaspoon minced
    garlic
½ teaspoon salt
⅛ teaspoon freshly
    ground white pepper

Mashed Avocado

Place the avocados in a medium bowl and mash with the back of a fork. Fold in the remaining ingredients, mixing until blended and creamy. Cover and refrigerate until ready to serve, up to 2 hours.

4 quarts water
2 lemons, cut in half
1 small yellow onion,
    peeled and quartered
1 rib celery, cut into
    2-inch pieces
2 garlic cloves, peeled
    and crushed
3 tablespoons salt
1 teaspoon Zatarain's
    Liquid Crab and
    Shrimp Boil
    (see Source Guide,
    page 333)
½ pound peeled and
    deveined medium
    shrimp
½ pound squid (bodies
    only), cut into
    ¼-inch-wide rings

Poached Seafood

1. Combine the water, lemons, onion, celery, garlic, salt, and crab boil in a large pot and bring to a boil. Add the shrimp and cook until just pink and cooked through, 1½ to 2 minutes. Remove with a strainer, refresh under cold running water, and drain. Add the squid to the pot and cook until firm, 30 to 45 seconds. Drain, rinse under cold running water, and drain again.

2. Cover and refrigerate until ready to serve.

SOUPS, GUMBOS, AND CHOWDERS

Oysters Rockefeller Bisque with Fried Oysters and Brie

6 slices bacon, each cut into 4 pieces

1 tablespoon minced garlic

¼ teaspoon fennel seeds

1 cup chopped yellow onions

1 cup chopped celery

1 cup chopped green onions (green parts only)

½ cup plus ¼ cup Herbsaint or other anise-flavored liqueur, such as Pernod or Ricard

1 cup Rich Chicken Stock (page 21)

2 cups heavy cream

36 freshly shucked oysters, with their liquor

2 tablespoons fresh lemon juice

2 teaspoons Worcestershire sauce

1 teaspoon salt

¼ teaspoon cayenne

¼ teaspoon freshly ground white pepper

1 pound spinach, tough stems removed, well rinsed, and patted dry

¼ cup chopped fresh parsley

1 recipe Fried Oysters and Brie

Oysters Rockefeller was created many years ago at the venerable New Orleans restaurant Antoine's. Because of its richness, the dish was named for the wealthy Rockefeller family. Chef Dave brings this already incredible dish to higher heights by turning it into a soup and pairing it with crunchy fried oysters and creamy Brie.

When making the soup, keep in mind the salinity of the oysters you're using. If the oysters are very salty, you won't need to use the amount of salt called for in the recipe. The soup will keep, refrigerated, for up to 3 days. Simply reheat it gently over medium heat to serve.

1. Cook the bacon in a large heavy pot over medium-high heat until crisp, about 6 minutes. Remove half of the bacon with a slotted spoon and drain on paper towels; reserve for the fried oyster garnish.

2. Reduce the heat to medium, add the garlic and fennel seeds, and cook, stirring, until fragrant, about 15 seconds. Add the onions, celery, and green onions, and cook, stirring, until soft, about 5 minutes. Add ½ cup of the Herbsaint and cook for 2 minutes to evaporate the alcohol. Add the chicken stock and bring to a boil. Reduce the heat to medium-low and simmer until the stock is reduced by half, about 8 minutes.

3. Add the cream, the oysters and their liquor, the lemon juice, Worcestershire, salt, cayenne, and white pepper and simmer for 25 minutes, stirring occasionally.

4. Remove from the heat, add the spinach and parsley, and stir well to blend. With a hand-held immersion blender, or in batches in a food processor, purée the soup.

5. To serve, ladle into large shallow soup bowls. Place 3 fried oysters in each bowl and drizzle 1 tablespoon of the remaining Herbsaint over each serving. Serve immediately.

4 cups vegetable oil for deep-frying
½ cup yellow cornmeal
½ cup masa harina
1 tablespoon Emeril's Original Essence or Creole Seasoning (page 28), plus more for seasoning
12 freshly shucked large oysters, drained
12 pieces cooked bacon (reserved from preceding recipe)
¼ pound Brie, cut into 12 thin slices

Fried Oysters and Brie

While Chef Dave uses these as a garnish to the bisque, these fried oysters are delicious on their own as an hors d'oeuvre or appetizer.

1. Preheat the oven to 400°F.

2. Heat the oil in a medium heavy pot or in a deep-fryer to 360°F. Combine the cornmeal, masa harina, and Essence in a medium bowl. Dredge the oysters in the breading and shake to remove any excess. Add to the hot oil, in batches, and fry until golden brown, about 2 minutes. Remove with a slotted spoon and drain on paper towels. Season lightly with Essence to taste and transfer to a baking sheet.

3. Place 1 piece of bacon on top of each oyster and top with a slice of Brie, skewering them with a toothpick to hold in place. Bake until the cheese is melted, about 3 minutes. Remove from the oven, remove the toothpicks, and serve hot.

NOLA food bar

Crawfish Vichyssoise with Lemon-Poached Leeks and French Bread Croutons

MAKES 6 CUPS; 6 TO 8 SERVINGS

- **1 pound live crawfish (or ½ pound cooked and peeled crawfish tails plus 1 pound shrimp shells) or 1 pound shrimp in the shells**
- **3 quarts water**
- **2 tablespoons salt**
- **¼ cup Zatarain's Liquid Crab and Shrimp Boil (see Source Guide, page 333)**
- **1 cup coarsely chopped yellow onions**
- **¾ cup coarsely chopped celery**
- **3 lemons, peel and white pith removed; peel from ½ lemon reserved for the Lemon-Poached Leeks**
- **3 bay leaves**
- **10 black peppercorns**
- **1 pound leeks**
- **4 tablespoons unsalted butter**
- **2 pounds Idaho potatoes, peeled and cut into 1-inch cubes**
- **Freshly ground black pepper**
- **2 cups heavy cream**
- **1 recipe Lemon-Poached Leeks**
- **1 recipe Large Croutons (page 33)**

If you can't get live crawfish at your local market, substitute whole shrimp in their shells and boil them until just pink, about 3 minutes.

Keep in mind that you'll use the stock to make the Vichyssoise as well as the Lemon-Poached Leeks. These leeks make a great accompaniment to fish and other seafood dishes. To make the dish without crawfish stock, just substitute Shrimp Stock (page 24) or Rich Chicken Stock (page 21), or follow the directions in the recipe to make your own here.

1. If using live crawfish, put them in a large container filled with salted water and let sit for 30 minutes. Drain and rinse under cold running water until the water runs clear.

2. To make the crawfish stock, combine the water, salt, crab boil, onions, celery, lemons, bay leaves, and peppercorns in a heavy 8-quart stockpot. Bring to a boil and cook for 5 minutes. Add the crawfish to the pot, and cook until they turn bright red, 10 to 12 minutes. Using tongs or a strainer, transfer the crawfish to a baking sheet and spread out to cool. (Alternatively, if live crawfish are not available, add the 1 pound shrimp shells to the boiling liquid. Boil for 30 minutes to make a rich shrimp stock. Strain and discard the shells.) Strain the cooking liquid through a fine-mesh strainer into a clean container. Set aside 4 cups of the stock for the soup, 2 cups for the leeks, and reserve the rest for another use or discard.

3. Meanwhile, trim the leeks, discarding the roots and green tops. Cut the whites crosswise into ½-inch slices and put in a bowl of ice water to soak for 5 minutes. Drain, place in fresh ice water, and soak again for 5 minutes. Drain well.

4. When the crawfish are cool enough to handle, peel them, reserving the tails and discarding the shells. Cover and refrigerate.

5. Melt the butter in a Dutch oven or other large heavy pot over medium-high heat. Add the drained leeks and cook, stirring, until soft, about 5 minutes. Add 4 cups of the strained stock and the potatoes, reduce the heat to medium-low, and simmer, stirring occasionally, until the potatoes are soft, about 25 minutes. Remove from the heat.

6. Purée the soup with a hand-held immersion blender, or in batches in a food processor or blender, until smooth. Adjust the seasoning to taste with salt and pepper.

7. Scald the cream in a small saucepan over medium-high heat. Remove from the heat and add to the puréed soup, stirring well. Cover and chill thoroughly before serving.

8. To serve, ladle the soup into bowls. Arrange 8 to 12 chilled crawfish tails or shrimp around the edge of each bowl. Place 1 heaping tablespoon of the poached leeks in the center of each bowl, and serve with the croutons.

Lemon-Poached Leeks

MAKES 6 TO 8 SERVINGS
AS A GARNISH

1 large leek
2 cups strained crawfish stock (reserved from above), Shrimp Stock (page 24), or Rich Chicken Stock (page 21)
½ cup dry white wine
Peel from ½ lemon (reserved from preceding recipe), coarsely chopped
2 bay leaves
⅛ teaspoon freshly ground black pepper

1. Trim the leek, discarding the root and green tops. Cut into thin strips and place in a bowl of ice water to soak for 5 minutes. Drain, place in fresh ice water and soak again for 5 minutes. Drain well.

2. Combine the stock, wine, lemon peel, bay leaves, and pepper in a medium saucepan and bring to a boil. Reduce the heat to medium-low, add the leeks, and simmer until tender, about 10 minutes. Remove from the heat and let the leeks sit in the poaching liquid for 10 to 15 minutes.

3. Drain the leeks in a fine-mesh strainer. Discard the bay leaves, and reserve the poaching liquid, if desired, for another use. Set the leeks aside until ready to serve.

SOUPS, GUMBOS, AND CHOWDERS

1 pound boneless pork butt,
  cut into ½-inch cubes
2 teaspoons Emeril's
  Original Essence or Creole
  Seasoning (page 28)
1 teaspoon Worcestershire
  sauce
1 teaspoon Emeril's Kick It
  Up Red Pepper Sauce or
  other hot pepper sauce
1 cup vegetable oil
1 cup all-purpose flour
1 pound andouille sausage,
  cut into ¼-inch slices
¼ pound tasso, diced
1½ cups chopped yellow
  onions
1 cup chopped celery
1 cup chopped green bell
  peppers
6 cups Rich Chicken Stock
  (page 21)
One 12-ounce bottle dark
  beer
1½ teaspoons salt
¼ teaspoon cayenne
3 bay leaves
1 recipe White Rice
  (page 19), for serving
½ cup chopped green
  onions (green parts only),
  for garnish
¼ cup chopped fresh
  parsley, for garnish

Kick-Butt Gumbo

Traditional Louisiana gumbos are usually made with seafood, or chicken and sausage, and some have okra—but hey, everyone has his own recipe for gumbo. Over the years, I've had the privilege of eating and making thousands and thousands of gumbos. Taste this one, and you'll know how it got its name! It will send you reeling! (Note that the pork must marinate overnight.)

1. Put the pork in a bowl and season with the Essence, Worcestershire, and hot sauce. Cover with plastic wrap and refrigerate overnight.

2. Heat the oil in a Dutch oven or other large heavy pot over medium heat. Add the flour and cook, stirring constantly with a large wooden spoon, to make a dark chocolate brown roux, 30 to 35 minutes.

Food of Love

3. Add the pork, sausage, and tasso and cook, stirring, until caramelized, 6 to 7 minutes. Add the onions, celery, and bell peppers and cook, stirring constantly, until soft, 7 to 10 minutes. Add the stock, stirring constantly to prevent lumps from forming, and bring to a boil. Add the beer, salt, cayenne, and bay leaves and stir to blend. Reduce the heat and simmer, uncovered, stirring occasionally, until the pork is tender, 1½ to 2 hours. Remove from the heat and remove the bay leaves.

4. Ladle the gumbo into eight large soup bowls. Spoon the rice into the center of the gumbo, and sprinkle each serving with the green onions and parsley. Serve immediately.

Kevin Delaune at Emeril's Delmonico

Tchoupitoulas Gumbo

While most gumbos freeze well, we don't suggest freezing this one since the beans would make the texture slightly mealy upon reheating. However, if the popularity of this full-flavored gumbo at Delmonico Steakhouse is any indication, we don't think you'll have any leftovers!

½ cup all-purpose flour
1 tablespoon plus
    2 teaspoons Emeril's
    Original Essence or Creole
    Seasoning (page 28)
¼ pound lamb stew meat,
    such as shoulder or shank,
    cut into 1-inch cubes
¼ pound veal stew meat,
    such as shoulder or
    shank, cut into 1-inch
    cubes
¼ pound beef stew meat,
    such as chuck, cut into
    1-inch cubes
½ pound pork butt, cut into
    1-inch cubes
½ pound bacon, cut into
    ¾-inch pieces
¼ pound andouille sausage,
    cut into ½-inch cubes
¼ cup vegetable oil
1 cup chopped yellow onions
½ cup chopped green bell
    peppers
½ cup chopped celery
1 tablespoon minced garlic
½ pound dry white lima
    beans or butter beans,
    rinsed and picked over
2 to 2½ quarts Rich Chicken
    Stock (page 21) or canned
    low-sodium chicken broth
1 tablespoon Worcestershire
    sauce
1 tablespoon Emeril's Kick It
    Up Red Pepper Sauce or
    other hot pepper sauce
4 cups White Rice (page 19),
    for serving

1. Combine the flour and 2 teaspoons of the Essence in a shallow dish. In batches, dredge all the cubed meat in the flour, shaking to remove any excess. Set aside.

2. Cook the bacon in a Dutch oven or other large heavy pot over medium-high heat until browned, about 5 minutes. Add the sausage and cook, stirring occasionally, until browned, about 4 minutes. Remove the bacon and sausage with a slotted spoon and drain on paper towels.

3. Add half the meat to the fat in the pot and cook, stirring, until evenly browned an all sides. With a slotted spoon, transfer the meat to a platter. Add the vegetable oil, and when it is hot, add the remaining meat and cook, stirring, until browned. Transfer to the platter.

4. Add the onions, bell peppers, celery, garlic, and the remaining tablespoon of Essence to the pot and cook, stirring and scraping the bottom of the pot, until the vegetables are soft, about 3 minutes. Add the bacon, sausage, and the beans and cook until the beans are warmed through and wrinkly, about 3 minutes. Add the browned meats and 2 quarts of the chicken stock and bring to a boil. Reduce the heat to medium-low and simmer, stirring occasionally, for 2 hours, adding up to an additional 2 cups stock if the gumbo gets too thick. Remove from the heat and stir in the Worcestershire and hot sauces.

5. Spoon the white rice into eight large soup bowls. Ladle the gumbo over the rice, and serve immediately.

Creole Seafood Courtbouillon

MAKES 1½ QUARTS; 6 SERVINGS

½ cup plus 3 tablespoons
  vegetable oil
¾ cup all-purpose flour
1 cup chopped yellow
  onions
1 cup chopped green bell
  peppers
½ cup chopped celery
1 tablespoon minced
  garlic
2 bay leaves
¼ cup tomato paste
½ cup dry sherry
5 cups Fish Stock
  (page 23) or Shrimp
  Stock (page 24)
One 14½-ounce can
  diced tomatoes, with
  their juices
1 tablespoon sugar
1 tablespoon salt
½ teaspoon freshly
  ground black pepper
½ teaspoon red pepper
  flakes
3 redfish or trout fillets
  (each about 6 ounces),
  cut lengthwise in half
24 medium shrimp,
  peeled and deveined
36 freshly shucked
  oysters (about
  2 pints), drained
1 tablespoon Emeril's
  Original Essence or
  Creole Seasoning
  (page 28)
4 tablespoons cold
  unsalted butter, cut
  into small pieces
3 cups White Rice
  (page 19), for serving

In South Louisiana, the Acadians (Cajuns) favor a hearty court-bouillon (not to be confused with the French poaching liquid known as courtbouillon*) that is made with a roux and whatever fish—saltwater or freshwater—is available. Here is Delmonico Restaurant's adaptation of the classic courtbouillon using local Louisiana seafood—trout, shrimp, and oysters. The result is a hearty soup with lots of flavor, ideal for a cold winter's night supper. You will want to have lots of hot, crusty French bread to sop up every last drop in your bowl.*

1. Heat ½ cup of the oil in a Dutch oven or other large heavy pot over medium-high heat. Add the flour, reduce the heat to medium, and cook, stirring constantly with a large wooden spoon, to make a thick roux almost the color of milk chocolate, 15 to 20 minutes.

2. Add the onions, bell peppers, and celery and cook, stirring, for 1 minute. Add the garlic and bay leaves and cook, stirring, for 30 seconds. Place the tomato paste in a small bowl and whisk in the sherry to blend. Add to the pot and cook, stirring, for 30 seconds. Add the stock, whisking to blend. Add the tomatoes and their juices, the sugar, salt, black pepper, and red pepper and cook, stirring occasionally, for 20 to 25 minutes. Remove from the heat.

3. Season the redfish fillets, shrimp, and oysters with the Essence. In a Dutch oven or other large heavy pot, heat the remaining 3 tablespoons of oil over medium-high heat. Add the redfish and shrimp and cook for 2 minutes, then turn and cook for 1 minute. Add the courtbouillon and oysters and cook just until the oysters curl, 1 to 2 minutes. Add the butter bit by bit and stir gently to incorporate.

4. Divide the courtbouillon equally among large soup bowls. Spoon ½ cup of the rice into the center of each bowl, and serve immediately.

SOUPS, GUMBOS, AND CHOWDERS

Lobster and Corn Chowder

MAKES 6 QUARTS; 12 SERVINGS

Lobster Cooking Liquid
1 large yellow onion, peeled
  and quartered
2 ribs celery, chopped
1 sprig fresh thyme
1 head garlic, cut
  horizontally in half
½ cup kosher salt
1 tablespoon black
  peppercorns
1 cup dry white wine
Three 1¼-pound lobsters

8 tablespoons (1 stick)
  unsalted butter
3 cups finely chopped leeks
  (white parts only)
2 cups finely chopped celery
1 cup finely chopped yellow
  onions
1 cup finely chopped red bell
  peppers
1 cup finely chopped yellow
  bell peppers
1 cup finely chopped green
  bell peppers
¼ cup chopped green onions
  (white parts only) plus
  ¾ cup chopped green
  onions (green parts only)
3 ears corn, kernels cut off,
  corncobs reserved for
  Lobster-Corn Stock
2 cups peeled, seeded, and
  finely chopped tomatoes
1 tablespoon minced garlic
1 tablespoon salt
2 teaspoons freshly ground
  black pepper
2 teaspoons Emeril's
  Original Essence or Creole
  Seasoning (page 28)

I've made lots of chowders in my life, but this one has captured my heart. You can't go wrong combining rich lobster meat with sweet corn. And the fennel in the broth gives the dish an added depth of flavor.

1. To cook the lobsters, fill a large stockpot three-quarters full with water. Add the onion, celery, thyme, garlic, salt, peppercorns, and wine and bring to a boil. Plunge the lobsters head-first into the boiling water and cook, covered, for 5 minutes. With tongs, transfer the lobsters to a large bowl filled with ice water to cool. When the lobsters are cool enough to handle, drain, crack the shells, and remove the tail and claw meat. Coarsely chop, cover, and refrigerate. Reserve the shells for the stock.

2. To make the chowder, melt the butter in a large Dutch oven or other large heavy pot over medium heat. Add the leeks, celery, onions, bell peppers, and ¼ cup of the green onions and cook, stirring, until soft, about 4 minutes. Add the corn kernels, tomatoes, garlic, salt, pepper, Essence, and red pepper flakes and cook, stirring, for 3 minutes.

3. Add the flour and cook, stirring constantly, until the flour smells slightly toasted but has not browned, about 3 minutes. Add the Cognac and cook, stirring, for 2 minutes. Add the lobster-corn stock and cayenne, and stir. Bring to a boil, stirring occasionally. Reduce the heat to medium-low and simmer, uncovered, stirring occasionally, for 30 minutes.

4. Add the potatoes, stir well, and simmer until tender, about 15 minutes.

5. Add the cream, lobster meat, the remaining ¾ cup green onions, the herbs, and the lemon juice, and cook, stirring, for 5 minutes. Remove from the heat and adjust the seasoning to taste.

6. Ladle the chowder into bowls and serve.

½ teaspoon red pepper
flakes
1½ cups all-purpose flour
½ cup Cognac or other
brandy
1 recipe Lobster-Corn
Stock
½ teaspoon cayenne
2 pounds Idaho potatoes,
peeled and cut into
½-inch cubes
2½ cups heavy cream
½ cup chopped mixed
fresh soft herbs, such
as parsley, chervil,
basil, and chives
2 teaspoons fresh lemon
juice

MAKES 3 QUARTS

Shells from three 1¼-
pound lobsters
(reserved from above)
3 corncobs (reserved
from above)
2 ribs celery, quartered
2 tomatoes, coarsely
chopped
1 yellow onion, peeled
and quartered
1 carrot, peeled and
coarsely chopped
1 fennel bulb, stalks re-
moved and cut in half
1 head garlic, cut
horizontally in half
3 sprigs fresh thyme
1 tablespoon salt
1 teaspoon freshly
ground black pepper
About 6 quarts water

Lobster-Corn Stock

1. Preheat the oven to 400°F.

2. Spread the lobster shells in one layer on a baking sheet and roast for 30 minutes. Turn the shells and continue to roast for 30 minutes more. Remove from the oven.

3. Combine the lobster shells, corncobs, and the remaining ingredients in a large pot. Add enough water to cover by 2 inches, about 6 quarts, and bring to a boil. Reduce the heat to medium-low and simmer, uncovered, until reduced by half, about 3 hours, stirring occasionally. Remove from the heat and strain through a fine-mesh strainer. Set aside until ready to use.

SOUPS, GUMBOS, AND CHOWDERS

NEW ORLEANS FISH HOUSE

Spiny Lobster–Tomato Saffron Stew with Shaved Artichoke and Olive Salad

MAKES 6 SERVINGS

Two 1½-pound spiny lobsters or Maine lobsters
5 tablespoons unsalted butter
¼ cup all-purpose flour
1 teaspoon saffron threads
3 tablespoons fresh lemon juice
2 tablespoons dry sherry, such as manzanilla or fino
1 tablespoon olive oil
1½ cups thinly sliced yellow onions
1½ cups thinly sliced yellow bell peppers
1½ cups thinly sliced red bell peppers
1 cup thinly sliced and seeded poblano peppers
1 tablespoon minced shallots
2 teaspoons minced garlic
1 cup coarsely peeled, chopped, and seeded tomatoes
1½ tablespoons tomato paste
1 tablespoon achiote powder (available at Latin American or gourmet markets)
1 tablespoon salt
2 teaspoons freshly ground white pepper

Here we've managed to offer soup and salad in the same dish. The soup is hearty but not overpowering, and the artichoke and olive salad gives it a good kick. The spiny lobster habitat ranges along the lower eastern seaboard of the United States, and down the Caribbean to Brazil, and they are most abundant in Florida, the Bahamas, and Cuba. If they are unavailable, you can use Maine lobsters.

1. Fill a large stockpot three-quarters full with salted water and bring to a boil. Plunge the lobsters headfirst into the boiling water and cook for 3 minutes. Using tongs, transfer to a large bowl filled with ice water to cool.

2. When the lobsters are cool enough to handle, drain, crack the shells, and remove the meat from the tails if using spiny lobsters, or from the tails and claws if using Maine lobsters. Cut into bite-sized pieces, cover, and refrigerate. Discard the shells or reserve for another use.

3. Melt 4 tablespoons of the butter in a small saucepan over medium heat. Add the flour and cook, stirring constantly with a wooden spoon, to make a blond roux, 5 to 6 minutes. Remove from the heat and let cool.

4. Combine the saffron threads, lemon juice, and sherry in a small bowl and stir to blend. Set aside.

5. Heat the olive oil and the remaining 1 tablespoon butter in a large heavy stockpot or Dutch oven over medium-high heat. Add the onions, bell peppers, and poblano peppers and cook, stirring, until soft, about 4 minutes. Add the shallots and garlic and cook, stirring, for 1 minute. Add the tomatoes, tomato paste, achiote powder, salt, and pepper and cook over medium-low heat, stirring occasionally, for 15 minutes.

5 cups Shrimp Stock
(page 24)
1 recipe Shaved
Artichoke and Olive
Salad
½ cup finely sliced fresh
basil for serving
2 tablespoons extra-
virgin olive oil for
serving

6. Add the saffron mixture, stir, and bring to a boil. Add the shrimp stock and roux, whisking to dissolve the roux. Bring to a boil and boil for 3 minutes. Reduce the heat to low, add the reserved lobster meat, and simmer until just cooked through, about 3 minutes.

7. To serve, ladle about 1 cup of the stew into each of six large soup bowls. Garnish each with about 2 tablespoons of the olive salad, 1 heaping tablespoon of the basil, and 1 teaspoon extra-virgin olive oil. Serve.

MAKES ABOUT ¾ CUP

2 large artichokes, all
outer leaves removed,
leaving only the heart
and bottom, stems
trimmed
2 tablespoons fresh
lemon juice
1 cup brine-cured black
olives, such as
Kalamata, pitted and
quartered
½ cup chopped fresh
parsley
¼ cup extra-virgin
olive oil

Shaved Artichoke and Olive Salad

Slice the artichokes paper-thin using a vegetable slicer such as a mandoline. Place in a glass bowl and toss with the remaining ingredients. Let sit for 15 minutes before serving.

4 | SALADS

Chef Joel Morgan at NOLA

Arugula-Stuffed Vidalia Onion Ring Salad with Lemon Herb Vinaigrette

2 tablespoons chopped
   mixed fresh herbs, such
   as parsley, chives,
   tarragon, basil, and/or
   cilantro
1 tablespoon minced
   shallots
1 teaspoon minced garlic
3 tablespoons fresh lemon
   juice
2$\frac{1}{2}$ teaspoons salt
1$\frac{1}{4}$ teaspoons freshly
   ground black pepper
$\frac{1}{4}$ cup olive or vegetable oil
$\frac{1}{4}$ cup extra-virgin olive oil
3 cups rice flour (available at
   Asian markets and some
   supermarkets)
1 to 1$\frac{1}{2}$ cups cold seltzer or
   soda water
1 cup all-purpose flour
1 tablespoon Emeril's
   Original Essence or Creole
   Seasoning (page 28)
2 large Vidalia onions or
   other sweet onions, such
   as Oso Sweet, Walla
   Walla, or Maui, peeled
   and cut into $\frac{1}{2}$-inch-thick
   rings
6 cups vegetable oil, for
   deep-frying
10 ounces arugula, tough
   stems removed, rinsed,
   and patted dry
$\frac{1}{4}$ cup shaved Parmigiano-
   Reggiano
2 tablespoons balsamic
   vinegar

You wouldn't think to serve fried onion rings in a salad, but is this ever good! The herbed lemon vinaigrette tames the peppery arugula in an inspired match.

The onion ring batter is like tempura, using seltzer instead of the usual milk or tap water. Make sure the soda is cold before you start, or even add a few ice cubes as you're working.

1. Combine the herbs, shallots, garlic, lemon juice, $\frac{1}{2}$ teaspoon of the salt, and $\frac{1}{4}$ teaspoon of the pepper in a medium bowl and whisk to blend. Slowly add the olive oils in a thin, steady stream, whisking constantly until the vinaigrette thickens. Set aside.

2. Combine the rice flour, 1 cup of the seltzer, and the remaining 2 teaspoons salt and 1 teaspoon pepper in a medium bowl and whisk, adding more seltzer as needed, to form a smooth batter the consistency of pancake batter. Combine the all-purpose flour and Essence in a shallow bowl. Toss 12 of the largest outer onion rings in the seasoned flour, and dredge in the batter, shaking to remove any excess. (Save the remaining smaller onion rings for another use.)

3. Heat the oil in a large deep pot or deep-fryer to 350°F. Carefully add the onion rings to the hot oil and cook, turning occasionally to prevent them from sticking together, until golden on both sides, 2 to 3 minutes. Drain on paper towels, and season with salt and pepper.

4. Place the arugula in a large bowl and toss with the vinaigrette. Place 1 fried onion ring in the center of each salad plate and stuff with about $\frac{1}{2}$ cup of the dressed arugula. Top each with another ring and stuff it, then repeat, for a total of 3 onion rings and about 1$\frac{1}{2}$ cups arugula per salad, with the greens spilling out of the top. Garnish each with 1 tablespoon of the Parmesan and a generous drizzle of the balsamic vinegar, and serve immediately.

ORLANDO

Hearts of Palm Salad with Tomatoes, Orange Segments, Bibb Lettuce, Shaved Fennel, and Cucumber-Yogurt Dressing

2 heads Bibb lettuce, cored, quartered, rinsed, and patted dry
1 fennel bulb (about ½ pound), stalks removed, fronds reserved for garnish, bulb thinly shaved
One 14-ounce can hearts of palm, drained and cut on the bias into quarters
4 oranges, peeled and segmented
2 medium ripe tomatoes, each cut into eighths
1 recipe Cucumber-Yogurt Dressing
Freshly ground black pepper

At the restaurant, fresh hearts of palm are used, but we call for canned ones here, since they're more readily available. If you can find the fresh ones, by all means use them instead. This dressing also would make a good dip.

Arrange 2 lettuce quarters on each of four large plates. Top each with a portion of the shaved fennel. Arrange 2 sliced hearts of palm decoratively around the rim of each plate, and the orange segments around the lettuce. Place 4 tomato quarters around each salad, points out. Drizzle the dressing decoratively over the salads, and sprinkle with black pepper. Garnish with the reserved fronds and serve immediately.

Cucumber-Yogurt Dressing

1 cup plain yogurt
2 tablespoons honey
2 tablespoons fresh lime juice
⅛ teaspoon salt
⅛ teaspoon freshly ground white pepper
½ cup peeled, finely chopped, and seeded cucumbers

Combine the yogurt, honey, lime juice, salt, and pepper in a medium bowl. Whisk to blend. Add the cucumber and mix well. (The dressing can be made in advance and kept in an airtight container in the refrigerator for up to 8 hours. Whisk well before serving.)

SALADS

Caesar Salad

MAKES 4 SERVINGS

One 18-ounce bag hearts of
romaine lettuce, torn into
pieces or left whole, as
desired
1 recipe Creamy Parmesan
Dressing
1 cup Small Croutons
(page 33)
½ cup finely grated
Parmigiano-Reggiano

*We're always being asked for the recipe for the terrific salad
dressing that is made tableside at the Steakhouse, so here you
go! Ours isn't as garlicky or cheesy as some, but that's really
more a matter of personal preference. If you're in the mood, go
ahead and kick up yours to suit your tastes!*

Put the lettuce in a large bowl, toss with the dressing to taste,
and divide among four large salad plates, or arrange the hearts
on the plates and drizzle the dressing over the lettuce. Top with
the croutons and cheese, and serve.

MAKES ¾ CUP

1 large egg, at room
temperature
2 anchovy fillets, drained
½ teaspoon minced garlic
¼ teaspoon kosher salt
¼ teaspoon freshly ground
black pepper
2 tablespoons freshly grated
Parmigiano-Reggiano
1 tablespoon fresh lemon
juice
1 teaspoon Dijon mustard
¼ cup extra-virgin olive oil
1 teaspoon Worcestershire
sauce
2 drops Emeril's Kick It Up
Red Pepper Sauce or
other hot pepper sauce

Creamy Parmesan Dressing

1. Bring a small saucepan of water to a boil. Add the egg and
cook for 30 seconds. Drain.

2. Combine the anchovies, garlic, salt, and pepper in a small
bowl and mash to a paste with a fork. Break the egg into the
mixture and whisk well to blend. Add the cheese, lemon juice,
and mustard and whisk well. Add the olive oil in a steady
stream, whisking constantly to form a thick emulsion. Add the
Worcestershire and pepper sauces and whisk well to combine.
Cover tightly and refrigerate until ready to use. (The dressing
will keep refrigerated for up to 1 day.)

Sliced Tomato Salad with Herb Vinaigrette, Red Onions, and Maytag Blue Cheese

3 large ripe tomatoes, each cut into 4 thick slices

1 teaspoon salt

1 teaspoon freshly ground black pepper

1/2 recipe Herb Vinaigrette

Twelve 1/8-inch-thick slices red onion or sweet onion

1/2 cup crumbled Maytag blue cheese (about 3 ounces)

This is a great way to start your meal if you're diving into a big hearty steak, like folks do at the Steakhouse. Use sweet onions, such as Vidalia, Maui, or Walla Walla, rather than red onions when they are in season.

1. Place the tomatoes in a large shallow bowl and season on both sides with the salt and pepper. Add 2 tablespoons of the vinaigrette and toss lightly to coat.

2. Place 1 tomato slice on each of four salad plates and top with an onion slice. Repeat to make 3 layers each of tomatoes and onions, ending with onions. Crumble 2 tablespoons of the cheese on top of each stack, drizzle with the remaining vinaigrette, and serve.

Herb Vinaigrette

1 tablespoon champagne vinegar

1 1/2 teaspoons fresh orange juice

3/4 teaspoon fresh lemon juice

3/4 teaspoon fresh lime juice

3/4 teaspoon fresh grape-fruit juice

1/2 cup vegetable oil

1/2 cup extra-virgin olive oil

1/2 cup chopped mixed fresh thyme, parsley, chives, and basil

1/4 teaspoon salt

1/4 teaspoon freshly ground black pepper

Serve with any tomato salad or mixed greens.

Combine the vinegar and citrus juices in a medium bowl and whisk together. Add the vegetable and olive oils in a slow stream, whisking constantly to form an emulsion. Add the herbs, salt, and pepper and whisk well to incorporate. (The dressing keeps refrigerated for up to 2 days.)

SALADS

Bibb Lettuce Wedges with Warm Black-Eyed Pea and Bacon Vinaigrette, Balsamic Braised Onions, Spiced Walnuts, Pears, and Roquefort Cheese

MAKES 4 SERVINGS

2 heads Bibb lettuce (about 6 ounces each), cored, quartered, rinsed, and patted dry

1 recipe Black-Eyed Pea and Bacon Vinaigrette

1 recipe Balsamic Braised Onions

1 Bartlett or d'Anjou pear, cored and thinly sliced

¼ pound Roquefort cheese, crumbled

½ recipe Spiced Walnuts

You might think there's too much going on here, but believe me, this salad comes together perfectly. To simplify things, cook the black-eyed peas a day ahead of time (or just use 1 cup canned peas, rinsed well and drained). You also can make the dressing in advance; it holds well in the refrigerator for up to 3 days (gently reheat to serve). And the spiced walnuts? You'll probably want to make a double batch—they're positively addictive and you'll want to put them in everything!

Arrange 2 lettuce quarters on each of four serving plates. Drizzle each wedge with warm vinaigrette to taste, and top with the onions, sliced pear, cheese, and walnuts. Serve immediately.

Emeril's New Orleans food bar

7 slices bacon, 6 slices diced, 1 left whole
1 tablespoon chopped shallots
½ teaspoon minced garlic
1 small bay leaf
1 sprig fresh thyme
⅜ teaspoon freshly ground black pepper
½ cup dried black-eyed peas, rinsed and picked over
1½ cups water
¼ cup red wine vinegar
2 tablespoons light brown sugar
¼ cup canola or vegetable oil
¼ teaspoon salt

Black-Eyed Pea and Bacon Vinaigrette

1. For the peas, cook the whole slice of bacon in a medium saucepan over medium-high heat until almost crisp, about 3 minutes. Add the shallots, garlic, bay leaf, thyme, and ¼ teaspoon of the pepper and cook, stirring, for 1 minute. Add the peas and water and bring to a boil. Reduce the heat to medium-low, cover, and simmer until the peas are just tender, about 30 minutes. Remove from the heat and let the peas cool in their cooking liquid.

2. Drain the peas and discard the bacon. (The peas can be cooked up to a day ahead and kept refrigerated.)

3. To make the vinaigrette, cook the diced bacon in a medium skillet over medium-high heat until crisp, about 5 minutes. Remove and drain on paper towels.

4. Drain off the fat from the pan and return to medium heat. Add the vinegar and stir to deglaze the pan. Add the sugar and stir to dissolve. Remove from the heat and let cool slightly.

5. Add the oil, black-eyed peas, cooked bacon, salt, and the remaining ⅛ teaspoon pepper, and stir to mix well. Serve warm. (Any leftover vinaigrette can be refrigerated for up to 3 days; reheat gently before using.)

1 large yellow onion, peeled and trimmed
½ cup balsamic vinegar
½ cup water
½ teaspoon fresh thyme leaves
⅛ teaspoon freshly ground black pepper

Balsamic Braised Onions

1. Preheat the oven to 350°F.

2. Combine all the ingredients in a loaf pan. Cover tightly with aluminum foil and bake for 30 minutes. Remove the foil (be careful of hot steam), turn the onion, re-cover, and continue baking until tender, about 45 minutes longer. Remove from the oven and let stand until cool enough to handle.

3. Thinly slice the onion and place in a small bowl. Transfer the cooking liquid to a medium skillet and bring to a boil. Cook until reduced by about three-quarters to a thick glaze, 7 to 8 minutes. Toss with the sliced onions. Let cool slightly before using.

SALADS

Spiced Walnuts

1. Line a baking sheet with aluminum foil. Melt the butter in a large skillet over medium-high heat. Add the walnuts and cook, stirring, until lightly toasted and fragrant, 3 minutes. Add the sugar and Essence and cook, stirring, until the nuts are caramelized and evenly coated, about 2 minutes.

2. Transfer the nuts to the baking sheet, separating them with a fork. Let stand until the nuts have cooled and the sugar has hardened.

*2 tablespoons unsalted
    butter*
*1½ cups (4 ounces) walnut
    pieces*
*2 tablespoons light brown
    sugar*
*½ teaspoon Emeril's
    Original Essence or Creole
    Seasoning (page 28)*

*(Left to right) Trevor Wisdom,
chef Dave McCelvey, and
Charlotte Armstrong Martory
testing recipes at Emeril's
Homebase*

HOMEBASE

Caramelized Grapefruit with Watercress, Endive, Blue Cheese, and Basil-Caramel Vinaigrette

¼ cup sugar
2 Ruby Red grapefruit, halved and seeded
2 heads Belgian endive, split lengthwise, cores removed, and cut crosswise into ½-inch-wide slices
2 bunches watercress, tough stems removed, rinsed, and patted dry
1 recipe Basil-Caramel Vinaigrette
½ cup (about 3 ounces) crumbled Maytag blue cheese

Sweet caramelized grapefruit and Belgian endive give this salad an intense balance of flavors. A propane torch is best for caramelizing the sugar, but a broiler will do. The basil dressing is also a fine accompaniment to a tomato-onion salad or chilled lobster or shrimp.

1. Sprinkle 1 tablespoon of the sugar evenly over each grapefruit half. Using a blowtorch, carefully caramelize the sugar to a mahogany color. (Alternatively, place the grapefruit on a baking sheet directly under a preheated broiler for about 4 minutes; however, the sugar will simply melt, not caramelize.)

2. Combine the endive and watercress in a large bowl and toss with the vinaigrette to taste. Mound the greens in the middle of four serving plates and place a grapefruit half on top of each. Sprinkle the cheese over the greens and drizzle with additional vinaigrette, if desired. Serve immediately.

Basil-Caramel Vinaigrette

½ cup sugar
½ cup rice wine vinegar
½ cup heavy cream, at room temperature
¼ cup fresh orange juice
10 fresh basil leaves, thinly sliced
1 tablespoon chopped shallots
1 teaspoon Dijon mustard
½ teaspoon minced garlic
½ teaspoon salt
½ teaspoon freshly ground black pepper
½ cup vegetable oil

1. Combine the sugar and vinegar in a medium deep heavy saucepan, bring to a boil, and cook, stirring, until the sugar is dissolved. Continue to cook, without stirring, until the caramel is an amber color, 3 to 5 minutes. Add the heavy cream (be careful, as the mixture will foam) and swirl the pan to incorporate. Cook for 2 minutes longer, without stirring. Remove from the heat and let cool to room temperature.

2. Combine the cooled caramel, orange juice, basil, shallots, mustard, garlic, salt, and pepper in a blender or food processor and purée until well blended. With the machine running, gradually add the oil, processing until emulsified. (The dressing will keep refrigerated for up to 3 days.)

SALADS

Arugula with Pears, Smithfield Ham, Blue Cheese, Toasted Brioche, and Warm Fig Vinaigrette

2 ripe but firm Bartlett or d'Anjou pears
1 pound arugula, tough stems removed, rinsed, and patted dry
1 recipe Fig Vinaigrette
½ teaspoon salt
¼ teaspoon freshly ground black pepper
½ cup thinly sliced Smithfield ham
½ cup crumbled blue cheese
4 slices fig brioche, Brioche (page 34), or French bread, lightly toasted

4 tablespoons unsalted butter
2 tablespoons sugar
2 tablespoons white wine vinegar
2 tablespoons fig preserves
¼ cup vegetable oil
2 tablespoons balsamic vinegar
Salt and freshly ground black pepper

The sweet ham, pears, and fig vinaigrette tame the spicy arugula and the bite of the blue cheese in this elegant salad. Matter of fact, I like this one so much, a whole bowl makes a great dinner for just me!

1. Halve and core the pears and cut each half lengthwise into ⅛-inch-thick slices, keeping the slices together.

2. Combine the arugula with the vinaigrette to taste, salt, and pepper in a medium bowl, tossing to coat. Divide the salad among four plates and top with the ham and blue cheese. Fan a sliced pear half on each plate, garnish with a slice of toasted brioche, and serve.

Fig Vinaigrette

1. Melt the butter in a small skillet over medium heat, then cook until golden brown. Transfer to a food processor, scraping all the solids from the pan with a wooden spoon.

2. Combine the sugar, wine vinegar, and fig preserves in the same pan, and cook over medium heat, stirring, just until the sugar is dissolved. Add to the food processor and process until blended. With the machine running, add the oil in a steady stream, processing until the mixture is emulsified and thick. Add the balsamic vinegar and process until well blended. Season to taste with salt and pepper.

Kentucky Limestone Bibb Lettuce with Warm Sweet Potato–Bourbon Dressing, Candied Pecans, and Bacon

4 strips thick-cut apple-smoked bacon, cut into ¼-inch-thick pieces

2 heads Bibb lettuce, preferably Kentucky Limestone, halved lengthwise, cored, rinsed, and patted dry

½ recipe Candied Pecans (page 20)

½ cup Sweet Potato–Bourbon Dressing

So you want a taste of the South for dinner? Try this one on for size! Chef Dave is a native Kentuckian, which explains his love of ingredients indigenous to that state. He particularly stresses the importance of using a good-quality Kentucky bourbon in this dressing.

The dressing recipe makes more than you will need here, but the dressing is also good served cold with chilled seafood. Or, to serve any leftover dressing warm, heat very gently over low heat, whisking. The dressing will keep for up to 1 week.

1. Cook the bacon in a large skillet over medium-high heat until crisp and golden, about 5 minutes. Drain on paper towels.

2. Place the lettuce halves cut side up on four plates. Sprinkle with the candied pecans and bacon. Drizzle 2 tablespoons of the warm dressing over each salad and serve.

Emeril's Orlando food bar

SALADS

Sweet Potato–Bourbon Dressing

1. Preheat the oven to 350°F.

2. Place the sweet potato on a baking sheet. Bake until tender and starting to ooze sugary syrup, about 1 hour and 20 minutes. Remove from the oven and let sit until cool enough to handle.

3. Cut a slit down the potato and scoop the flesh into a bowl. Discard the skin.

4. Put the cream in a small saucepan and bring to a low simmer over medium heat. Remove from the heat.

5. Combine the brown sugar, corn syrup, butter, and water in a small saucepan. Bring to a boil and boil for 1 minute. Add the hot cream and boil for 1 minute. Remove from the heat and let cool slightly.

6. Combine the sweet potato, warm sugar mixture, vinegar, bourbon, shallots, allspice, salt, and pepper in a food processor and purée for 30 seconds. Gradually add the oil, pulsing to blend. Serve warm. (Leftover dressing can be kept in an airtight container in the refrigerator for up to 1 week.)

1 large sweet potato
  (about ¾ pound)
½ cup heavy cream
½ cup packed light brown
  sugar
¼ cup dark corn syrup
4 tablespoons unsalted
  butter
2 tablespoons water
¼ cup apple cider vinegar
¼ cup Kentucky bourbon or
  other bourbon
1 tablespoon chopped
  shallots
⅛ teaspoon ground allspice
1 teaspoon salt
½ teaspoon freshly cracked
  black pepper
½ cup vegetable oil

Fried Green Tomatoes with Lump Crabmeat and Two Rémoulade Sauces

1 cup all-purpose flour
¼ cup Emeril's Original
  Essence or Creole
  Seasoning (page 28),
  plus more for dusting
½ cup buttermilk
2 large eggs
1 cup yellow cornmeal
½ to 1 cup vegetable oil,
  for panfrying
2 pounds (6 medium)
  green tomatoes, cut
  crosswise into ½-
  inch-thick slices
  (discard the ends; you
  should have 24 slices)
1 pound lump crabmeat,
  picked over for shells
  and cartilage
1 tablespoon fresh
  lemon juice
½ teaspoon salt
4 cups thinly sliced
  mesclun or other baby
  greens
1 recipe White
  Rémoulade Sauce
1 recipe Red Rémoulade
  Sauce

Talk about a twist! Here we've got fried green tomatoes, that big Southern favorite, with my tweak on shrimp rémoulade. Instead of shrimp, I use sweet lump crabmeat, and not one but two (!) rémoulade sauces. And don't be reluctant to make the two sauces; while you won't use all of them for this dish, they keep for several days refrigerated. They go well with just about everything, from seafood to chicken to vegetables. This is very popular at Delmonico, and one bite will tell you why.

1. Combine the flour and 1 tablespoon of the Essence in a shallow bowl. In another shallow bowl, whisk together the buttermilk and eggs. Put the cornmeal in another shallow bowl and season with 1 tablespoon of the Essence.

2. Heat ½ cup of the vegetable oil in a large heavy skillet until hot but not smoking.

3. Season both sides of each tomato slice with ⅛ teaspoon of the Essence. Dredge the tomatoes in the flour, coating evenly on both sides and shaking to remove any excess, then dip in the egg wash, letting the excess drip off, and then dredge in the cornmeal, shaking to remove any excess. Add several tomato slices at a time to the hot oil and fry until golden brown, about 2 minutes per side. Remove with a slotted spoon and drain on paper towels. Sprinkle lightly with Essence. Repeat with the remaining tomatoes, adding more oil to the pan as necessary.

4. Place the crabmeat in a medium bowl and toss gently with the lemon juice and salt, being careful not to break up the lumps of crab.

5. To serve, arrange the lettuce in the center of six plates and top with the crabmeat. Arrange the fried green tomatoes around the crabmeat and spoon the two sauces over the tomatoes. Serve.

SALADS

White Rémoulade Sauce

¾ cup mayonnaise,
   homemade (page 31) or
   store-bought
2 tablespoons finely
   chopped green onions
   (green parts only)
2 tablespoons finely
   chopped yellow onions
2 tablespoons finely
   chopped celery
2 teaspoons finely chopped
   fresh parsley
2 teaspoons Dijon mustard
1 teaspoon prepared horseradish
1 teaspoon powdered
   mustard
½ teaspoon minced garlic
½ teaspoon Worcestershire
   sauce
¼ teaspoon salt
¼ teaspoon freshly ground
   white pepper

Combine all the ingredients in a bowl and whisk to blend. Cover and refrigerate until needed. (Stored in an airtight container, this will keep for up to 2 days.)

Red Rémoulade Sauce

Combine all the ingredients in a bowl and whisk lightly to blend. Cover and refrigerate until needed. (Stored in a airtight container, this will keep for up to 2 days.)

1/3 cup mayonnaise, homemade (page 31) or store-bought
2 tablespoons ketchup
2 tablespoons finely chopped celery
1 tablespoon finely chopped yellow onions
1 tablespoon finely chopped green onions (green parts only)
1 tablespoon Creole mustard or other whole-grain mustard
1½ teaspoons red wine vinegar
1½ teaspoons rice wine vinegar
1½ teaspoons paprika
1½ teaspoons minced fresh parsley
1 teaspoon prepared horesradish
1 teaspoon Emeril's Kick It Up Red Pepper Sauce or other hot pepper sauce
½ teaspoon minced garlic

General manager Fred Sutherland at NOLA's entrance

SALADS

Blue Crab, Smoked Salmon, and Caviar Salad with Dilled Buttermilk Dressing

1 large head Bibb lettuce (about 8 ounces), cored, quartered, rinsed, and patted dry

¾ cup Dilled Buttermilk Dressing

½ pound jumbo lump crabmeat, picked over for shells or cartilage

6 ounces Home-Smoked Salmon (page 19) or store-bought hot-smoked salmon, flaked (or store-bought cold-smoked salmon, diced)

½ cup thinly sliced red onions

2 tablespoons snipped fresh chives

2 tablespoons champagne vinegar

2 tablespoons canola oil

¼ teaspoon salt

¼ teaspoon freshly ground black pepper

1 ounce good quality American caviar (see headnote), such as bowfin, paddlefish, American sturgeon, or salmon roe

At NOLA we use choupique caviar, the roe of the bowfin, a prehistoric bony freshwater fish indigenous to South Louisiana. Choupique is the Cajun name for bowfin, and the fish's black eggs resemble those of the sturgeon, with a distinctive, lively flavor. Should you use this roe in other recipes, be forewarned that choupique caviar turns red when heated or cooked. If you're feeling extravagant, use Beluga or Sevruga caviar instead of the choupique. Salmon roe also makes a great substitute.

1. Place the lettuce on four large salad plates and drizzle lightly with the buttermilk dressing to taste.

2. Combine the crabmeat, salmon, onions, chives, vinegar, oil, salt, and pepper in a large bowl and toss gently. Arrange on the lettuce and drizzle each serving with 3 tablespoons of the dressing. Place about 1 teaspoon of the caviar in the center of each salad, and serve.

Dilled Buttermilk Dressing

1 large egg
2 tablespoons fresh lemon juice
1½ teaspoons chopped fresh dill
1 cup canola oil
½ cup buttermilk
¾ teaspoon salt
¼ teaspoon freshly ground black pepper

Combine the egg, lemon juice, and dill in a food processor or blender and process for 15 seconds. With the machine running, add the oil in a thin, steady stream, processing until an emulsion forms. Transfer to a bowl and whisk in the buttermilk, salt, and pepper. (Leftover dressing will keep refrigerated for up to 1 day.)

Delmonico Steakhouse dining room

SALADS

Warm Watercress Salad with Stir-Fried Beef and Kimchee

MAKES 4 SERVINGS

2 tablespoons soy sauce
2 tablespoons chopped garlic
1 tablespoon sesame oil
1 tablespoon sugar
2 teaspoons minced ginger
½ teaspoon freshly ground
   black pepper
½ teaspoon fish sauce
   (nuoc nam)
½ pound flank steak, sliced
   into ⅛-inch-thick 2-inch-
   long slivers
1 tablespoon vegetable oil
3 Roma (plum) tomatoes,
   quartered
1 bunch green onions, cut
   into 2-inch pieces (green
   and white parts)
4 cups watercress, tough
   stems removed, rinsed,
   and patted dry
1 cup Kimchee
¼ cup chopped fresh cilantro

Kimchee is a Korean spicy pickled cabbage served as a condiment. It needs to be made at least twenty-four hours in advance for the flavors to develop, and it gets even better after several days. Mrs. Hay Nguyen, one of our original NOLA kitchen team members, inspired this Asian-style salad. The first time she made kimchee, it was so good we put it on the menu!

1. Whisk together the soy sauce, garlic, sesame oil, sugar, ginger, pepper, and fish sauce in a medium bowl. Add the steak and toss to coat with the marinade. Cover with plastic wrap and marinate in the refrigerator for at least 8 hours, or overnight.

2. Heat the oil in a wok or large skillet over high heat. Add the beef, tomatoes, and green onions and cook, stirring, until the beef is cooked to medium, 2 to 3 minutes.

3. Place the watercress in a large bowl and toss with the beef mixture and kimchee. Divide among four plates and garnish with the cilantro. Serve immediately.

½ pound carrots, peeled and julienned
½ large daikon radish (about ½ pound), peeled and julienned
1 jalapeño, seeded and minced
2 cups white distilled vinegar
1 cup sugar
2 tablespoons salt
2 tablespoons minced garlic

Kimchee

1. Combine the carrots, radish, and jalapeño in a large bowl.

2. Combine the remaining ingredients in a small saucepan and bring to a boil, stirring to dissolve the sugar. Remove from the heat and let cool to room temperature.

3. Add the cooled vinegar mixture to the vegetables and stir well. Cover with plastic wrap and let sit at room temperature for 24 hours, then refrigerate until ready to serve. (The kimchee will keep refrigerated for up to 1 week.)

General manager Brian Molony, Emeril's Delmonico

SALADS

Duck Confit Salad with Dried Berries, Stilton Cheese, Arugula, and Vanilla-Shallot Vinaigrette

Duck confit is easier to make than you might imagine, so we've included a recipe in the Basics chapter. Don't let the fact that it takes a couple of days to make scare you off—there are only a few ingredients involved, the procedure is easy, and the slow cooking time ensures an amazingly rich flavor and texture. The amount we call for here is the equivalent of three duck legs.

¾ pound Duck Confit (page 16), removed from the bones and shredded (about 1½ cups meat)

½ pound radicchio, cored, rinsed, patted dry, and coarsely chopped

4 ounces Belgian endive (1 large or 2 small heads), cores removed and leaves separated

4 ounces arugula (about 6 cups), tough stems removed, rinsed, and patted dry

1 recipe Vanilla-Shallot Vinaigrette

⅛ teaspoon salt

¼ teaspoon freshly ground black pepper

¼ pound Stilton cheese, crumbled

2 tablespoons dried cherries

Combine the duck confit, radicchio, endive, arugula, vinaigrette, salt, and pepper in a large bowl and toss to mix. Add the cheese and cherries and toss. Divide among four salad plates and serve.

Entrance to Emeril's New Orleans Fish House

Vanilla-Shallot Vinaigrette

4 shallots (about 3 ounces), peeled and trimmed
1 teaspoon olive oil
¾ teaspoon salt
⅜ teaspoon freshly ground white pepper
1 vanilla bean
¼ cup plus 1 tablespoon extra-virgin olive oil
1 tablespoon champagne vinegar
1 teaspoon fresh lemon juice
¼ teaspoon freshly ground black pepper
⅛ teaspoon sugar

1. Preheat the oven to 300°F.

2. Place the shallots in a small baking pan. Add the olive oil, ½ teaspoon of the salt, and ¼ teaspoon of the white pepper and toss to coat. Roast until the shallots are tender and just beginning to color, 30 to 35 minutes. Remove from the oven and let cool.

3. Thinly slice the shallots and place in a medium bowl.

4 Split the vanilla bean lengthwise in half. With the tip of a sharp knife, scrape out the seeds and add them to the shallots. (Reserve the vanilla pod for another use.) Add the olive oil, vinegar, lemon juice, the remaining ¼ teaspoon salt, the black pepper, the remaining ⅛ teaspoon white pepper, and the sugar to the bowl with the shallots, and whisk well to blend. (The dressing will keep refrigerated in an airtight container for up to 5 days.)

Charlotte Armstrong Martory testing recipes at Emeril's Homebase

SALADS

Fried Rabbit Salad with Buttermilk-Parmesan Dressing

¾ *pound boneless rabbit meat, cut into 1-inch pieces*

3½ *tablespoons Emeril's Original Essence or Creole Seasoning (page 28)*

1 *large egg*

¼ *cup whole milk*

½ *cup all-purpose flour*

1 *cup fine dry bread crumbs*

4 *cups vegetable oil, for deep-frying*

6 *cups mesclun greens or baby lettuces, rinsed and patted dry*

½ *to ¾ cup Buttermilk-Parmesan Dressing*

In 1983, a couple of local chefs and I hooked up to form a cooperative, and I then discovered a great farmer, Dan Crutchfield. Dan supplied me with farm-raised rabbits and they were the inspiration for this great salad. The buttermilk dressing can be used on a variety of things—toss it with greens or use it as a dip for vegetables.

1. Place the rabbit in a medium bowl and toss with 1 tablespoon of the Essence.

2. Combine the egg, milk, and 1½ teaspoons of the Essence in a shallow bowl and whisk to blend. Combine the flour with 1½ teaspoons of the Essence in another shallow bowl, and the bread crumbs with another 1 tablespoon of Essence in another shallow bowl.

3. Heat the oil to 350°F in a medium heavy pot or deep-fryer.

4. Dredge the rabbit, in batches, in the flour, tossing to coat, then dip in the egg wash, shaking to remove any excess, and dredge in the bread crumbs, shaking to remove any excess. Deep-fry, in batches, until golden brown and cooked through, 2 to 2½ minutes. Remove and drain on paper towels. Season with the remaining 1½ teaspoons Essence.

5. Place the greens in a large bowl and toss with about ½ cup of the dressing. Divide among four plates and top with the fried rabbit. Drizzle with a little additional dressing, and serve.

Buttermilk-Parmesan Dressing

1 large egg
1 teaspoon fresh lemon juice
¾ teaspoon salt
½ cup vegetable oil
¼ cup buttermilk
¼ cup chopped green onions (green parts only)
¼ cup freshly grated Parmigiano-Reggiano
1 teaspoon minced garlic
1 teaspoon freshly ground black pepper

Place the egg, lemon juice, and salt in a food processor or blender and process for 30 seconds. With the motor running, add the oil in a slow, steady stream, processing until an emulsion forms. With the motor running, add the buttermilk, green onions, cheese, garlic, and pepper and process for 15 seconds. Transfer to an airtight container and refrigerate until ready to serve. (The dressing will keep refrigerated for 1 day.)

Manager Raul Gonzalez and chef Shannon Rowland at Emeril's Orlando evening pre-meal meeting

SALADS

117

5 | BRUNCH

Sunday jazz brunch,
Emeril's Delmonico

Emeril's ORLANDO

Bacon Pancakes with Walnut Butter and Caramelized Onions

MAKES 18 PANCAKES; 6 SERVINGS

6 slices thick-cut bacon, chopped
2 cups all-purpose flour
2 teaspoons baking powder
¼ teaspoon salt
1 large egg, beaten
2¼ cups buttermilk
1 to 2 tablespoons vegetable oil
1 recipe Walnut Butter, thinly sliced
½ recipe Caramelized Onions (page 271)

These pancakes make an unusual appetizer or brunch dish. And for a kicked-up breakfast version, try serving these drizzled with my morning favorite, Steen's 100% Pure Cane syrup!

1. Cook the bacon in a large skillet over medium-high heat until crisp, about 5 minutes. Remove from the pan and drain on paper towels.

2. Sift the flour, baking powder, and salt into a large bowl. Add the egg and buttermilk and stir until just blended, being careful not to overmix. Add the bacon and stir to blend.

3. Heat 2 teaspoons of the oil in a large nonstick skillet over medium-high heat. Ladle 2 tablespoons of the batter for each pancake into the pan, without crowding, and cook until golden brown on both sides, 2 to 3 minutes per side. Transfer to a plate and cover to keep warm. Repeat with the remaining batter, adding more oil to the pan as needed.

4. To serve, place three pancakes on each plate. Top each pancake with a slice of the walnut butter and some onions, and serve immediately.

Emeril's New Orleans dining room

½ cup walnut pieces
8 tablespoons (1 stick)
unsalted butter, cut
into pieces, at room
temperature
1 tablespoon minced
shallots
½ teaspoon salt

Walnut Butter

1. Preheat the oven to 400°F.

2. Spread the walnuts on a baking sheet and lightly toast in the oven for 5 to 7 minutes. Remove from the oven and let cool, then coarsely chop.

3. Combine the butter, walnuts, shallots, and salt in a medium bowl and mix well with a rubber spatula. Spoon the butter mixture into the center of a sheet of plastic wrap or wax paper, forming a log about 1 inch in diameter. Fold the wrap over the butter and gently push in and under to form a smooth cylinder. Twist the ends to seal. Refrigerate until firm, about 1 hour. (Refrigerate for up to 1 week or freeze for up to 1 month.)

Dinner ready to leave
Emeril's New Orleans Fish
House kitchen

BRUNCH

Savory Leek and Prosciutto Tart

1 recipe Flaky Butter
   Crust (page 36)
8 leeks
4 tablespoons unsalted
   butter
1 teaspoon chopped
   garlic
1 teaspoon salt
$1/2$ teaspoon freshly
   ground black pepper
Pinch of grated nutmeg
2 large eggs
$1/4$ cup heavy cream
4 ounces prosciutto, cut
   into medium dice
$1/2$ cup freshly grated
   Parmigiano-Reggiano
$1/2$ cup grated Gruyère

This tart is quite dense, as it uses only one-quarter cup of cream and two eggs, compared to the usual proportion of 1 cup of cream and three eggs used in savory tarts. The leek, prosciutto, and two cheeses pack an intense flavor that makes this a delicious brunch dish or appetizer. Or pair it with a large salad and fruit for a light main course.

1. On a lightly floured surface, roll out the dough to an 11-inch circle. Fit it into a 9-inch fluted tart pan with a removable bottom and trim the edges. Refrigerate for at least 30 minutes.

2. Preheat the oven to 400°F.

3. Line the pastry with parchment paper and fill with pie weights or dried beans. Bake until the crust is set, about 12 minutes. Remove the paper and weights and bake until golden brown, 8 to 10 minutes. Remove from the oven and let cool on a wire rack. Leave the oven on.

4. Trim off the root ends and green parts from the leeks. Cut the leeks lengthwise in half and then crosswise into $1/4$-inch-thick slices. Place in a bowl of cold water and rinse well. Drain, place in fresh water, and soak again. Drain well.

5. Melt the butter in a large skillet over medium-high heat. When it is foamy, add the leeks, garlic, salt, pepper, and nutmeg and stir well to mix. Reduce the heat to low, cover, and cook until the leeks are very soft but not browned, about 15 minutes, stirring occasionally. Remove from the heat and drain in a fine-mesh strainer.

6. Combine the eggs and cream in a medium bowl and whisk well. Add the prosciutto and two cheeses and whisk well. Add the leeks and whisk to combine. Pour into the tart shell and bake until golden brown, 40 to 45 minutes. Let cool for at least 20 minutes on a wire rack before serving. Serve warm or at room temperature.

MAKES 6 SERVINGS

4 phyllo pastry sheets (each
    about 12 × 18 inches),
    thawed if frozen
8 tablespoons (1 stick)
    unsalted butter, melted
1 recipe Mushroom Duxelles
3 Boiled Artichokes
    (page 14)
3 tablespoons unsalted
    butter
24 spears Blanched
    Asparagus (page 14)
6 ounces lump crabmeat,
    picked over for shells and
    cartilage
½ teaspoon salt
¼ teaspoon freshly ground
    white pepper
1 recipe Poached Eggs
1 recipe Béarnaise Sauce

Poached Eggs Erato

This is my take on the heavenly egg dishes served at the old-line New Orleans restaurants for brunch, and sometimes at lunch, too. You know the type of dish I mean: Eggs Benedict, Eggs Sardou, Eggs Hussarde, and such. In my opinion, this is the richest one yet. We serve our poached eggs in a baked phyllo pastry basket, on a nest of mushroom duxelles, sautéed artichoke hearts, and lump crabmeat. It's all then topped with a classic béarnaise sauce and garnished with asparagus spears. Heaven! Instead of making the phyllo baskets, you could substitute toast rounds or store-bought or Homemade English Muffins (page 75), but don't skimp on the other ingredients!

1. Preheat the oven to 350°F.

2. Lay the phyllo on a work surface and cover with a damp kitchen towel to keep it from drying out.

3. Turn a 12-cup muffin pan upside down on the work surface. Using a pastry brush, lightly butter the outside of every other cup with melted butter. (Alternatively, butter the outsides of six ramekins placed on a baking sheet.)

4. Place a sheet of phyllo on the work surface and brush with butter. Lay a second sheet on top and brush with butter, then repeat with the remaining phyllo, to make a stack of 4 sheets. Cut into 6 equal rectangles, each about 4 × 6 inches. Drape each stack over a buttered muffin cup and gently shape it into a cup.

5. Bake the cups on the muffin tin until golden and crisp, 12 to 15 minutes. Remove from the oven and carefully lift the cups from the pan, twisting gently to loosen them. Let cool on a wire rack.

6. Arrange the phyllo cups on six large plates. Place 2 tablespoons of the mushroom duxelles in each; set aside.

7. Pull off the large outer leaves from the artichokes, and discard or reserve for another use. Remove and discard the spiky inner leaves. Scrape the hairy choke from each heart, and cut the hearts into ¼-inch-thick slices.

BRUNCH

8. Melt the butter in a large skillet over medium-high heat. Add the artichoke hearts, asparagus, crabmeat, salt, and pepper and cook, stirring, until warmed through, 1 to 2 minutes. Remove from the heat.

9. Divide the artichoke hearts and crabmeat among the phyllo cups. Arrange 4 asparagus spears, tips up, spacing them evenly in each phyllo cup. Place 2 poached eggs on top of the crabmeat mixture in each cup, and spoon ¼ cup of the béarnaise sauce on top of each serving. Serve immediately.

MAKES ABOUT 1 CUP

2 tablespoons unsalted butter
¼ cup minced shallots
1 teaspoon minced garlic
1 pound white button mushrooms, stemmed, wiped clean, and finely chopped
¼ teaspoon salt
¼ teaspoon freshly ground white pepper
⅓ cup dry white wine
1 teaspoon soy sauce
1 teaspoon balsamic vinegar
1 teaspoon Worcestershire sauce

Mushroom Duxelles

1. Heat the butter in a large skillet over medium-high heat. Add the shallots and garlic and cook, stirring, for 30 seconds. Add the mushrooms, salt, and white pepper and cook, stirring, until all the liquid has evaporated and the mushrooms begin to caramelize, about 12 minutes.

2. Add the wine and cook, stirring to deglaze the pan, until all the liquid has evaporated. Add the soy sauce, balsamic vinegar, and Worcestershire, stir to mix, and cook for 1 minute. Remove from the heat.

1 tablespoon white distilled
    vinegar
12 large eggs

Poached Eggs

1. Pour about 2 inches of cold water into a large deep skillet. Bring to a simmer over high heat, then reduce the heat so that the surface of the water barely shimmers. Add the vinegar.

2. Break 4 of the eggs into individual saucers, then gently slide them one at a time into the water and, with a large spoon, lift the whites over the yolks. Repeat the lifting once or twice to completely enclose each yolk. Poach until the whites are set and the yolks feel soft when gently touched, 3 to 4 minutes. Remove the eggs with a slotted spoon and serve immediately, or place in a shallow pan or large bowl of cold water. Repeat with the remaining eggs, adding more water as needed to keep the depth at 2 inches and bringing the water to a simmer before adding the eggs.

3. If necessary, just before serving, reheat the eggs, in batches, by slipping them into simmering water for 30 seconds to 1 minute.

2 tablespoons chopped
    shallots
4 sprigs fresh tarragon, plus
    2 tablespoons chopped
    tarragon
¼ cup dry white wine
¼ cup dry vermouth
4 large egg yolks
1 cup melted Clarified Butter
    (page 15) or 16 table-
    spoons (2 sticks) unsalted
    butter, melted
1 teaspoon fresh lemon juice
½ teaspoon salt
⅛ teaspoon freshly ground
    white pepper

Béarnaise Sauce

1. Combine the shallots, tarragon sprigs, white wine, and vermouth in a small saucepan, bring to a boil, and cook until reduced to 4 teaspoons. Strain through a fine-mesh sieve and let cool.

2. Whisk the egg yolks and reduced wine in the top of a double boiler, or in a metal bowl set over a pot of simmering water, until ribbons start to form when the whisk is lifted. Whisking constantly, drizzle in the melted butter, a bit at a time, until the mixture thickens. Remove from the heat, add the lemon juice, chopped tarragon, salt, and pepper, and whisk to blend. Adjust the seasoning to taste.

3. Serve immediately, or keep warm, covered, over a pot of simmering water for 5 to 10 minutes. Whisk before serving.

BRUNCH

Shrimp Toast with Creole Tomato Glaze, Green Onion Slaw, and Smoked Almonds

MAKES 8 SERVINGS

½ **pound peeled and deveined shrimp (about 9 ounces unpeeled)**

1 **large egg**

1 **large egg white**

2 **tablespoons minced green onions (green parts only)**

2 **tablespoons minced fresh cilantro**

1 **teaspoon minced garlic**

½ **teaspoon salt**

⅛ **teaspoon freshly ground white pepper**

3 **ounces cream cheese, cut into pieces**

¼ **cup heavy cream**

8 **slices Brioche (page 34) or home-style white bread**

½ **cup vegetable oil or melted Clarified Butter (page 15) for panfrying**

1 **recipe Green Onion Slaw**

1 **recipe Creole Tomato Glaze**

¼ **cup smoked almonds**

This is a fun addition to any brunch menu. Make the shrimp mixture and the Creole Tomato Glaze on Saturday, and Sunday brunch will be a breeze. The glaze is extremely versatile and will keep for 2 weeks, covered, in the refrigerator.

At Delmonico, the almonds are home-smoked. While the procedure is not difficult, for the small amount called for here, it's easier to use the smoked almonds available at the supermarket. There they leave the almonds whole, but you can roughly chop them and sprinkle over the toast. The recipe for the mayonnaise makes a little more than is needed for the slaw. Use the leftover mayo as a dip for vegetables or boiled artichokes, or mix it with boiled seafood for a terrific salad, or with heavy cream to make a salad dressing.

1. Combine the shrimp, egg, egg white, green onions, cilantro, garlic, salt, and white pepper in a food processor and process until blended but still slightly chunky. Add the cream cheese and pulse until smooth and thick. Add the cream and pulse just until blended, being careful not to overprocess.

2. Spread ¼ cup of the shrimp mixture on each slice of bread, spreading it to the edges and smoothing the top.

3. Heat the vegetable oil to 360°F in a large deep skillet. Add the shrimp toast, in batches, coated side down, and fry until golden on the first side, 2 to 2½ minutes. Turn and cook until golden on the second side, about 1½ minutes. Drain on paper towels.

4. To serve, cut each toast diagonally into quarters. Place ½ cup slaw in the middle of each of eight plates. Lean the shrimp toast quarters up against the slaw, and drizzle each serving with 2 tablespoons of the tomato glaze. Top with the almonds and serve immediately.

*2 cups thinly sliced green
    cabbage*
*1 cup thinly sliced red
    cabbage*
½ cup thinly sliced fennel
*¼ cup chopped green onions
    (green parts only)*
*½ cup Green Onion
    Mayonnaise*
¼ teaspoon salt
*¼ teaspoon freshly ground
    black pepper*

Green Onion Slaw

Combine the green and red cabbages, fennel, and green onions in a large bowl. Add the mayonnaise, salt, and pepper and toss to coat. Cover and refrigerate for at least 30 minutes, or up to 3 hours, before serving.

1 large egg
*¼ cup chopped green onions
    (green parts only)*
*1 tablespoon rice wine
    vinegar*
1 teaspoon Dijon mustard
¼ teaspoon salt
*¼ teaspoon freshly ground
    black pepper*
1 cup vegetable oil

Green Onion Mayonnaise

Combine the egg, green onions, vinegar, mustard, salt, and pepper in a food processor or blender and process for 30 seconds. With the machine running, add the oil in a thin, steady stream and process until the mayonnaise becomes smooth and thick. Transfer to an airtight container and refrigerate until ready to use. (The mayonnaise will keep refrigerated for up to 1 day.)

1 cup sugar

¼ cup Emeril's Kick It Up
   Red Pepper Sauce or
   other hot pepper sauce

¼ cup apple cider
   vinegar

2 tablespoons tomato
   paste

2 tablespoons Creole
   mustard or other
   whole-grain mustard

1 teaspoon kosher salt

½ teaspoon minced
   garlic

½ teaspoon freshly
   ground black pepper

¼ teaspoon celery salt

2 bay leaves

Creole Tomato Glaze

*We call this Creole Glaze not because it's made with Creole toma-
toes, a tomato hybrid indigenous to South Louisiana, but because
of the spiciness of the glaze. At Delmonico it's paired with the Pan-
Roasted Quail (page 214) as well as the shrimp toasts, but it is also
an excellent accompaniment to grilled chicken or shrimp.*

Combine all the ingredients in a medium saucepan. Bring to a simmer over medium-high heat, whisking to dissolve the sugar and
tomato paste, and cook for 3 minutes. Remove from the heat and
let cool to room temperature. Remove the bay leaves before serving. (The glaze will keep refrigerated for up to 2 weeks. Bring to
room temperature before serving.)

Delmonico Steakhouse
interior

Chicken Breast Florentine with Dijon Mustard Cream Sauce and Lyonnaise Potatoes

8 boneless, skinless chicken breast halves (6 ounces each)

4 teaspoons Emeril's Original Essence or Creole Seasoning (page 28)

1 tablespoon plus 1 teaspoon olive oil

8 slices (about 6 ounces) smoked ham

1 recipe Sautéed Spinach

½ pound Brie, cut into 8 thin wedges

1 recipe Lyonnaise Potatoes

1 recipe Dijon Mustard Cream Sauce

The Emeril's Delmonico menu is known for its clever reinterpretations of classic dishes. This dish combines spinach with a Dijon cream sauce in a delicious way that's not too much work. If the Lyonnaise Potatoes seem like too much effort, try a simpler preparation, such as Herb-Roasted Potatoes (page 263).

1. Preheat the oven to 400°F.

2. Season each chicken breast half with ½ teaspoon of the Essence. Heat the olive oil in a large skillet over medium-high heat. Add the chicken, in batches, and sear until lightly colored, 1 to 1½ minutes per side.

3. Transfer the chicken to a baking sheet and roast until cooked through, about 6 minutes. Remove from the oven (leave the oven on), and top each breast half with a slice of ham and a spoonful of spinach. Place a wedge of Brie in the center of each portion of spinach. Return to the oven and cook until the cheese is melted, 4 to 5 minutes. Remove from the oven.

4. To serve, divide the potatoes among four large dinner plates. Arrange 2 chicken breast halves each on top of the potatoes and drizzle with the Dijon cream sauce. Serve immediately.

Sautéed Spinach

2 tablespoons unsalted butter

1 teaspoon minced garlic

1½ pounds spinach, tough stems removed, washed, and finely chopped

¼ teaspoon salt

⅛ teaspoon freshly ground black pepper

Melt the butter in a large skillet over medium-high heat. Add the garlic and cook, stirring, for 30 seconds. Add the spinach, salt, and pepper and cook until the spinach has wilted, 1 to 2 minutes. Remove from the heat and cover to keep warm.

BRUNCH

Lyonnaise Potatoes

1 pound Yukon Gold
  potatoes, peeled and
  cut into ¼-inch-thick
  slices
¼ cup olive oil
1 teaspoon salt
½ teaspoon freshly
  ground black pepper
2 tablespoons unsalted
  butter
2 cups thinly sliced
  yellow onions

1. Bring a medium pot of salted water to a boil. Add the potatoes and cook until just tender, about 3½ minutes. Drain in a colander.

2. Heat the oil in a large skillet over medium-high heat. Add the potatoes, salt, and pepper and cook, shaking the pan occasionally, until golden brown on both sides, about 8 minutes. Remove from the heat.

3. Melt the butter in a large skillet over medium-high heat. Add the onions and cook, stirring occasionally, until golden, about 15 minutes. Add the potatoes and toss. Remove from the heat and cover to keep warm.

Dijon Mustard Cream Sauce

1 teaspoon vegetable oil
1 tablespoon minced
  shallots
1 teaspoon minced garlic
1 tablespoon soy sauce
1 tablespoon
  Worcestershire sauce
1 tablespoon balsamic
  vinegar
1 tablespoon Dijon
  mustard
1 teaspoon chopped
  fresh rosemary
1 cup heavy cream

Heat the oil in a small saucepan over medium heat. Add the shallots and garlic and cook, stirring, for 1 minute. Add the soy sauce, Worcestershire, vinegar, mustard, and rosemary and bring to a boil, stirring to loosen any browned bits on the bottom of the pan. Add the cream and simmer until thick enough to coat the back of a spoon, about 3 minutes. Remove from the heat and cover to keep warm.

Souffléd Spinach and Brie Crêpes with Artichoke Cream Sauce, Sautéed Portobellos and Artichoke Hearts, Fennel Fries, and Asparagus

MAKES 6 SERVINGS

12 Crêpes
1 recipe Spinach Soufflé
¾ pound Brie, cut into ¼-inch-thick slices
3 tablespoons heavy cream
1 recipe Artichoke Cream Sauce
1 recipe Sautéed Portobellos and Artichoke Hearts
1 recipe Fennel Fries
18 stalks Blanched Asparagus (page 14), warmed

This is a main course on the dinner menu at Delmonico Restaurant, but it also makes a great brunch dish. If you're in the mood for something different, a variation of this dish is served at Delmonico's brunch. To make that one, oysters simmered in the artichoke sauce are spooned over the crêpes, and fried leeks (page 49) are served on the side instead of fennel fries.

1. Preheat the oven to 400°F.

2. Lay the crêpes out on a work surface. Cut the spinach soufflé into 12 equal portions. Lay one portion in the center of each crêpe, top with a slice of Brie, and roll up into a log. Place the crêpes seam side down on a large baking sheet. Using a pastry brush or your fingers, paint the top of each crêpe with 1 teaspoon cream.

3. Bake until the crêpes are golden brown, the filling is warmed through, and the cheese is melted, about 15 minutes.

4. To serve, drizzle ⅓ cup of the artichoke cream sauce in a circular pattern on six large plates. Place 2 crêpes each on top of the sauce. Top with the sautéed mushrooms and artichoke hearts and the fennel fries. Place 3 warm asparagus spears on the side of each plate, and serve.

BRUNCH

**7 tablespoons unsalted
butter**
**2 tablespoons fine dry
bread crumbs**
**2 tablespoons finely
chopped yellow onions**
**2 tablespoons all-purpose
flour**
1 cup whole milk
¼ teaspoon salt
**⅛ teaspoon freshly
ground white pepper**
Pinch of grated nutmeg
**½ cup chopped green
onions (green parts
only)**
**1¼ pounds spinach,
tough stems removed
and well rinsed**
8 large eggs, separated

Spinach Soufflé

1. Preheat the oven to 375°F. Butter the bottom and sides of a 10-inch square baking dish with 1 tablespoon of the butter, and coat evenly with the bread crumbs.

2. Melt 2 tablespoons of the butter in a medium saucepan over medium heat. Add the onions and cook until soft, about 2 minutes. Add the flour and cook, stirring constantly, until it starts to form a light roux, about 1 minute. Gradually add the milk, whisking constantly, and bring to a boil. Reduce the heat to medium-low, add the salt, pepper, and nutmeg, and simmer, whisking, until thickened, about 5 minutes. Remove from the heat.

3. Melt the remaining 4 tablespoons butter in a large skillet over medium-high heat. Add the green onions and spinach, one-third at a time, letting the spinach wilt after each addition, and cook, stirring, until tender, 4 to 5 minutes. Remove from the heat and let stand briefly.

4. When it is cool enough to handle, place the spinach in a fine-mesh strainer and press with a large spoon to remove the excess liquid. Transfer to a food processor. Add the white sauce and egg yolks, and process until smooth.

5. Whip the egg whites in a large bowl until stiff peaks form. Fold in the spinach mixture. Pour into the prepared dish and bake until risen and golden brown, about 30 minutes. Remove from the oven and let cool completely, then refrigerate until thoroughly chilled, at least 3 hours, or overnight.

Crêpes

MAKES 12 CREPES

¾ **cup all-purpose flour**
3 **large eggs, beaten**
2 **tablespoons unsalted
    butter, melted**
¾ **cup plus 3 tablespoons
    whole milk**

There are a couple of tricks to making crêpes. First, make sure your pan is good and hot. Then give it only a light coating of melted butter, so the crêpes won't be greasy. (We find that an old pastry brush is a good way to grease the pan lightly.) And don't overcook the crêpes; they don't take much time at all. To simplify things, these crêpes can be made up to a day in advance, stacked between sheets of wax paper, tightly wrapped in plastic wrap, and stored in the refrigerator.

1. Whisk together the flour, eggs, 1½ tablespoons of the butter, and the milk in a bowl to make a smooth thin batter. Cover and refrigerate for at least 30 minutes.

2. Heat a heavy 6-inch skillet or crêpe pan over medium-high heat until hot. Brush lightly with a light coating of the remaining butter, and ladle about ¼ cup of the batter into the pan, tilting the skillet to coat the pan evenly with batter. Cook until the bottom is golden brown and the top is beginning to look dry, 1 to 2 minutes. Using a spatula, carefully turn the crêpe, and cook just until the bottom colors slightly, about 30 seconds. Transfer to a plate and cover loosely to keep warm. Repeat with the remaining batter.

Artichoke Cream Sauce

MAKES 2 CUPS

2 **Boiled Artichokes
    (page 14)**
1 **tablespoon olive or
    vegetable oil**
¼ **cup chopped yellow
    onions**
¼ **cup chopped parsnips**
¼ **cup chopped celery**
¼ **cup chopped leeks (white
    parts only), well rinsed
    and patted dry**
1 **teaspoon chopped garlic**
1 **cup dry white wine**
2 **cups heavy cream**
¾ **teaspoon salt**
⅜ **teaspoon freshly ground
    white pepper**

1. Pull off the large outer leaves from the artichokes and set aside. Remove and discard the spiky inner leaves. Scrape the hairy choke from the hearts, and reserve the hearts for the Sautéed Portobellos and Artichoke Hearts.

2. Heat the oil in a medium heavy pot over medium-high heat. Add the onions, parsnips, celery, and leeks and cook, stirring, for 2 minutes. Add the garlic and cook, stirring, for 30 seconds. Add the artichoke leaves and wine. Bring to a boil and cook, stirring, until the wine is almost evaporated, about 5 minutes. Add the cream, salt, and pepper and lower the heat. Simmer for 5 minutes. Remove from the heat.

3. Transfer to a food processor and process to make a thick paste, about 1 minute. In small batches, pass through a fine-mesh strainer set over a bowl, pressing with a rubber spatula to extract as much sauce as possible. Cover the sauce to keep warm until ready to serve.

BRUNCH

2 Boiled Artichokes
(page 14), plus the
2 hearts reserved
from the Artichoke
Cream Sauce
2 tablespoons olive oil
2 tablespoons minced
shallots
3 large portobello
mushroom caps,
wiped clean and cut
into ¼-inch-thick
slices
¼ teaspoon salt
⅛ teaspoon freshly
ground white pepper
2 tablespoons water

Sautéed Portobellos and Artichoke Hearts

1. Remove the leaves and chokes from the cooked artichokes, as described in the cream sauce recipe above. Slice the 4 artichoke hearts into ½-inch-thick slices.

2. Heat the oil in a large skillet over medium-high heat. Add the shallots, mushrooms, salt, and pepper and cook, stirring, for 2 minutes. Add the artichokes and cook, stirring, for 2 minutes. Add the water and cook for 1 minute, stirring to deglaze the pan. Remove from the heat and cover to keep warm until ready to serve.

4 cups vegetable oil, for
deep-frying
1 cup all-purpose flour
1 teaspoon salt
¼ teaspoon freshly
ground white pepper
1 cup buttermilk
1 large fennel bulb,
stalks trimmed,
tough core removed,
and cut crosswise into
⅛-inch-thick slices

Fennel Fries

1. Heat the oil in a large deep heavy pot or deep-fryer to 350°F.

2. Combine the flour, salt, and pepper in a shallow bowl. Pour the buttermilk into another bowl. In batches, dip the fennel slices in the buttermilk, then dredge in the seasoned flour. Fry until golden brown on both sides, about 2½ minutes. Remove with a slotted spoon and drain on paper towels.

3. Lightly season with salt, and serve.

Twice-Cooked Veal Grillades with Creole Meunière Sauce, Creamy Grits, and Roasted Tomatoes

MAKES 6 SERVINGS

2 pounds veal stew meat, such as shoulder, neck, or shank, cut into 2-inch cubes

2 tablespoons plus 2 teaspoons Emeril's Original Essence or Creole Seasoning (page 28), plus extra for garnish

1¾ teaspoons salt

2 tablespoons vegetable oil

1 cup chopped yellow onions

½ cup chopped celery

½ cup chopped green bell peppers

1 teaspoon minced garlic

1½ cups peeled, seeded, and diced tomatoes

1 teaspoon tomato paste

6 cups Reduced Veal Stock (page 25)

9 Roma (plum) tomatoes (about 1½ pounds), cored and cut lengthwise in half

¾ teaspoon freshly ground black pepper

¼ cup all-purpose flour

2 large eggs

½ cup whole milk

1½ cups fine dry bread crumbs

6 cups vegetable oil, for deep-frying

1 recipe Creole Meunière Sauce

1 recipe Creamy Grits

½ cup chopped fresh parsley, for garnish

Grillades (pronounced "gree-yahds") is a southern Louisiana dish using pounded beef or veal, browned and braised in a sauce with onions, bell peppers, tomatoes, and just the right amount of spices. While the traditional preparation is superb, at the Fish House, they kicked it up another notch by forming the grillades into small cakes, then breading and panfrying them. Holy smokes—are these good, and rich, rich, rich!

Having the grillades as cold as possible before cooking them the second time is essential. And make sure you cook the grillades as long as the recipe specifies, or they may not set up in the refrigerator; they must be firm before moving on to the next step. These are a lot of work but worth every minute of it.

1. Season the meat on all sides with 2 teaspoons of the Essence and 1 teaspoon of the salt. Heat the 2 tablespoons oil in a large Dutch oven or other large pot over medium-high heat. Cook the meat, in batches, turning often, until evenly browned, about 10 minutes. Return all the meat to the pan. Add the onions, celery, and bell peppers and cook, stirring often, until soft, about 3 minutes. Add the garlic and cook, stirring, for 1 minute. Add the diced tomatoes, tomato paste, and 1 teaspoon of the Essence and cook, stirring, for 3 minutes. Add the veal stock and bring to a low simmer. Cover the pan and cook over medium-low heat, stirring occasionally, until the meat is almost falling-apart tender, about 2 hours.

2. Remove from the heat and let sit, covered, for 20 minutes, then remove the meat from the liquid and spread on a plate until cool enough to handle. Set the pan aside.

3. Shred the meat and return it to the cooking liquid, mixing well, then transfer to a large baking dish. Cover and refrigerate until set and firm, at least 3 hours.

4. Preheat the oven to 350°F.

5. Place the tomatoes cut sides up on a baking sheet. Sprinkle with the remaining ¾ teaspoon salt and the pepper. Roast until they have released most of their liquid and are slightly caramelized around the edges, about 1 hour. Set aside.

6. Meanwhile, place the dish of grillades in the freezer until very firm, 20 to 30 minutes.

7. In a medium shallow bowl, combine the flour with 1 teaspoon of the Essence. Whisk together the eggs and milk in a shallow bowl. Combine the bread crumbs with the remaining 4 teaspoons Essence in another shallow bowl.

8. Remove the grillades from the freezer. With a 2-inch cookie cutter, cut out 12 rounds. Place on a baking sheet and refrigerate. Bread 2 grillades rounds at a time, keeping the remaining rounds refrigerated.

9. One at a time, dredge the rounds in the seasoned flour, shaking to remove any excess, then dip into the egg wash and the bread crumbs. Dip again in the egg wash and bread crumbs, coating evenly on all sides, place on a baking sheet or dish, and return them to the refrigerator. Refrigerate the breaded rounds for at least 1 hour so that they are very cold before cooking.

10. Heat the vegetable oil to 375°F in a deep heavy pot or a deep-fryer. In batches, carefully slip the breaded rounds into the hot oil and fry, turning once, until golden brown, 2 to 3 minutes total. Remove from the oil with a slotted spoon and drain on paper towels.

11. To serve, spoon about ⅓ cup of the warm Meunière sauce onto each of six dinner plates, and top with the grits. Place 2 grillade cakes on top of the grits and arrange 2 tomato halves at the top of each plate. Garnish the plates with a sprinkling of Essence and the chopped parsley, and serve immediately.

MAKES ABOUT 2 CUPS

*¼ cup Creole Meunière Base
    (page 28)*
3 tablespoons heavy cream
*¾ pound (3 sticks) cold
    unsalted butter, cut into
    pieces*

Creole Meunière Sauce

Combine the meunière base and heavy cream in a small saucepan and bring to a boil over medium-high heat. Reduce the heat to low and slowly add the cold butter about 1 tablespoon at a time, whisking constantly, adding each new piece before the previous is completely incorporated. Continue until all the butter is incorporated and the sauce coats the back of a spoon, pulling the pan from the heat occasionally to prevent the sauce from breaking. Do not allow to boil. Keep warm in a double boiler until ready to serve.

MAKES ABOUT 5½ CUPS;
6 SERVINGS

2¼ cups water
2¼ cups whole milk
*1 cup regular grits
    (not instant)*
2 teaspoons salt
*1 teaspoon freshly ground
    white pepper*
2 tablespoons cream cheese
*2 tablespoons mascarpone
    cheese*

Creamy Grits

1. Combine the water and milk in a large heavy pot and bring to a boil. Slowly add the grits, salt, and pepper, whisking constantly. Bring to a boil, then reduce the heat to low and simmer, stirring occasionally, until thickened, about 20 minutes.

2. Add the cream cheese and mascarpone and simmer for 5 minutes, stirring occasionally. Remove from the heat and adjust the seasoning to taste. Cover to keep warm until ready to serve.

6 | PASTA, RICE, AND RISOTTO

*Chef Dave McCelvey testing
recipes at Emeril's Homebase*

½ pound angel hair pasta
2 tablespoons olive oil
½ cup chopped tasso
1 tablespoon chopped green
    onions (white parts only)
    plus 3 tablespoons
    chopped green onions
    (green parts only), for
    garnish
1 tablespoon chopped
    shallots
1 teaspoon chopped garlic
1 recipe Smoked Mushrooms
2½ cups heavy cream
2 teaspoons Worcestershire
    sauce
1 teaspoon Emeril's Kick It
    Up Red Pepper Sauce or
    other hot pepper sauce
½ teaspoon salt
2 tablespoons cold unsalted
    butter, cut into pieces
3 tablespoons freshly grated
    Parmigiano-Reggiano

Smoked Mushrooms and Tasso over Angel Hair

In 1983, when I was at Commander's Palace in New Orleans, I really got into making homemade tasso and sausage, adding them to some of the new dishes I put on the menu at the restaurant. At the time, we weren't allowed to have smokers in the Garden District where Commander's is located, so I would toss the mushrooms with a seasoning blend, put them in a wire basket, and shake them over a hot grill to get the smoky flavor I loved. The combination of the smoked mushrooms and tasso is awesome, and it's been on the menu at Emeril's since Day One—and our customers still won't let us take it off the menu!

1. Bring a large pot of salted water to a boil. Add the pasta and cook until just al dente, about 3 minutes. Drain in a colander, return to the pot, and toss with 1 tablespoon of the oil.

2. Meanwhile, heat the remaining tablespoon of oil in a large skillet over medium-high heat. Add the tasso and cook, stirring, for 2 minutes. Add the green onion whites, the shallots, and garlic and cook, stirring, until fragrant, 30 seconds. Add the smoked mushrooms, stir well, and cook for 1 minute. Add the cream and cook until reduced by half, about 10 minutes. Add the Worcestershire, hot sauce, and salt, then stir in the cold butter.

3. Divide the pasta among four or six plates and spoon the sauce evenly over the top. Garnish with the remaining green onions and the cheese and serve.

Smoked Mushrooms

1 pound button
mushrooms,
stemmed, wiped
clean, and quartered
2 tablespoons olive oil
2 tablespoons Emeril's
Original Essence or
Creole Seasoning
(page 28)

1. Combine the mushrooms with the oil and Essence in a medium bowl and toss to coat evenly.

2. Prepare a stovetop smoker according to the manufacturer's instructions. Place the mushrooms on the grill pan, and partially cover the smoker, leaving the lid ajar by 1 inch. Place over medium heat. When it begins to smoke, close the lid completely and cook until the mushrooms are tender, about 25 minutes. Remove from the smoker.

Alain Joseph during recipe testing at Emeril's Homebase

1 pound angel hair pasta
5 slices bacon, cut into
    ¼-inch dice
1½ cups thinly sliced yellow
    onions
2 teaspoons chopped garlic
2 cups fresh or thawed
    frozen green peas
½ cup extra-virgin olive oil
1½ teaspoons salt
½ teaspoon freshly ground
    black pepper
½ cup freshly grated
    Parmigiano-Reggiano
2 tablespoons chopped fresh
    basil
2 tablespoons chopped fresh
    parsley
1 teaspoon chopped fresh
    thyme

Pasta and Peas

Before I opened Emeril's Restaurant, I thought I knew the long hours it took to be in the restaurant business—but when the restaurant is your own it takes even more. That said, this dish was created after a full day and a long night of cooking. And since there were always pasta, bacon, and peas on hand in the kitchen, this became the perfect late, late night snack.

1. Bring a large pot of salted water to a boil. Add the pasta and cook until just al dente, about 3 minutes.

2. Meanwhile, heat a large skillet over medium-high heat. Add the bacon and cook, stirring, until golden, 4 to 5 minutes. Add the onions and garlic and cook, stirring, until soft, about 4 minutes. Add the peas and olive oil and simmer for 2 minutes. Remove from the heat, add the salt and pepper, and cover to keep warm.

3. Drain the pasta and place in a large bowl. Add the sauce, cheese, basil, parsley, and thyme and toss gently to coat. Serve immediately.

Clams, Mussels, Shrimp, and Oysters with Piri Piri Sauce and Chorizo over Fettuccine

One 1½-pound Maine lobster
1 pound fresh or dried fettuccine
¼ cup strained Piri-Piri oil plus ¼ cup Piri Piri Sauce
½ cup freshly grated Parmigiano-Reggiano
¼ cup thinly sliced basil leaves
2 teaspoons salt
¼ teaspoon freshly ground white pepper
12 medium shrimp, peeled and deveined
1 tablespoon Emeril's Original Essence or Creole Seasoning (page 28)
¼ cup olive oil
6 ounces chorizo, removed from casings and coarsely chopped
3 tablespoons minced shallots
1 tablespoon minced garlic
12 clams, scrubbed
12 mussels, scrubbed and debearded
1 cup peeled, seeded, and coarsely chopped tomatoes
3 cups Shrimp Stock (page 24)
12 freshly shucked oysters, with their liquor

Piri Piri sauce separates if it sits for any length of time. We take advantage of this by skimming the oil from some of the sauce and tossing the pasta in it, then using the remaining thick sauce in the seafood broth. Talk about a marriage made in heaven!

1. Fill a medium stockpot three-quarters full with salted water and bring to a boil. Plunge the lobster headfirst into the boiling water and cook, covered, for 7 minutes. With tongs, transfer to a large bowl filled with ice water to cool.

2. When the lobster is cool enough to handle, drain, crack the shell, and remove the meat from the tail and claws. Discard the shells. Coarsely chop the meat and set aside.

3. Bring a large pot of salted water to a boil. Add the pasta and cook, stirring occasionally, until al dente, about 5 minutes for fresh pasta or 8 minutes for dry pasta. Drain in a colander and return to the pot. Add the piri piri oil, ¼ cup of the cheese, 2 tablespoons of the basil, 1 teaspoon of the salt, and the white pepper and toss well to coat.

4. Meanwhile, season the shrimp with the Essence and the remaining 1 teaspoon salt. Heat the olive oil in a large sauté pan or medium pot over high heat. Add the chorizo and cook, stirring occasionally, until browned, about 2 minutes. Add the shrimp and cook, stirring, for 1 minute. Add the shallots and garlic and cook, stirring, for 1 minute. Add the clams, mussels, tomatoes, piri piri sauce, and shrimp stock, cover, and simmer until the clams and mussels open, about 4 minutes. Add the oysters with their liquor and the chopped lobster. Cook, stirring, until the oysters start to curl around the edges, about 2 minutes. Discard any unopened clams or mussels.

5. To serve, pile the pasta into the center of four large plates and arrange equal amounts of the seafood around the edges. Pour the broth over the pasta, garnish with the remaining ¼ cup cheese and 2 tablespoons basil, and serve immediately.

PASTA, RICE, AND RISOTTO

Piri Piri Sauce

This spicy Portuguese sauce is an awesome addition to any dish. Serve it as a condiment for seasoning soups or other pasta dishes to totally kick them up.

¾ cup olive oil

2 jalapeño peppers, coarsely chopped (including stems and seeds)

1 poblano pepper, coarsely chopped (including stem and seeds)

1½ teaspoons red pepper flakes

½ teaspoon salt

¼ teaspoon freshly ground black pepper

1½ teaspoons minced garlic

1. Combine all of the ingredients except the garlic in a medium heavy saucepan and cook, stirring, over high heat for 4 minutes. Add the garlic, remove from the heat, and let cool to room temperature.

2. Pour into a food processor or blender and pulse until smooth. Strain through a fine-mesh strainer. Refrigerate in an airtight container for 7 days before using.

Decadent Angel Hair Pasta Alfredo with Lump Crabmeat and White Truffle Oil

Yes, this is definitely decadent! Your love of rich food will dictate just how large your portions will be.

1 pound angel hair pasta
4 cups heavy cream
2 teaspoons dried basil
1 teaspoon minced garlic
2½ teaspoons salt
½ teaspoon freshly ground white pepper
1 pound jumbo lump crabmeat, picked over for shells and cartilage
2 tablespoons white truffle oil, plus about 2 tablespoons for garnish
1 cup freshly grated Parmigiano-Reggiano plus about ½ cup for serving
3 tablespoons snipped fresh chives

1. Bring a large heavy pot of salted water to a boil. Add the pasta and cook, stirring to separate the strands of pasta, until just barely al dente, about 3 minutes. Drain in a colander.

2. Combine the cream, basil, garlic, salt, and white pepper in the same pot. Bring to a boil and cook for 2 minutes, or until slightly thickened. Add the pasta, toss to coat, and simmer for 2 minutes, stirring occasionally. Add the crabmeat and 2 tablespoons of the truffle oil, stir gently so as to not break up the lumps of crabmeat, and cook for 1 minute. Add 1 cup of the cheese and gently stir to blend.

3. Divide the pasta among six or eight pasta bowls. Drizzle 1 teaspoon of truffle oil over each serving and sprinkle each with 1 tablespoon Parmesan cheese. Garnish with the chopped chives, and serve immediately.

PASTA, RICE, AND RISOTTO

Shrimp Ragout with Noodles

2 pounds medium heads-on
   shrimp in their shells
2 teaspoons Emeril's
   Original Essence or Creole
   Seasoning (page 28)
10 tablespoons (1¼ sticks)
   unsalted butter
½ cup chopped yellow
   onions
¼ cup chopped celery
¼ cup chopped carrots
2 teaspoons paprika
½ cup dry sherry
6 cups water
¼ cup plus 3 tablespoons
   all-purpose flour
1 tablespoon tomato paste
½ teaspoon salt
¼ teaspoon freshly ground
   white pepper
½ cup heavy cream
¾ pound egg noodles
¼ cup chopped fresh
   parsley, for garnish

An exceedingly rich and delicious treat, this is a play on classic Seafood Newburg, which uses lobster shells. Here we make a rich stock from shrimp shells, and the shells are then puréed with the stock to make the sauce. Be sure to use a very fine-mesh strainer, so that no bits of shell pass into the final dish.

I was inspired to make this when I moved near Lake Pontchartrain in New Orleans a few years ago and was able to buy fresh shrimp caught in the lake at neighborhood seafood markets. This became a dish I could count on for an impressive dinner, and it eventually found its way onto the special menu at Emeril's New Orleans and Emeril's Orlando.

1. Peel and devein the shrimp; reserve the heads and shells for the stock. Toss the shrimp with the Essence, cover, and refrigerate.

2. Melt 2 tablespoons of the butter in a large pot over high heat. Add the shrimp shells and heads and cook, stirring constantly, for 5 minutes, or until they are orange-red. Add the onions, celery, and carrots, and cook for 5 minutes. Add the paprika and sherry and cook until most of the liquid has evaporated, about 5 minutes. Add the water and simmer, uncovered, until reduced by nearly half, to about 3½ cups, about 1 hour.

3. Meanwhile, melt 6 tablespoons butter in a small pot. Whisk in the flour and stir to blend. Cook over medium heat, stirring constantly, to make a blond roux, about 5 minutes. Add the tomato paste, salt, and pepper and cook for 2 minutes. Transfer to a shallow bowl and refrigerate until cold.

4. Pour the cream into a small saucepan and bring to a simmer over medium heat. Remove from the heat.

5. Add the cooled roux to the shrimp stock and whisk to blend. With a hand-held immersion blender, or in batches in a blender, purée the stock mixture, including the shells. Strain through a very fine-mesh strainer into a clean pot, pressing hard on the solids with the back of a spoon to extract as much liquid as possible. Add the hot cream and the shrimp, stir to mix, and cook over medium heat until the shrimp are cooked through, about 8 minutes. Remove from the heat and whisk in the remaining 2 tablespoons butter. Remove from the heat and cover to keep warm.

6. Bring a large pot of salted water to a boil. Add the egg noodles and cook until tender, 5 to 7 minutes. Drain in a colander.

7. To serve, divide the egg noodles among four or six pasta bowls. Top with the ragout, garnish with the chopped parsley, and serve immediately.

Upstairs dining room at NOLA

Roasted Red Peppers Stuffed with Mozzarella, Basil, and Angel Hair Pasta in a Garlic–White Wine Broth

2 heads garlic
2 tablespoons plus 2
   teaspoons olive oil
1½ teaspoons salt
1⅛ teaspoons freshly
   ground black pepper
4 large red bell peppers
½ pound fresh mozzarella,
   preferably buffalo
   mozzarella, thinly sliced
1 tablespoon unsalted butter
2 cups dry white wine
6 ounces angel hair pasta
¼ cup extra-virgin olive oil
2 teaspoons minced garlic
¼ cup thinly sliced fresh
   basil leaves

This is a great vegetarian dish with a cool presentation. Take care when roasting, peeling, and seeding the peppers in order to keep them from falling apart. For a nonvegetarian version, kick it up and add some lump crabmeat and sautéed shrimp to the broth.

1. Preheat the oven to 400°F.

2. Cut off the top quarter of each head of garlic, and set the garlic on a small foil-lined baking sheet. Drizzle 2 teaspoons of the oil over the tops and sprinkle with ¼ teaspoon salt and ⅛ teaspoon pepper. Turn cut side down and roast until the cloves are tender but still firm enough to slice, 30 to 35 minutes. Remove from the oven and let stand until cool enough to handle. Leave the oven on.

3. Meanwhile, roast the peppers over an open gas flame, turning frequently with tongs, until all sides are charred black, 7 to 10 minutes. (Alternatively, the peppers can be roasted under a broiler, or on a gas or charcoal grill.) Place the blackened peppers in a plastic or paper bag, seal tightly, and let stand until cool enough to handle, about 15 minutes.

4. Peel the peppers. Make a slit down one side of each one and open flat. Remove the seeds and stems. Season each pepper with a pinch of salt and pepper. Reserve 4 slices of mozzarella for garnish, and stuff the peppers with the remaining cheese. Set aside.

5. Squeeze the garlic cloves from the skins, and cut into slivers.

6. Melt the butter with the remaining 2 tablespoons oil in a large ovenproof skillet over medium heat. Add the garlic slivers and cook, stirring, for 1 minute. Add the white wine and cook for 1 minute. Remove from the heat.

7. Bring a large saucepan of salted water to a boil. Add the pasta and cook until al dente, about 3 minutes. Drain in a colander.

8. Meanwhile, heat the extra-virgin olive oil in a large ovenproof skillet over medium-high heat. Add the minced garlic and cook, stirring, for 30 seconds. Add the pasta and basil and toss to coat evenly. Add the remaining 1¼ teaspoons salt and 1 teaspoon pepper and toss well. Remove from the heat.

9. With tongs, stuff the peppers with the pasta. Fold the peppers over to enclose the stuffing. Place the reserved mozzarella on top of the pasta. Arrange the peppers in the skillet with the roasted garlic–wine broth and cover tightly with aluminum foil. Roast for 10 minutes. Remove the foil and roast for 5 minutes longer.

10. With a slotted spoon, transfer each pepper to a large pasta bowl. Ladle the broth over the peppers, and serve immediately.

Richard Ziegler, general manager, Delmonico Steakhouse

PASTA, RICE, AND RISOTTO

1½ pounds lean ground
    lamb
1 cup chopped yellow onions
1 tablespoon chopped garlic
2 ounces prosciutto, diced
2 tablespoons tomato paste
¼ cup pine nuts, lightly
    toasted
One 28-ounce can diced
    tomatoes, with their
    juices
One 14-ounce can diced
    tomatoes, with their
    juices
2 teaspoons chopped fresh
    oregano
1 teaspoon chopped fresh
    rosemary
¾ teaspoon salt
½ teaspoon freshly ground
    black pepper
1 pound ricotta cheese or
    Homemade Ricotta
    (page 241)
6 ounces feta cheese,
    crumbled
1¼ packed cups freshly
    grated Parmigiano-
    Reggiano
1 pound lasagna noodles

Lamb and Feta
Cheese Lasagna

The combination of the lamb and feta in this eastern Mediterranean-influenced lasagna is fabulous. If you want to use the Homemade Ricotta for this lasagna, note that you'll need to increase the recipe by half. Oh, and this cooking method doesn't require that the noodles be precooked before assembly. They cook in the sauce, tightly covered.

1. Preheat the oven to 350°F.

2. Heat a large deep skillet over medium-high heat. Add the lamb and cook, stirring to break up the meat, for 2 minutes. Drain in a colander.

3. Discard the fat from the pan, return the meat to the pan, and cook over medium-high heat for 3 minutes. Add the onions and cook, stirring, for 3 minutes. Add the garlic and cook, stirring, for 30 seconds. Add the prosciutto and tomato paste, stir well, and cook for 1 minute. Stir in the pine nuts. Add the tomatoes with their juices and bring to a boil. Reduce the heat to medium-low and simmer, stirring occasionally, for 25 minutes.

4. Add the oregano, rosemary, salt, and pepper and stir well. Remove from the heat and let cool.

5. Combine the ricotta, feta, and 1 cup of the Parmesan in a medium bowl and mix well.

6. Place a layer of lasagna noodles in the bottom of a 9-inch square baking dish, spread one-third of the lamb mixture over the noodles, and top with one-third of the cheese mixture. Repeat with the remaining ingredients, for three layers in all. Sprinkle the top with the remaining ¼ cup Parmesan.

7. Cover tightly with aluminum foil and bake for 50 minutes. Uncover and bake until bubbling and golden brown, about 15 minutes longer. Remove from the oven and let stand for 15 minutes before serving.

Creole Boiled Shrimp Cocktail (page 44)

Poached Oysters in Herbsaint Cream with Black Pepper Crème Fraîche, Beluga Caviar, and Deep-Fried Spinach (page 50)

Firecracker-Roll Wontons with Dipping Sauce (page 58)

Home-Smoked Salmon Cheesecake with Sweet Onion and Mirliton Slaw, Creamy Ravigote, and Marinated Black Beans (page 60)

Spiny Lobster–Tomato Saffron Stew with Shaved
Artichoke and Olive Salad (page 92)

Arugula-Stuffed Vidalia Onion Ring Salad
with Lemon Herb Vinaigrette (page 96)

Hearts of Palm
Salad with
Tomatoes, Orange
Segments, Bibb
Lettuce, Shaved
Fennel, and
Cucumber-Yogurt
Dressing
(page 97)

Bibb Lettuce
Wedges with
Warm Black-Eyed
Pea and Bacon
Vinaigrette,
Balsamic Braised
Onions, Spiced
Walnuts, Pears,
and Roquefort
Cheese
(page 100)

Sliced Tomato Salad with Herb Vinaigrette, Red Onions, and Maytag Blue Cheese (page 99)

Caramelized Grapefruit with Watercress, Endive, Blue Cheese,
and Basil-Caramel Vinaigrette (page 103)

Warm Watercress
Salad with Stir-
Fried Beef and
Kimchee
(page 112)

Poached Eggs
Erato
(page 123)

Souffléd Spinach and Brie Crêpes with Artichoke Cream
Sauce, Sautéed Portobellos and Artichoke Hearts, Fennel
Fries, and Asparagus (page 131)

Shrimp Toast with Creole Tomato Glaze, Green
Onion Slaw, and Smoked Almonds (page 126)

Shrimp and
Coconut Milk
Risotto with
Summer Squash,
Peas, and Roasted
Red Pepper Sauce
(page 152)

Roasted Red
Peppers Stuffed
with Mozzarella,
Basil, and Angel
Hair Pasta in a
Garlic–White Wine
Broth (page 148)

Roasted Pumpkin Stuffed with Duck and Mushroom Risotto (page 156)

Cedar-Planked Fish with Citrus Horseradish
Crust and Citrus Butter Sauce (page 160)
with Vietnamese seafood salad

Potato-Crusted
Pompano on
Warm Chanterelle
and Lump
Crabmeat Salad,
with Fava Bean
Cream and
Crawfish Foam
(page 165)

Grilled Whole Fish
Emeril-Style
(page 168)

Poached Grouper with Mango Salsa, Smashed Avocado, Coconut-Cilantro Rice Pilaf, Black Bean Sauce, and Tortilla Chips (page 169)

Yellowfin Tuna Niçoise (page 184)

Roasted Poussins with Spiced Butternut Squash Purée, Crispy Sage Leaves, and Fresh Huckleberry Syrup (page 197)

Roasted Garlic–Glazed Chicken with Lemon Herb Sauce, Creole Rice Pilaf, and Vegetable Brochettes (page 199)

Funky Chicken Roulade with Parslied Rigatoni (page 205)

Cumin-Rubbed
Duck Breast with
Cilantro Sticky
Rice, Smoky Black
Beans, and Rock
Shrimp Salsa
Fresca (page 212)

Tasso-and-
Cornbread–
Stuffed
Quail with
Fig Glaze
(page 217)

Ingredients for Dry-Aged Rib-Eyes with
Emeril's Maître d'Hôtel Butter (page 230)

Seared Beef
Tournedos with
Herb-Roasted
Potatoes and
Sauce au Poivre
(page 232)

Panéed Veal
Medallions with
Lump Crabmeat
Ravioli, Red
Pepper Cream
Sauce, and
Asparagus
(page 247)

Grilled Veal Chops with Herb Cheese, Wild Mushroom–Tomato Bordelaise, and Prosciutto-Wrapped Asparagus (page 244)

Pork Tenderloin en Croûte (page 253)

Scalloped Potatoes (page 262)

Sour Cream Toffee Fudge Cake (page 289)

Caramelized Apple Cheesecake with Spiced Crème Anglaise and Butterscotch Sauce (page 294)

White Chocolate Raspberry Mascarpone Cream Pie in a Pistachio Crust (page 304)

Banana Boston Cream Pie (page 300)

Dessert Pizzas with Fresh Strawberries, Armagnac-
Scented Goat Cheese, and Mint (page 312)

Chicory Coffee Crème Brûlée with Brown
Sugar Shortbread Cookies (page 315)

Pecan Lace
Cookies
(page 317)

Bananas Foster
(page 318)

Strawberries Romanoff with Mint Syrup (page 327)

Fig-and-Balsamic Syrup Mille-Feuille (page 320)

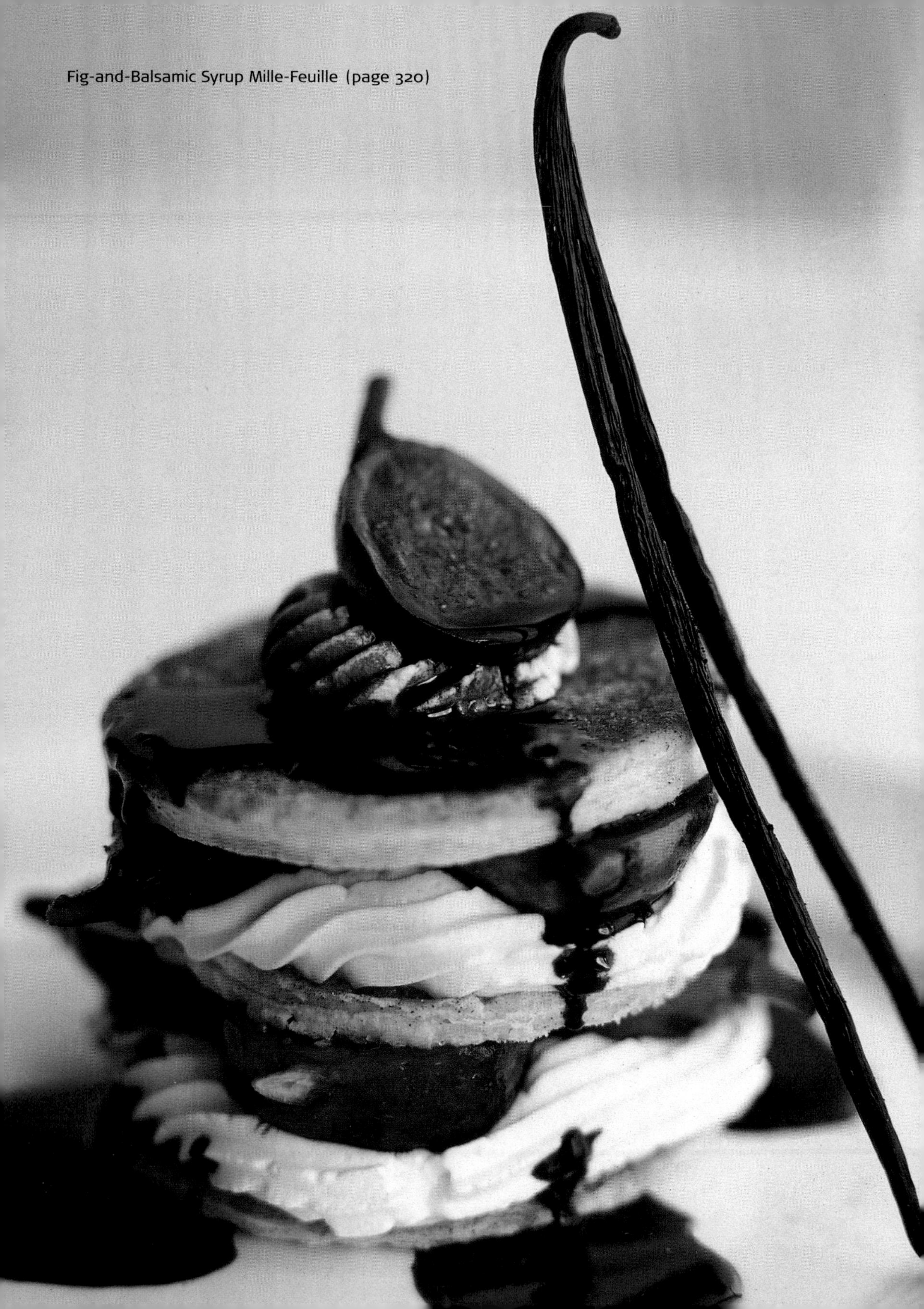

3 tablespoons canola or
    vegetable oil
1 teaspoon sesame oil
1½ teaspoons minced
    garlic
1½ teaspoons minced
    ginger
¼ cup plus 2 tablespoons
    thinly sliced on the
    bias green onions
    (green parts only)
½ cup chopped yellow
    onions
½ cup chopped carrots
½ cup chopped green
    bell peppers
½ cup chopped zucchini
½ cup chopped button
    mushrooms
3 cups cooked White Rice
    (page 19)
¼ cup soy sauce
2 tablespoons sugar
¼ teaspoon freshly
    ground black pepper
1 recipe Chinese Omelet
¼ cup roasted peanuts
2 tablespoons chopped
    fresh cilantro
½ cup mung bean sprouts

2 large eggs
1 teaspoon canola oil or
    vegetable oil

Emeril's Vegetable and Egg Fried Rice

Here's a great family dish that everybody will love. The sugar and ginger are unusual additions to fried rice, but the sweet note they add is a terrific surprise. If you like things hotter, kick this up with about ½ teaspoon of red pepper flakes or a touch of cayenne. One more thing: The secret to this dish's success is cooking the rice one day ahead of time.

1. Heat the canola and sesame oils in a wok or very large skillet over high heat until smoking hot. Add the garlic, ginger, and green onions and stir-fry for 15 seconds, using a Chinese spatula. Add the onions and carrots and stir-fry for 30 seconds. Add the bell peppers, zucchini, and mushrooms and cook for 30 seconds. Add the rice and stir-fry until hot, about 1 minute. Add the soy sauce, sugar, and black pepper and mix well. Gently fold in the omelet strips and remove from the heat.

2. Divide the rice among bowls or plates. Garnish with the peanuts, cilantro, and bean sprouts. Serve immediately.

Chinese Omelet

1. Beat the eggs in a bowl until frothy.

2. Heat the oil in a wok over medium heat until hot. Swirl the oil around to evenly coat the sides, then add the eggs and swirl around in the same fashion; the eggs will cook almost instantly. Carefully peel the omelet from the sides of the pan and lift out onto a cutting board or plate. Roll the omelet into a cylinder and cut into ¼-inch-wide strips.

Shrimp and Coconut Milk Risotto with Summer Squash, Peas, and Roasted Red Pepper Sauce

1 pound medium shrimp in their shells

4 cups water

2 cloves garlic, peeled and smashed, plus 2 teaspoons minced garlic

½ cup dry white wine

¼ cup fresh lime juice

One 14-ounce can unsweetened coconut milk

3 tablespoons olive oil

1 cup finely chopped yellow onions

¾ cup finely chopped leeks, well rinsed (white parts only)

2 cups Arborio rice

2 teaspoons salt

1 teaspoon freshly ground white pepper

½ teaspoon freshly ground black pepper

2 cups fresh or thawed frozen green peas

2 cups cubed yellow summer squash

1 cup freshly grated Parmigiano-Reggiano

4 tablespoons unsalted butter, cut into pieces

¼ cup chopped fresh cilantro

1 recipe Roasted Red Pepper Sauce

Chef Chris devised this dish for a recipe contest a few years back and now it appears periodically on the menu at Emeril's New Orleans. The flavors of the coconut milk and red pepper sauce together make this version of risotto one you won't soon forget. Chef Chris won that contest—make this, and you'll see why!

1. To make the stock, peel the shrimp and set aside. Place the shells in a medium saucepan. Add the water, smashed garlic cloves, white wine, and lime juice and bring to a boil. Reduce the heat to medium-low and simmer until reduced by half.

2. Remove the stock from the heat and add the coconut milk. Strain through a fine-mesh strainer into a clean saucepan, cover, and keep warm over very low heat.

3. Heat the oil in a medium saucepan over medium heat. Add the onions and leeks and cook, stirring, until soft, about 3 minutes. Add the 2 teaspoons minced garlic and cook, stirring, for 30 seconds. Add the rice, stir to coat with the oil, and cook for 1 minute. Add enough of the shrimp stock just to cover the rice, about 2 cups, then add the salt, white pepper, and black pepper and stir well. Simmer, stirring constantly, adding more stock as it is absorbed by the rice.

4. When the rice is almost completely cooked but still retains a slight crunch, about 12 minutes, add the peas, squash, and shrimp. Simmer, adding more stock as necessary, until the shrimp are cooked through and the vegetables are tender, about 6 minutes. Add the cheese, butter, and cilantro and stir to combine. Cook, stirring, until all the liquid has been absorbed and the rice is tender but not mushy, about 10 minutes longer.

5. Remove from the heat and adjust the seasoning to taste. Spoon the risotto into six or eight serving bowls, drizzle the red pepper sauce around it, and serve.

Roasted Red Pepper Sauce

**2 large red bell peppers
(about 1 pound)**
**1 cup extra-virgin
olive oil**
**3 tablespoons minced
shallots**
10 fresh cilantro leaves
4 fresh basil leaves
**¼ teaspoon balsamic
vinegar**
½ teaspoon salt
**¼ teaspoon freshly
ground white pepper**

1. Roast the peppers over an open gas flame, turning them frequently with tongs until all sides are charred black, 7 to 10 minutes. (Alternatively, the peppers can be roasted under a broiler, or on a gas or charcoal grill.) Place the blackened peppers in a plastic or paper bag, seal tightly, and let stand until cool enough to handle, about 15 minutes.

2. Peel the peppers, remove the seeds and stems, and coarsely chop.

3. Heat 2 tablespoons of the oil in a small skillet over medium heat. Add the shallots and cook, stirring, for 1 minute. Add the peppers and cook for 5 minutes. Transfer to a food processor or blender.

4. Add the cilantro, basil, vinegar, salt, and pepper to the peppers and process for 20 seconds. With the machine running, add the remaining ¾ cup plus 2 tablespoons oil in a slow, steady stream, processing until thick and smooth. Serve warm, or transfer to a bowl or other container, cover, and refrigerate for up to 3 days. Reheat gently before serving.

Delmonico Steakhouse kitchen daily specials board

PASTA, RICE, AND RISOTTO

Arancini

Arancini are stuffed and fried rice balls that are made from risotto that has been allowed to cool. These make a wonderful late-night snack, side dish, or hors d'oeuvre when served with the Creole Tomato Marinara Sauce (page 242).

3¾ to 4 cups chicken stock
4 tablespoons unsalted butter
¾ cup finely chopped yellow onions
1 cup Arborio or Carnaroli rice
½ cup dry white wine
½ cup finely grated Parmigiano-Reggiano
⅓ cup heavy cream
1½ tablespoons chopped fresh herbs, such as basil, thyme, parsley, or chives
1½ teaspoons salt
½ teaspoon freshly ground black pepper
3 large eggs
⅓ cup cubed mozzarella, Cheddar, Muenster, or Swiss cheese
⅓ cup chopped ham, prosciutto, pepperoni, salami, or other fully cooked meat or sausage
Vegetable oil, for deep-frying
5½ teaspoons Emeril's Original Essence or Creole Seasoning (page 28)
½ cup all-purpose flour
1 cup fine dry bread crumbs
1 recipe Creole Tomato Marinara Sauce (page 242), optional

1. To make the risotto, bring the stock to a simmer in a saucepan. Reduce the heat to low and cover to keep warm.

2. Melt 3 tablespoons of the butter in a large saucepan over medium-high heat. Add the chopped onions and cook, stirring, until soft, about 3 minutes. Add the rice and cook, stirring constantly, until the rice is opaque, 2 minutes. Add the white wine and cook, stirring, until the liquid is nearly all evaporated, about 2 minutes. Add ½ cup of the hot stock, and cook, stirring constantly, until nearly all the liquid is absorbed. Continue adding more stock ½ cup at a time as the previous addition is nearly absorbed, until all the stock has been added and the rice is just tender and the risotto is creamy, 18 to 20 minutes. Add the Parmesan cheese, heavy cream, herbs, 1 teaspoon of the salt, and the pepper, and stir to combine well. Transfer to a large bowl to cool. Refrigerate until well chilled, at least 4 hours or overnight.

3. To make the arancini, stir 1 egg into the chilled risotto, mixing well. Using a small scoop or large spoon, divide the risotto into equal portions on a baking sheet, about 3 tablespoons each. With your hands, form into rough balls. With your thumb, press a hole into the center of each ball and stuff with cubed cheese and chopped ham. Seal the opening and roll the ball between your hands until smooth. Place on a baking sheet.

4. Heat enough oil to come 2 inches up the sides of a large saucepan to 360°F.

5. In a shallow bowl, make an egg wash by beating the remaining 2 eggs with 2 teaspoons of the Essence. In another shallow bowl, combine the flour and 1½ teaspoons of Essence. In a third bowl, combine the bread crumbs, the remaining 2 teaspoons Essence, and ½ teaspoon salt.

6. Lightly coat each risotto ball with flour. Dip in the egg wash, then dredge in the bread crumbs, turning to coat completely and shaking to remove any excess. Transfer to a baking sheet.

7. Fry the balls in two batches, eight at a time, turning once to brown evenly, about 2 minutes. Transfer to paper towels to drain.

8. Serve immediately with the marinara sauce, if desired.

Chef Drew Knoll in Emeril's
Delmonico kitchen

**4 to 6 pie pumpkins
(2 pounds each)**
**½ pound (2 sticks) unsalted
butter**
¼ cup sugar
**2 teaspoons grated orange
zest**
**1½ teaspoons ground
cinnamon**
1 teaspoon salt
½ teaspoon ground allspice
2 tablespoons vegetable oil
**2 teaspoons Emeril's
Original Essence or Creole
Seasoning (page 28)**
**1 recipe Duck and Mushroom
Risotto**
**½ cup freshly grated
Parmigiano-Reggiano**

Roasted Pumpkin Stuffed with Duck and Mushroom Risotto

Chef Dave liked to serve this autumn dish at NOLA when he was the chef there. We call for small pie pumpkins here, which are sweeter than the big Halloween jack-o'-lanterns. They are available in the fall and early winter. The pumpkins may take a little more time to bake than specified, depending on how fresh they are. If you can't get pie pumpkins, substitute butternut or acorn squash weighing about 1¼ pounds each. Simply reduce the cooking time as necessary. You can fill these pumpkins with your favorite soup or use them to serve the Thanksgiving stuffing, if you're looking for a different holiday presentation.

When making the risotto, the quality and variety of Arborio rice will determine the cooking time and volume of liquid needed.

1. Preheat the oven to 350°F.

2. With a sharp heavy knife, carefully remove the top third of each pumpkin. Remove the seeds and fibers from the insides and tops, discarding the fibers; reserve the seeds. Place the pumpkins and lids on two large baking sheets. Place 4 tablespoons of the butter inside each pumpkin.

3. In a small bowl, combine the sugar, zest, cinnamon, salt, and allspice and mix well. Divide the mixture among the pumpkins and cover tightly with foil. Bake the pumpkins for 1 hour and 15 minutes, and the lids for about 1 hour.

4. Meanwhile, place the reserved pumpkin seeds in a large colander, rinse well under cold running water, and pat dry. Place in a large bowl, add the vegetable oil and Essence, and stir well to coat. Spread evenly on two baking sheets and toast until golden brown and fragrant, about 1 hour. Remove from the oven, stir with a spatula to prevent the seeds from sticking, and cool on the baking sheet.

5. Remove the pumpkins and lids from the oven, uncover, and bake until tender, about 15 minutes longer. Remove from the oven and let stand until cool enough to handle, then drain the butter from the pumpkins and reserve ⅓ cup for the risotto.

6. Spoon the risotto into the cooked pumpkins and garnish with the Parmesan cheese. Replace the lids on the pumpkins. Sprinkle four large serving plates with the pumpkin seeds, top with the pumpkins, and serve immediately.

Duck and Mushroom Risotto

MAKES 4 TO 6 SERVINGS

4 to 6 cups Duck Stock (page 22) or Rich Chicken Stock (page 21)
1 tablespoon salt
1/2 teaspoon freshly ground black pepper
2 tablespoons unsalted butter
2 tablespoons extra-virgin olive oil
1/2 cup chopped shallots
1 tablespoon minced garlic
1 duck liver (reserved from the Roast Duck), chopped
4 cups sliced mixed wild mushrooms, such as oyster, stemmed shiitake, and cremini (about 3/4 pound)
1 1/2 cups Arborio rice
1 cup Pinot Noir or other dry red wine
2 cups shredded Roast Duck meat (page 17)
1/3 cup butter reserved from the pumpkins
1 teaspoon minced fresh thyme
1 teaspoon minced fresh oregano
1/2 cup freshly grated Parmigiano-Reggiano

1. Bring the stock, salt, and pepper to a simmer in a medium heavy pot over medium-high heat. Reduce the heat to low and cover to keep warm.

2. Melt the butter with the oil in a large saucepan over medium-high heat until foamy. Add the shallots, garlic, and duck liver and cook, stirring, for 1 minute. Add the mushrooms and cook, stirring, until they give off their liquid, about 3 minutes. Add the rice, stirring to coat with oil, and cook, stirring constantly, for 2 minutes. Add the wine, stirring to deglaze the pan, bring to a boil, and cook until reduced by half, about 4 minutes. Reduce the heat to medium, add 1 cup of the hot stock, and cook, stirring constantly, until it has been absorbed. Continue adding more stock 1/2 cup at a time, stirring, until the previous addition is nearly absorbed before adding more, until all the stock has been added and the rice is tender yet still slightly firm, 16 to 18 minutes total cooking time. Fold in the pumpkin butter, thyme, and oregano, mixing well. Add the cheese and mix well. Serve hot.

7 | SEAFOOD

Emeril's New Orleans Fish House

Cedar-Planked Fish with Citrus Horseradish Crust and Citrus Butter Sauce

MAKES 4 SERVINGS

½ pound horseradish root, peeled and grated
1 teaspoon grated orange zest
1 teaspoon grated lemon zest
1 teaspoon grated lime zest
2 teaspoons fresh orange juice
1 teaspoon fresh lemon juice
1 teaspoon fresh lime juice
1 tablespoon chopped fresh cilantro
1 tablespoon sugar
½ teaspoon kosher salt
Four 8-ounce skinless redfish, drum, red snapper, or trout fillets
2 teaspoons Emeril's Original Essence or Creole Seasoning (page 28)
2 teaspoons olive oil
1 recipe Citrus Butter Sauce

Four 10-inch untreated cedar planks (see headnote)

Believe it or not, you can purchase untreated cedar planks, or cedar siding, from your local hardware or home improvement store. Just make sure they're untreated.

Now, the only way for this recipe really to work is to use fresh horseradish, not the prepared kind sold in jars. It looks like a big root and can be found in the produce section of your local supermarket or specialty market. Keep in mind that you'll want to work quickly, as, when you grate it, your sinuses and tear ducts will open and the heat will make your skin tingle.

Keep an eye on the fish while it's broiling, as each broiler is different and yours may get hotter faster. You want the crust to brown, but not burn or char. Depending upon your oven and how close the rack is to the broiler element, the process could take anywhere from 3 to 7 minutes.

1. Preheat the oven to 375°F.

2. Combine the horseradish, citrus zests and juices, cilantro, sugar, and salt in a bowl and stir well to blend. Season both sides of each fillet with ½ teaspoon of the Essence.

3. Rub the top of each plank with ½ teaspoon of the olive oil. Place 1 fish fillet on each plank. Divide the crust among the fillets, spreading the crust evenly over them. Place the planks on a large baking sheet and bake for 15 minutes.

4. Increase the heat to broil and, watching carefully, broil until the crust is golden brown and just starting to brown around the edges, about 5 minutes.

5. Transfer the planks to four large dinner plates. Drizzle the fish with the butter sauce, and serve immediately.

¼ *cup dry white wine*
2 *tablespoons fresh*
   lemon juice
2 *tablespoons fresh*
   orange juice
2 *tablespoons chopped*
   shallots
1 *bay leaf*
½ *teaspoon black*
   peppercorns
½ *teaspoon chopped*
   fresh thyme
¼ *cup heavy cream*
½ *pound (2 sticks) cold*
   unsalted butter, cut
   into pieces

Citrus Butter Sauce

Combine the wine, lemon juice, orange juice, shallots, bay leaf, peppercorns, and thyme in a medium saucepan and bring to a boil. Cook until reduced by half, 2 to 3 minutes. Add the cream and return to a boil. Cook until reduced by half, 2 to 3 minutes. Reduce the heat to medium-low. Whisk in the butter about 1 tablespoon at a time, adding each new piece before the previous one has been completely incorporated, removing the pan from the heat periodically to prevent the sauce from getting too hot and breaking; the sauce should be thick enough to coat the back of a spoon. Strain through a fine-mesh strainer into a bowl and cover to keep warm, or keep warm in a double boiler.

Bringing dinner to the main dining room at NOLA

SEAFOOD

Redfish Amandine

¼ cup Creole Meunière Base
   (page 28)
3 tablespoons heavy cream
½ pound (2 sticks) cold
   unsalted butter, cut into
   pieces
Four 10-ounce redfish fillets
2 tablespoons plus
   1 teaspoon Emeril's
   Original Essence or Creole
   Seasoning (page 28)
1 teaspoon kosher salt
1 cup all-purpose flour
2 large eggs
1 tablespoon water
About 2 cups vegetable oil
1 recipe Brabant Potatoes
   (page 18)
½ cup sliced almonds,
   lightly toasted, for
   garnish

Sautéing or panfrying fish with almonds is referred to as aman-dine, meaning garnished with almonds. It's a traditional French method, and the dish is found on the menus of old-line New Orleans restaurants. With Delmonico's emphasis on classic Cre-ole cuisine, it's no surprise that this rich favorite is found on its menu, served with the customary Brabant potatoes. However, we kick up our sauce by adding our Creole Meunière Base and heavy cream to the usual butter.

Triple coating the fish before it hits the pan ensures a crunchy, light texture. Just make sure that the oil comes halfway up the sides of the fish so it browns evenly. If redfish isn't avail-able, substitute trout or another sweet, firm, white-fleshed fish.

1. To make the sauce, combine the meunière base and heavy cream in a small saucepan and bring to a boil over medium-high heat. Reduce the heat to medium-low and slowly add the cold butter about 1 tablespoon at a time, whisking constantly, adding each new piece before the previous addition is com-pletely incorporated, removing the pan from the heat periodi-cally to prevent the sauce from getting too hot and breaking. Keep warm in a double boiler.

2. Season each fillet on both sides with 1 teaspoon of the Essence and ¼ teaspoon of the salt.

3. Combine the flour and the remaining tablespoon of Essence in a shallow bowl. Beat the eggs with the water in another shallow bowl. One at a time, dredge the fish in the flour and then the egg wash, then dredge again in the flour and egg wash, and finish with a third coating of flour.

4. Pour 1 inch of oil into a large deep sauté pan or skillet and heat to 350°F over medium-high heat. Add 2 of the fish fillets and cook for 3 minutes. Carefully turn with a large spatula and cook for 3½ minutes on the second side. Remove and drain on paper towels. Add more oil as needed, and cook the remaining fish.

5. Spoon about ¼ cup of sauce onto each of four large dinner plates. Place the potatoes in the center of the plates, place the fish on top of the potatoes, and sprinkle with the almonds. Serve immediately.

ORLANDO

Grilled Florida Pompano with Lemon-Poached Leeks and Shrimp–Lemon Butter Sauce

MAKES 4 SERVINGS

2 teaspoons olive oil
2 teaspoons Emeril's Original Essence or Creole Seasoning (page 28)
Four 5- to 6-ounce pompano fillets
1 recipe Shrimp–Lemon Butter Sauce
1 recipe Lemon-Poached Leeks (page 85)

The Emeril's Orlando menu highlights fresh Florida products, such as the delicious pompano. This fish has a high oil content, so the fine-textured, meaty flesh has a buttery flavor that's well suited to this shrimp–lemon butter sauce. Pompano ranges from one to five pounds in weight, but we prefer the smaller two-pound fish, which yields two six- to eight-ounce fillets. You could substitute snapper fillets.

1. Preheat a grill to medium-high (or preheat the oven to 375°F).

2. Combine the oil and Essence in a small bowl. Lightly rub both sides of each fillet with the mixture.

3. Place the fish flesh side down on the grill and cook for 2 minutes. Turn the fillets a quarter turn to make decorative grill marks and cook for 2 minutes more. Turn over and cook until the fish flakes easily, about 4 minutes. (Alternatively, place the seasoned fish on a nonstick baking sheet and roast until golden brown and cooked through, 10 to 12 minutes.)

4. Place the fish on four serving plates. Top with the butter sauce and leeks, and serve immediately.

SEAFOOD

1 cup dry white wine
3 lemons, peeled, white pith
removed, and quartered
1 tablespoon minced
shallots
1 tablespoon minced garlic
½ cup heavy cream
½ pound (2 sticks) cold
unsalted butter, cut into
pieces, plus 1 teaspoon
butter
1 teaspoon salt
⅛ teaspoon freshly ground
white pepper
1 tablespoon finely chopped
fresh parsley
5 ounces peeled and
deveined shrimp, chopped
(about 10 ounces in the
shell)
1 teaspoon Emeril's Original
Essence or Creole
Seasoning (page 28)

Shrimp–Lemon Butter Sauce

1. Combine the wine, lemons, shallots, and garlic in a medium saucepan and bring to a boil. Reduce the heat to medium-low and simmer, stirring occasionally and mashing the lemons with the back of a spoon to break them up into pieces, until reduced by half, about 20 minutes. Add the cream and cook until reduced by half, about 3 minutes.

2. Reduce the heat to medium-low. Whisk in the butter, about 1 tablespoon at a time, adding each piece before the previous one has been completely incorporated, removing the pan from the heat periodically to prevent the sauce from getting too hot and breaking; the sauce should be thick enough to coat the back of a spoon. Add the salt and pepper and whisk to blend. Remove from the heat and strain, pressing down with the whisk, through a fine-mesh strainer into a bowl. Fold in the parsley and cover to keep warm.

3. Season the shrimp with the Essence. Melt the remaining 1 teaspoon butter in a medium nonstick skillet over medium-high heat. Add the shrimp and cook, stirring, until pink and cooked through, 2 to 3 minutes. Fold into the sauce. Serve immediately.

Emeril's Orlando general manager Gabriel Orozco

NEW ORLEANS FISH HOUSE

Potato-Crusted Pompano on Warm Chanterelle and Lump Crabmeat Salad, with Fava Bean Cream and Crawfish Foam

MAKES 6 SERVINGS

2 large Idaho potatoes (about 1½ pounds), peeled

3 tablespoons Dijon mustard

Six 6-ounce pompano fillets

1 tablespoon salt

1 tablespoon freshly ground white pepper

1 cup vegetable oil

1 recipe Fava Bean Cream

1 recipe Warm Chanterelle and Lump Crabmeat Salad

1 recipe Crawfish Foam

¼ cup plus 2 tablespoons chopped mixed fresh herbs, including chives, basil, chervil, and parsley, for garnish

Though light in texture, the crawfish foam that sauces this pompano is packed with flavor. Why a foam? After a long cooking time to concentrate the crawfish flavors, the reduction is strained, then blended in a food processor to a frothy spray.

The best way to make the crawfish foam base is to roughly chop live crawfish before sautéing them. However, we have written the recipe using cooked crawfish for those of you who might find this step offensive. But if you are not squeamish, go ahead and use live crawfish for better flavor.

The warm mushroom and crabmeat salad would be a great accompaniment to other fish, or delicious on its own or tossed with cooked pasta. You can substitute snapper or speckled trout fillets for the pompano.

1. Using a mandoline or a sharp heavy knife, slice the potatoes as thin as possible.

2. Rub 1½ teaspoons of the mustard onto the flesh side of each fillet, and season each one on both sides with ¼ teaspoon of the salt and ¼ teaspoon of the white pepper. Arrange the potato slices over the mustard in an overlapping pattern to resemble fish scales.

3. Heat ½ cup of the oil in each of two large nonstick skillets over high heat. When the oil is hot, carefully add the fillets, potato side down, being careful to keep the potato crust intact, and cook until the potatoes are crispy and golden brown, 3 to 4 minutes per side. Remove from the heat.

4. To serve, spoon enough of the fava bean cream to cover the bottom of six plates. Spoon the crabmeat salad on top of the cream, and lay the fish, potato side up, on top. Pour the foam around the fish, and garnish with the fresh herbs. Serve immediately.

SEAFOOD

Fava Bean Cream

1 pound fresh fava beans,
shelled (about 1 cup)
2 tablespoons unsalted
butter
1½ teaspoons finely
chopped shallots
¼ teaspoon minced garlic
¼ teaspoon salt
⅛ freshly ground white
pepper
1 cup Vegetable Stock
(page 27), plus more as
needed
¼ cup heavy cream

1. Bring a large pot of salted water to a boil. Add the fava beans and cook until crisp-tender, about 2 minutes. Drain in a colander, rinse under cold running water, and drain again. Slip off the outer skin from each bean and discard. Transfer the beans to a medium bowl.

2. Melt 1 tablespoon of the butter in a medium saucepan over medium-high heat. Add the shallots and garlic and cook, stirring, for 30 seconds. Add the fava beans, salt, and pepper, reduce the heat to low, and cook, stirring occasionally, until the beans are soft, about 8 minutes. Add the stock and cream, bring to a simmer, and cook until the beans begin to break up and the liquid reduces by one-quarter, about 5 minutes.

3. Transfer to a food processor or blender and add the remaining 1 tablespoon butter. Process until smooth, adding more vegetable stock as needed. Transfer to a bowl and cover to keep warm.

Warm Chanterelle and Lump Crabmeat Salad

3 tablespoons unsalted
butter
3 tablespoons olive oil
¾ cup thinly sliced yellow
onions
¾ teaspoon salt
¼ teaspoon freshly ground
white pepper
2 teaspoons minced garlic
1 pound small chanterelle
mushrooms, stems
trimmed and wiped
cleaned
¾ pound lump crabmeat,
picked over for shells and
cartilage
1½ teaspoons snipped fresh
chives

1. Melt the butter with the olive oil in a large skillet over medium-high heat. Add the onions, salt, and pepper and cook, stirring, until the onions are soft, about 3 minutes. Add the garlic and cook, stirring, until fragrant, about 30 seconds. Add the mushrooms and cook until they are tender and their liquid has evaporated, about 6 minutes.

2. Add the crabmeat and chives and stir gently to blend, being careful not to break up the crabmeat. Cook until warmed through, about 2 minutes. Remove from the heat and cover to keep warm.

Crawfish Foam

2 pounds boiled whole crawfish in their shells or raw whole shrimp in their shells
2 tablespoons olive oil
½ cup chopped yellow onions
¼ cup chopped carrots
¼ cup chopped celery
½ teaspoon salt
¼ teaspoon freshly ground white pepper
1 tablespoon chopped garlic
½ cup brandy
1½ tablespoons tomato paste
1 bay leaf
1 sprig thyme
4 cups Shrimp Stock (page 24), Fish Stock (page 23), or bottled clam juice
1 cup heavy cream
3 tablespoons cold unsalted butter

1. With a large heavy knife, roughly chop the crawfish (or shrimp).

2. Heat the olive oil in a large pot over medium-high heat. Add the crawfish (or shrimp) and cook, stirring constantly, until aromatic, about 5 minutes. Add the onions, carrots, celery, salt, and pepper and cook until the vegetables are soft, about 3 minutes. Add the garlic and cook, stirring, for 30 seconds.

3. Remove the pan from the heat and add the brandy, then return to high heat and stir to deglaze the pan, scraping up any browned bits sticking to the bottom. Add the tomato paste and cook, stirring, for 2 minutes. Add the bay leaf, thyme, shrimp stock, and heavy cream and bring to a boil. Reduce the heat to medium-low and simmer until reduced by half, about 30 minutes.

4. Strain the sauce in batches through a fine-mesh strainer into a clean container, pressing down on the solids with the back of a heavy spoon to extract as much liquid as possible; discard the solids. Transfer, in two batches, to a food processor or blender, add the butter in equal amounts, and process until smooth and foamy, about 3 minutes. Transfer to a saucepan and adjust the seasoning to taste. Cover to keep warm until ready to serve.

5. Immediately before serving, whisk the sauce for 1 minute to re-create the foam.

One 4- to 5-pound red
  snapper, cleaned and
  scaled, fins removed
1¼ cups extra-virgin
  olive oil
1 cup dry white wine
1 cup thinly sliced yellow
  onions
1 cup chopped mixed fresh
  herbs, such as parsley,
  tarragon, mint, chives,
  chervil, and basil
¼ cup chopped garlic
1 tablespoon red pepper
  flakes
1 tablespoon grated lemon
  zest
1 tablespoon grated lime
  zest
1 tablespoon cracked black
  pepper
2 tablespoons kosher salt
2 lemons, cut into wedges

Grilled Whole Fish Emeril-Style

I've always been a fan of preparing whole fish, and I created this dish for a Super Bowl tailgating segment on Emeril Live. *The presentation just can't be beat. At the restaurants, we generally present this tableside and then fillet it for the guests.*

I have a great relationship with my pals at the New Orleans Fish House, and when they supply me with a nice, whole fish, this is the way to go. American Red Snapper ranges from two to twenty-five pounds and the season is very limited. Commercial fishermen can only catch them during the first week of each month from January 1 to July 1, with no weekend fishing. Talk about limited availability! (Though sports fishermen can, of course, catch them anytime.)

Other snappers are available year-round, including the Beliner, Lane, and the Mangrove Snapper. Or you could substitute whole striped bass, or adapt the recipe to smaller fish for individual portions. Redfish, another sportfish, also would be great tossed on the grill, as it has a firm skin that can take the heat.

---

1. Score the fish all over in a ⅛-inch-deep grid pattern. Place the fish in a large resealable plastic storage bag on a baking sheet.

2. Combine 1 cup of the oil and all the remaining ingredients except the salt and lemon wedges in a bowl. Pour into the bag with the fish and seal tightly. Refrigerate for 24 hours, turning the bag occasionally.

3. Preheat a grill to medium-high and preheat the oven to 375°F.

4. Remove the fish from the bag and sprinkle with the salt. Place on the hot grill and cook for 2 minutes per side. Transfer to a baking sheet and bake until firm and cooked through, about 20 minutes.

5. Remove from the oven and place on a large platter. Drizzle with the remaining ¼ cup olive oil and garnish with the lemon wedges. Serve.

Emeril's ORLANDO

Poached Grouper with Mango Salsa, Smashed Avocado, Coconut-Cilantro Rice Pilaf, Black Bean Sauce, and Homemade Tortilla Chips

MAKES 4 SERVINGS

Four 6- to 7-ounce grouper fillets
1 teaspoon salt
½ teaspoon freshly ground white pepper
4 cups Vegetable Stock (page 27)
¼ cup sweetened flaked coconut
1 recipe Black Bean Sauce
1 recipe Coconut-Cilantro Rice Pilaf
1 recipe Mango Salsa
1 recipe Smashed Avocado
1 recipe Homemade Tortilla Chips

In this dish, you'll taste the flavors of the tropics—from the mild Gulf fish to the bright mango salsa, rich coconut-flavored rice, and creamy black bean sauce—that typify our Orlando style. And all of these sides stand well on their own.

Grouper can range from one to one hundred pounds, depending upon the species. It is a firm white-fleshed fish (some species have a slightly pink tone) with a subtle flavor and not at all oily. It retains a lot of moisture and is ideally suited to the poaching method used in this recipe. Good substitutes would include Red Snapper, Hake, Monkfish, and Black Drum.

1. Preheat the oven to 350°F.

2. Season each fillet on both sides with ¼ teaspoon of the salt and ⅛ teaspoon of the white pepper.

3. Bring the vegetable stock to a simmer in a saucepan or deep skillet large enough to hold 2 fillets. Add 2 of the fillets and poach over medium heat until cooked through, about 5 minutes. Transfer to a baking dish, add 2 tablespoons of the poaching liquid, and cover with foil to keep warm while you cook the remaining fillets.

4. Meanwhile, spread the coconut on a baking sheet and bake until lightly toasted and golden, about 5 minutes. Set aside.

5. To serve, spoon a portion of the black bean sauce into the middle of each plate, top with about ½ cup of the rice, and place a grouper fillet on top. Arrange the mango salsa and smashed avocado decoratively around the beans, and stand several tortilla chips in each. Sprinkle all with the toasted coconut and serve immediately.

SEAFOOD

2 tablespoons olive oil
One ¾-pound ham hock
½ cup chopped yellow
  onions
½ cup finely chopped celery
¼ cup finely chopped carrots
1½ teaspoons minced garlic
½ pound dried black beans,
  rinsed and picked over
¼ cup chopped fresh
  cilantro
½ teaspoon ground cumin
2 tablespoons fresh lime
  juice
1½ teaspoons salt

Black Bean Sauce

1. Heat the oil in a large saucepan over medium-high heat. Add the ham hock, onions, celery, and carrots and cook, stirring, until the vegetables are soft, about 3 minutes. Add the garlic and cook, stirring, for 30 seconds. Add the beans, cilantro, cumin, and enough water to cover by 1 inch and bring to a boil. Reduce the heat to medium-low, cover, and simmer until the beans are tender, about 1 hour and 45 minutes, stirring occasionally and skimming any foam that rises to the surface.

2. Remove from the heat. Remove and discard the ham hock. Add the lime juice and salt. With a slotted spoon, transfer the beans to a food processor, add about ½ cup of the cooking liquid, and process to a smooth purée, adding more cooking liquid as needed. Transfer to a bowl and cover to keep warm until ready to serve.

2 tablespoons olive oil
½ cup chopped yellow
  onions
¼ cup chopped red bell
  peppers
2 tablespoons minced
  shallots
1 teaspoon minced garlic
1¼ cups long-grain white
  rice
1½ cups Vegetable Stock
  (page 27)
½ cup canned unsweetened
  coconut milk
½ cup Coco Lopez
1 teaspoon salt
½ teaspoon freshly ground
  white pepper
3 tablespoons chopped fresh
  cilantro

Coconut-Cilantro Rice Pilaf

Heat the oil in a large heavy saucepan over medium-high heat. Add the onions, bell peppers, shallots, and garlic and cook, stirring, for 2 minutes. Add the rice, stirring to coat with the oil, and cook for 1 minute. Add the vegetable stock, coconut milk, Coco Lopez, salt, and pepper and bring to a gentle boil. Reduce the heat to low, cover, and simmer until the rice is tender and all the liquid is absorbed, 20 to 22 minutes. Remove from the heat and let sit for 10 minutes. Fluff the rice with a fork, stir in the cilantro, and serve.

1 ripe mango, peeled,
    seeded, and diced
¼ cup finely chopped
    poblano peppers
¼ cup finely chopped red
    bell peppers
¼ cup finely chopped red
    onions
1½ teaspoons minced
    garlic
½ cup rice wine vinegar
2 tablespoons finely
    chopped fresh cilantro
⅛ teaspoon salt

Mango Salsa

Combine the mango, poblanos, bell peppers, onions, and garlic in a nonreactive bowl and stir to mix. Add the vinegar, cilantro, and salt and stir well. Adjust the seasoning to taste and serve. (The salsa can be made up to 4 hours in advance and refrigerated in an airtight container.)

1 ripe Hass avocado,
    peeled, seeded, and
    diced
2 tablespoons minced
    red onions
1 tablespoon fresh lime
    juice
⅛ teaspoon salt
⅛ teaspoon freshly
    ground white pepper

Smashed Avocado

Combine all the ingredients in a small nonreactive bowl and gently stir to blend. Adjust the seasoning to taste. Cover tightly and refrigerate until ready to serve, or up to 2 hours.

4 yellow corn tortillas
4 cups vegetable oil, for
    deep-frying
1 teaspoon Emeril's
    Original Essence or
    Creole Seasoning
    (page 28)
¼ teaspoon salt

Homemade Tortilla Chips

1. Cut the tortillas into eighths.

2. Heat the vegetable oil to 350°F in a large heavy saucepan or deep-fryer. Add the tortillas, in batches, being careful not to over-crowd, and cook, turning once, until golden brown, 45 seconds to 1 minute. Drain on paper towels and sprinkle with the Essence and salt. Serve hot.

SEAFOOD

NOLA

Roasted Atlantic Salmon with Herbed Potato Cakes, Granny Smith Apple Butter, Citrus Fennel Salad, and Salmon Roe

MAKES 4 SERVINGS

½ teaspoon olive oil
Four 6-ounce salmon fillets
½ teaspoon salt
½ teaspoon freshly ground white pepper
1 recipe Herbed Potato Cakes
1 recipe Granny Smith Apple Butter
1 recipe Citrus Fennel Salad
1 ounce salmon roe

Salmon's rich, pronounced flavor makes it a popular mainstay on all of our menus. While there are a number of wild salmon species from around the world, Atlantic salmon are farm-raised and available year-round.

The tart notes in the apple butter, which is actually a butter sauce (or beurre blanc*), really complement the fish, as do the bright flavors and crunch of the citrus fennel salad. And, hey, you can't go wrong with a little salmon roe on top, can you? Also try the herbed potato cakes with roasted meats or poultry, if you're looking for a different type of potato dish.*

1. Preheat the oven to 350°F.

2. Grease a baking sheet with the oil. Season both sides of the salmon fillets with the salt and pepper and place on the sheet. Roast just until the center is still slightly pink, about 10 minutes. Remove from the oven.

3. Place one potato cake on each plate and top with a salmon fillet. Drizzle with the apple butter. Spoon about ½ cup of the salad onto the sauce and top with about 1 teaspoon of the caviar. Serve immediately.

Herbed Potato Cakes

**2 Idaho potatoes (about
1½ pounds), peeled
and grated**

2 large eggs

**1 tablespoon chopped
fresh parsley**

**1 tablespoon chopped
fresh tarragon**

**1 tablespoon chopped
fresh basil**

½ teaspoon salt

**¼ teaspoon freshly
ground black pepper**

**6 tablespoons Clarified
Butter (page 15) or
vegetable oil**

1. Rinse the potatoes in a large bowl of cold water and drain well. Transfer to a dish towel and wring dry; if necessary, wring again in a second towel. Place in a large bowl and add all the remaining ingredients except the butter. Stir to mix well.

2. Heat 3 tablespoons of the clarified butter in a large skillet over medium-high heat. Divide the potato mixture into quarters. Form each portion into a 4-inch round cake about ½ inch thick, squeezing out any excess moisture. Place 2 cakes in the hot pan and cook, turning once, until golden brown, 5 to 6 minutes per side. Remove from the pan and drain on paper towels. Wipe the pan clean with a paper towel and repeat with the remaining butter and potato cakes. Serve hot.

Granny Smith Apple Butter

**1 Granny Smith apple,
peeled, cored, and cut
into small dice**

**¼ cup apple cider
vinegar**

**2 tablespoons light
brown sugar**

¼ cup heavy cream

**½ pound (2 sticks) cold
unsalted butter, cut
into pieces**

¼ teaspoon salt

**⅛ teaspoon freshly
ground white pepper**

Combine the apples, vinegar, and sugar in a medium saucepan and cook over medium-high heat until the apples are translucent, about 5 minutes. Add the cream and cook until reduced by half, about 3 minutes. Reduce the heat to low. Whisk in the butter about 1 tablespoon at a time, adding each new piece before the previous one has been completely incorporated, and removing the pan from the heat periodically to prevent the sauce from getting too hot and breaking; the sauce should be thick enough to coat the back of a spoon. Add the salt and pepper. Keep warm in a double boiler.

SEAFOOD

Citrus Fennel Salad

MAKES 2 CUPS

1 lemon

1 orange

1 fennel bulb, stalks
    trimmed, tough core
    removed, and finely
    chopped

2 tablespoons extra-virgin
    olive oil

½ teaspoon salt

⅛ teaspoon freshly ground
    black pepper

With a sharp knife, slice off the top and bottom of the lemon and orange. Stand each one on a cutting board and slice off the peel and bitter white pith in strips, following the natural curve of the fruit. Working over a large nonreactive bowl to catch the juices, slice between the membranes to release the citrus segments, letting them drop into the bowl; discard the seeds. Add the fennel, oil, salt, and pepper and stir well to combine. Let sit at room temperature for 1 to 2 hours for the flavors to blend before serving.

*Chef Neal Swidler in the bar
of Emeril's Delmonico*

Grilled Salmon with Saffron Broth, Black Olive Mashed Potatoes, and Cured Artichokes

4 cups Fish Stock
 (page 23)
¼ cup thinly sliced
 fennel
¼ cup thinly sliced
 yellow onions
¼ cup thinly sliced green
 bell peppers
¼ cup peeled, seeded,
 and chopped tomatoes
½ teaspoon minced
 garlic
1 teaspoon salt
½ teaspoon freshly
 ground white pepper
1 teaspoon saffron
 threads
2 large artichokes (about
 10 ounces each), all
 outer leaves removed
 to expose only the
 heart and bottom, and
 hairy choke discarded
3 tablespoons fresh
 lemon juice
1 tablespoon kosher salt
Four 6-ounce salmon
 fillets, skin removed
1 tablespoon Emeril's
 Original Essence or
 Creole Seasoning
 (page 28)
1 recipe Black Olive
 Mashed Potatoes

I've tried to capture the sunny flavors of the Mediterranean and my Portuguese background by marrying artichokes, fennel, saffron, and tomatoes in the broth for the salmon. And, along with the black olive mashed potatoes, you know, I think I've got it! This creative dish would be an elegant addition to any dinner party. And once you're tried these black olive mashed potatoes, you'll want to serve them with roasted chicken, too!

1. Pour the fish stock into a medium saucepan and bring to a simmer. Add the fennel, onions, bell peppers, tomatoes, garlic, salt, pepper, and saffron threads and simmer until the vegetables are softened, about 12 minutes. Remove from the heat and cover to keep warm.

2. Using a vegetable slicer such as a mandoline, slice the artichokes paper-thin. Toss in a nonreactive bowl with the lemon juice and kosher salt; set aside.

3. Preheat a grill to medium-high.

4. Season the salmon on both sides with the Essence. Grill until firm and nearly cooked through but still pink in the middle, about 4 minutes per side. Remove from the grill.

5. To serve, mound the mashed potatoes in the center of four large bowls and place one fillet on top of each. Ladle the broth around the potatoes, garnish each serving with about ¼ cup of the artichokes, and serve.

SEAFOOD

Black Olive Mashed Potatoes

1½ pounds Red Bliss
  potatoes
1½ teaspoons salt
¼ cup coarsely chopped
  pitted black olives
¼ cup plus 2 tablespoons
  extra-virgin olive oil
1 tablespoon minced garlic
1 teaspoon chopped fresh
  oregano
½ teaspoon freshly ground
  black pepper

1. Put the potatoes in a medium heavy pot, cover with water by 1 inch, add 1 teaspoon of the salt, and bring to a boil. Cook until the potatoes are tender, 15 to 17 minutes. Drain in a colander.

2. Return the potatoes to the pot, set over low heat, and add the black olives, olive oil, garlic, oregano, remaining ½ teaspoon salt, and the pepper. Mash, using a potato masher. Serve immediately.

On the dinner line at
Emeril's New Orleans

HOMEBASE

Salmon Paillards with Lump Crabmeat, Corn Maque Choux, and Citrus-Tomato Marmalade

4 thin 4-ounce salmon fillets, sliced on an angle into 4-inch-wide pieces about ¼ inch thick

½ pound lump crabmeat, picked over for shells and cartilage

1 recipe Corn Maque Choux

1 teaspoon Emeril's Original Essence or Creole Seasoning (page 28)

1 recipe Citrus-Tomato Marmalade

This salmon cooks briefly (about 2 minutes) under the broiler, directly on the plate. Make sure you use heavy ovenproof plates, not your grandmother's good china, to make these! Also, you'll need to set the heavy plates on top of large base plates to avoid burning your dinner table.

When we make salmon paillards at the restaurants, we cut the fillets on the bias from a side of salmon in order to get them as thin as possible. Ask your fish market for salmon cut this way.

1. Place each salmon fillet between two sheets of plastic wrap. With the flat side of a meat pounder or the side of a cleaver, working from the outer edges in, gently pound each fillet to a thickness of ⅛ inch. Refrigerate, still between the plastic wrap, for 5 minutes.

2. Preheat the broiler.

3. Fold the crabmeat into the warm maque choux. Divide among four large ovenproof plates or shallow bowls, spreading evenly. Peel the top layer of plastic from the fish and season the top of each with ⅛ teaspoon of the Essence. Using the plastic as a guide, lay one piece of fish, seasoned side down, on each portion of maque choux. Peel the remaining plastic from the fish and season the top of the fish with the remaining Essence.

4. Broil just until the salmon is no longer opaque, about 2 minutes. Using thick oven mitts, remove the plates from the oven and place on large base plates. Drizzle the marmalade in a decorative pattern over the salmon, and serve immediately.

SEAFOOD

Corn Maque Choux

6 tablespoons unsalted
  butter
1 cup chopped yellow onions
1/2 cup chopped celery
1/2 cup chopped red bell
  peppers
1 teaspoon minced garlic
1 teaspoon Emeril's Original
  Essence or Creole
  Seasoning (page 28)
3 cups corn kernels
1 1/2 cups Rich Chicken Stock
  (page 21)
1 tablespoon light brown
  sugar
1/4 teaspoon salt

1. Melt 2 tablespoons of the butter in a large skillet over medium-high heat. Add the onions, celery, and bell peppers and cook, stirring, until soft, about 3 minutes. Add the garlic and Essence and cook, stirring, for 30 seconds. Add the corn and cook, stirring, until fragrant and just golden, about 5 minutes.

2. Add 1/4 cup of the chicken stock and cook until it has almost evaporated, about 2 minutes. Continue to cook and stir, adding the stock 1/4 cup at a time as it is absorbed. Add the remaining 4 tablespoons butter, the sugar, and salt and stir until the butter is melted. Serve warm.

Citrus-Tomato Marmalade

1 1/2 pounds Roma (plum)
  tomatoes, peeled,
  seeded, and chopped
1/2 cup chopped red onions
1/2 cup dry white wine
3 tablespoons sugar
2 teaspoons fresh lemon
  juice
1 teaspoon tomato paste
1 teaspoon Emeril's Kick It
  Up Red Pepper Sauce or
  other hot pepper sauce
1/2 teaspoon salt
1/2 teaspoon grated orange
  zest
1/2 teaspoon ground
  cinnamon
1/8 teaspoon cayenne
1/8 teaspoon ground
  coriander
1/8 teaspoon ground cloves

1. Combine all the ingredients in a medium heavy pot and bring to a boil. Reduce the heat and cook, uncovered, at a low boil until thickened and almost all the liquid has evaporated, about 10 minutes, stirring occasionally. Remove from the heat.

2. Transfer to a blender and process to a thick purée. Transfer to a bowl and cover to keep warm.

NOLA

MAKES 4 SERVINGS

1 tablespoon olive oil
1 cup chopped yellow
   onions
½ cup chopped celery
½ cup chopped red bell
   peppers
2 large eggs
1 tablespoon Creole
   mustard or other spicy
   whole-grain mustard
2 teaspoons Emeril's
   Kick it Up Red Pepper
   Sauce or other hot
   pepper sauce
2 teaspoons
   Worcestershire sauce
3 tablespoons Emeril's
   Original Essence or
   Creole Seasoning
   (page 28)
1½ cups vegetable oil
1½ cups plus 2
   tablespoons fine dry
   bread crumbs
1 pound jumbo lump
   crabmeat, picked over
   for shells and
   cartilage
½ cup all-purpose flour
½ cup whole milk
1 recipe Piquante Butter
   Sauce
1 recipe Pickled Sweet
   Pepper–Okra Relish

Louisiana Crab Cakes with Piquante Butter Sauce and Pickled Sweet Pepper–Okra Relish

The homemade mayonnaise gives these crab cakes a light, moist texture inside, and the three-way breading gives them an incredible crunchy crust. The pickled sweet pepper–okra relish is like a cross between hot pepper jelly and pickled okra—a real eye-opener! It's also a terrific side dish to grilled chicken or seafood.

1. Heat the olive oil in a large heavy skillet over medium-high heat. Add the onions, celery, and bell peppers and cook, stirring, until soft, about 3 minutes. Remove from the heat and let cool.

2. Combine 1 egg, the mustard, hot sauce, Worcestershire, and 1 tablespoon of the Essence in a food processor or blender and process for 15 seconds. With the machine running, add 1 cup of the vegetable oil in a slow, steady stream, processing until the mayonnaise thickens.

3. Combine the mayonnaise, cooked vegetables, ½ cup plus 2 tablespoons of the bread crumbs, and 1 tablespoon of the Essence in a large bowl and mix well. Gently fold in the crabmeat.

4. Combine the flour with 1½ teaspoons of the Essence in a shallow bowl, mixing well. Combine the remaining 1 cup bread crumbs with the remaining 1½ teaspoons Essence in another bowl. Whisk the remaining egg with the milk in another bowl.

5. Form the crabmeat mixture into 8 cakes, packing gently but firmly. Dredge each crab cake in the flour mixture, then in the egg wash, and then the bread crumb mixture, shaking to remove any excess breading.

6. Heat the remaining ½ cup vegetable oil in a large heavy skillet over medium heat. Panfry the crab cakes 3 or 4 at a time until golden brown, about 4½ minutes per side. Drain on paper towels.

7. To serve, spoon the butter sauce onto four plates and top each with 2 crab cakes. Spoon the relish on top and serve immediately.

SEAFOOD

Piquante Butter Sauce

MAKES 2¼ CUPS

1 tablespoon vegetable oil
½ cup chopped yellow
 onions
¼ cup chopped red bell
 peppers
¼ cup chopped celery
1 tablespoon minced garlic
2 teaspoons minced jalapeño
1 bay leaf
1 tablespoon Emeril's
 Original Essence or Creole
 Seasoning (page 28)
¼ teaspoon salt
¼ cup packed light brown
 sugar
One 14-ounce can tomato
 sauce
8 tablespoons (1 stick) cold
 unsalted butter, cut into
 pieces

1. Heat the oil in a large skillet over medium-high heat. Add the onions, bell peppers, and celery and cook, stirring, until soft, about 3 minutes. Add the garlic, jalapeño, bay leaf, Essence, and salt and cook, stirring, for 30 seconds. Add the brown sugar and cook, stirring, until the sugar is dissolved. Add the tomato sauce and bring to a boil. Reduce the heat to medium-low and simmer, stirring occasionally, until the sauce is thick enough to coat the back of a spoon, 8 to 10 minutes.

2. Whisk in the butter 1 tablespoon at a time, adding each piece before the previous one has been completely incorporated, removing the pan from the heat periodically to prevent the sauce from getting too hot and breaking; the sauce should be thick enough to coat the back of a spoon. Remove from the heat and remove the bay leaf. Cover to keep warm until ready to serve.

Pickled Sweet Pepper–Okra Relish

MAKES 3 CUPS

1 red bell pepper, cored,
 seeded, and chopped
1 green bell pepper, cored,
 seeded, and chopped
¼ pound okra, stem ends
 trimmed and cut
 lengthwise in half
1 tablespoon black
 peppercorns
1 cup red wine vinegar
¾ cup sugar
1 bay leaf
1½ teaspoons red pepper
 flakes

1. Combine the bell peppers and okra in a nonreactive large bowl, and set aside.

2. Place the peppercorns in the center of a 4-inch square of cheesecloth and tie tightly with kitchen twine.

3. Combine the vinegar, sugar, bay leaf, red pepper flakes, and black peppercorn pouch in a medium nonreactive saucepan and bring to a gentle boil. Pour over the peppers and okra. Cover and let stand for 2 hours.

4. Remove the peppercorns and bay leaf, cover, and refrigerate until cool, about 2 hours. (The relish will keep refrigerated in an airtight container for up to 1 week.) Serve cold.

ORLANDO

Seafood en Papillote: Clams, Scallops, and Gulf Shrimp Baked with Fingerling Potatoes and Fresh Herbs

½ **pound small fingerling potatoes or new potatoes**

8 **medium sea scallops**

16 **medium shrimp, peeled and deveined**

2 **teaspoons Emeril's Original Essence or Creole Seasoning (page 28)**

16 **clams, scrubbed**

1 **tablespoon plus 1 teaspoon minced garlic**

4 **sprigs fresh thyme**

¼ **cup chopped fresh parsley**

½ **teaspoon chopped fresh oregano**

½ **teaspoon minced fresh basil**

6 **tablespoons unsalted butter**

1 **cup dry white wine**

Traditionally cooking en papillote *referred to the French technique of wrapping meat, fish, or vegetables in a greased parchment paper pouch and then baking it. Today the pouches are just as often made of aluminum foil, as they are here. You'll find that cooking in a pouch renders the food very moist and tender, and opening the pouches at the table gives your guests a delicious whiff of the aromatic cooking juices. And, if you're trying to save calories, this is a good way to maximize flavors without adding fat to the dish.*

Here, the seafood juices and wine marry in the pouch to create a heady, flavorful broth that is an excellent vehicle for hot, crusty French bread. Chef Dave says this is an awesome lunch dish, particularly with a good Sancerre.

1. Preheat the oven to 350°F. Cut 4 large pieces of heavy-duty aluminum foil, each 30 inches long. Fold crosswise in half; set aside.

2. Place the potatoes in a medium saucepan, add salted water to cover by 1 inch, bring to a boil, and cook until just tender, about 10 minutes. Drain. When they are cool enough to handle, cut the potatoes into quarters.

3. Season the scallops and shrimp with the Essence. Divide the scallops, shrimp, clams, and potato quarters among the sheets of foil, arranging them in a circle on the bottom half of each. Place one-quarter of the garlic and herbs and 1½ tablespoons of butter in the center of each circle. Fold the foil over to enclose the seafood, and tightly crimp and fold over the edges of the foil on two sides, leaving one side open. Pour ¼ cup of the wine into each packet, then tightly crimp and seal the open side.

4. Place the packages on two large baking sheets and bake for 20 minutes. Transfer the packages to four serving plates.

5. With a small sharp knife, cut an X in each package, and open at the table.

Pan-Roasted Halibut in Lobster Chowder with Steamed Cherrystone Clams and Apple-Smoked Bacon

MAKES 6 SERVINGS

1¼ pounds thick-cut apple-smoked bacon, ¼ pound chopped (the rest left in strips)

Two 1½-pound Maine lobsters

3 cups diced peeled Idaho potatoes

4 tablespoons unsalted butter

3 medium leeks (white parts only), halved lengthwise, cut into ¼-inch slices, well rinsed, and patted dry (about 1 cup)

1 cup finely chopped yellow onions

1 teaspoon minced garlic

¼ cup all-purpose flour

2½ cups heavy cream

1½ cups Shrimp Stock (page 24) or bottled clam juice

1¼ teaspoons salt

1¼ teaspoons freshly ground white pepper

18 cherrystone clams, scrubbed

1 tablespoon olive oil

Six 6-ounce halibut fillets

½ cup chopped fresh parsley, for garnish

Here's a good example of the lengths we go to in capturing a particular flavor: not only are our stocks, sauces, dressings, and such "homemade," but at the Fish House we also smoke our own bacon. It's not as much trouble as you might imagine, if you have a little patience and access to a home smoker. If you're unable to smoke your own bacon, substitute high-quality, thick-cut apple-smoked bacon. The smokiness of the bacon really plays up the flavors of the fish and clams.

1. Heat a grill to high.

2. Place the sliced bacon on the grill and cook until crisp and brown, about 8 minutes. (Alternatively, cook the bacon in a large skillet over medium-high heat until crisp, 5 to 7 minutes.) Transfer to paper towels and set aside.

3. Fill a large stockpot three-quarters full with salted water and bring to a boil. Plunge the lobsters headfirst into the boiling water and cook, covered, for 7 minutes. With tongs, transfer to a large bowl filled with ice water to cool; set the pot aside.

4. Add the potatoes to the lobster water and return to a boil. Cook until just tender, 8 to 10 minutes. Drain in a colander, refresh under cold running water, and set aside.

5. When the lobsters are cool enough to handle, crack the shells and remove the meat from the tails and claws; discard the shells. Coarsely chop the meat and set aside.

6. Preheat the oven to 400°F.

7. Melt the butter in a large heavy saucepan over medium-high heat. Add the chopped bacon and cook until it begins to brown, about 5 minutes. Add the leeks and onions and cook, stirring, until soft, about 4 minutes. Add the garlic and cook, stirring, for 30 seconds. Add the flour and cook, stirring constantly, until a light blond roux forms, about 5 minutes. Add the cream, shrimp stock, and ½ teaspoon each of the salt and white pepper and bring to a simmer. Simmer for 10 minutes, stirring occasionally. Add the clams, lobster, and potatoes, and stir well. Reduce the heat to medium-low, cover, and simmer, stirring occasionally, until the clams open, 6 to 8 minutes. Remove from the heat. Discard any clams that did not open, and cover to keep warm.

8. Heat the olive oil in a large nonstick ovenproof skillet, or in two smaller skillets, over high heat. Season each halibut fillet on both sides with ⅛ teaspoon each of the remaining salt and white pepper. Place the fillets in the pan(s), reduce the heat to medium-low, and cook until a golden brown crust forms, about 3 minutes. Turn the fish, place in the oven, and roast until just cooked through, 4 to 5 minutes. Remove from the oven.

9. To serve, ladle the chowder into six rimmed soup bowls arranging 3 clams around the rim of each bowl. Place a halibut fillet in the center, and lay 3 strips of bacon on top of the fish. Garnish with the parsley, and serve immediately.

Yellowfin Tuna Niçoise

1 pound small red potatoes,
scrubbed and cut in half,
then into ¼-inch-thick
slices

6 ounces haricots verts or
small thin green beans,
ends trimmed

½ cup plus 1 tablespoon
olive oil

1 tablespoon plus 1 teaspoon
salt

2 teaspoons freshly ground
black pepper

2 teaspoons minced garlic

1 pound Roma (plum)
tomatoes, cut into 1-inch
cubes

½ cup halved and pitted
brine-cured black olives

½ cup halved and pitted
brine-cured green olives

½ cup Creamy Ravigote
(page 62)

2 hearts of romaine lettuce,
cored, separated into
leaves, rinsed, and patted
dry

¾ cup Creamy Parmesan
Dressing (page 98)

2½ pounds yellowfin tuna
loin, trimmed of sinew
and cut into 6 equal
rectangular portions,
about 1 × 1 × 4 inches
each (see headnote)

You'll want to buy the freshest fish you can find when making this salad because of the minimal cooking involved. Ask for "number one" Yellowfin Tuna or sashimi-grade tuna, and look for bright, firm, red flesh, almost the color of a fire engine; be sure that it hasn't been frozen. Yellowfin is widely available in the summer, making this an ideal summer salad with fresh haricots verts and tomatoes. Bigeye or Bluefin Tuna can be substituted for the Yellowfin; while their flesh also is red, the colors will differ slightly—the Bigeye will be paler and the Bluefin will be a dark burgundy color. If you can't get a tuna loin, use thick tuna steaks.

Since tunas are migratory with the Gulf Stream, the prices will be higher in the winter, but the quality will be higher because of the higher fat content the fish has when the water temperatures are colder. And you know what I say—fat is flavor!

At Delmonico, they use Picholine and Niçoise olives in this main-course salad, but you can use whatever you like best.

1. Bring two medium pots of salted water to a boil. Add the potatoes to one pot and cook until just tender, about 3½ minutes; drain in a colander. Add the green beans to the other pot and blanch until tender, about 4 minutes; drain in a colander.

2. Heat ¼ cup of the oil in a large skillet over medium-high heat. Add the potatoes, 1 teaspoon of the salt, and ½ teaspoon of the pepper and cook, shaking the pan occasionally, until the potatoes are golden brown on both sides, about 8 minutes. Add 1 more tablespoon oil, the garlic, and green beans and stir and cook for 1 minute. Add the tomatoes and olives and cook, stirring occasionally, until the tomatoes are warmed through, about 2 minutes. Remove from the heat, add the ravigote sauce, and stir to mix.

3. Combine the lettuce with the dressing in a bowl and toss to coat. Arrange 3 or 4 leaves on one side of each of six large plates. Spoon the vegetables onto the other side of the plates. Let sit while you cook the tuna.

4. Season each tuna portion with ½ teaspoon of the remaining salt and ¼ teaspoon of the remaining pepper. Heat the remaining ¼ cup oil in a large skillet, or two medium skillets, over medium-high heat. Add the tuna and sear for 15 seconds on each side. Remove from the pan.

5. Cut each portion of tuna crosswise into 4 slices. Arrange the tuna slices down the middle of the plates, and serve.

Chef Emeril Lagasse

Creole Bouillabaisse: Fresh Gulf Fish, Shrimp, Oysters, and Lump Crabmeat in an Herbsaint-Scented Broth

MAKES 4 SERVINGS

½ cup small red new potatoes cut into ⅛-inch-thick rounds

4 cups Shrimp Stock (page 24) or Fish Stock (page 23)

½ pound fish fillets, such as redfish, mahi-mahi, amberjack, or snapper, cut into ½-inch cubes

2 teaspoons Emeril's Original Essence or Creole Seasoning (page 28)

16 medium shrimp, peeled and deveined

1 tablespoon extra-virgin olive oil

1 teaspoon chopped garlic

½ teaspoon fennel seeds

½ teaspoon minced orange zest

½ cup thinly shaved fennel bulb

½ cup peeled, seeded, and chopped tomatoes

2 teaspoons saffron threads

¼ cup Herbsaint or other anise-flavored liqueur, such as Pernod or Ricard

½ teaspoon salt

½ teaspoon Emeril's Kick It Up Red Pepper Sauce or other hot pepper sauce

⅛ teaspoon freshly ground black pepper

⅛ teaspoon cayenne

16 freshly shucked oysters, with their liquor

Restaurants in the South of France serve bouillabaisse as two separate courses. First the broth is ladled into bowls and served with rouille croutons, then the seafood is served as a main course, with additional rouille on the side as a dipping sauce. Chef Dave's Creole version serves the seafood and broth together, topped by rouille croutons, for a hearty main course. Of course, if you're feeling French, go ahead and do it the other way!

1. Put the potatoes in a small pot, add salted water to cover by 1 inch, and bring to a boil. Reduce the heat to medium and cook until the potatoes are almost tender but still firm, 5 to 6 minutes. Drain in a colander and set aside.

2. Bring the shrimp stock to a simmer in a small saucepan over medium heat. Turn off the heat and cover to keep warm.

3. Put the fish cubes in a small bowl and season with 1 teaspoon of the Essence. Put the shrimp in a separate bowl and season with the remaining teaspoon of Essence. Set aside.

4. Heat the olive oil in a large saucepan over medium-low heat. Add the garlic, fennel seeds, and orange zest and cook for 15 seconds. Add the fennel, tomatoes, and drained potatoes, increase the heat to medium, and cook for 15 seconds. Add the saffron and Herbsaint and cook, stirring, for 15 seconds. Lay the fish cubes on top of the vegetables and simmer uncovered, for 1 minute. Turn the fish, gently spoon the cooking liquid over it, and simmer for 2 minutes. Add the warm shrimp stock, the salt, hot sauce, black pepper, cayenne, and shrimp, and bring to a boil. Lower the heat and simmer uncovered, for 3 minutes. Add the oysters and their liquor and simmer uncovered, for 3 minutes. Add the crabmeat, parsley, chervil, and lemon juice, stir gently, and cook uncovered, for 3 minutes. Remove from the heat and adjust the seasoning to taste.

½ *pound jumbo lump*
crabmeat, picked over
for shells and cartilage
1 *tablespoons chopped*
fresh parsley
½ *tablespoon chopped*
fresh chervil
1 *teaspoon fresh lemon*
juice
1 *recipe Rouille Croutons*

MAKES 8 CROUTONS

1 *medium Idaho potato*
1 *red bell pepper*
2 *large egg yolks*
1 *tablespoon fresh*
lemon juice
1 *tablespoon chopped*
garlic
1 *teaspoon salt*
½ *teaspoon cayenne*
1 *cup extra-virgin olive*
oil
8 *Large Croutons*
(page 33)

5. Ladle the bouillabaisse into large soup bowls and place 2 rouille croutons in each bowl. Serve immediately.

Rouille Croutons

1. Preheat the oven to 400°F.

2. Prick the potato with a fork and place on a baking sheet. Bake until tender, about 1 hour. Remove from the oven and let cool.

3. When the potato is cool enough to handle, remove and discard the skin. Grate enough of the potato to equal ½ cup; reserve the rest for another use.

4. Meanwhile, roast the pepper over an open gas flame, turning frequently with tongs, until all sides are charred black, 7 to 10 minutes. (Alternatively, roast the pepper under a broiler, or on a gas or charcoal grill.) Place the pepper in a plastic or paper bag, seal tightly, and let cool for about 15 minutes. Remove the seeds and stem from the pepper, and coarsely chop it.

5. Combine the bell pepper, egg yolks, lemon juice, garlic, salt, and cayenne in a blender and purée on high speed until smooth. With the machine running, gradually add the olive oil in a thin, steady stream, blending until the sauce thickens. Adjust the seasoning to taste and transfer to a bowl. Fold in the grated potato, blending until smooth.

6. Spread the rouille evenly on the croutons and serve.

SEAFOOD

Pan-Roasted Striped Bass with Wild Mushrooms, Potato Gnocchi, and Tarragon-Reggiano Cream Sauce

MAKES 4 SERVINGS

¾ **pound haricots verts or very small young tender green beans, ends trimmed**

5 tablespoons vegetable oil

2 tablespoons minced shallots

2 tablespoons minced garlic

1 pound wild mushrooms, such as shiitake, oyster, wood ear, or porcini, stems trimmed (remove the stems if using shiitake), wiped clean, and thinly sliced

1¾ teaspoons salt

1¾ teaspoons freshly ground black pepper

Four 6-ounce skin-on striped bass, rainbow trout, or speckled trout fillets

1 recipe Potato Gnocchi

1 recipe Tarragon-Reggiano Cream Sauce

1 tablespoon chopped fresh tarragon, for garnish

¼ cup freshly grated Parmigiano-Reggiano, for garnish

Most striped bass is farm-raised, so it is readily available in markets year-round, but wild fish can be found on the East Coast in winter and spring. The farm-raised fish average two to two and a half pounds, yielding two five- to nine-ounce fillets each; the wild fish run up to fifty pounds and have much thicker fillets.

In striped bass, there's a creamy layer of fat between the skin and flesh, and this is where the flavor is. This is why we serve bass with the skin on (scaled, of course) and it's how you'll want to buy yours too. A good substitute would be red snapper with the skin on, or trout.

And for all you gnocchi lovers who've been afraid to tackle the dish at home, follow the recipe exactly and you'll discover that these are fairly easy to make. And the light little puffs of potato air on your plate, perfectly napped with creamy cheese sauce, will be worth every single second!

1. Bring a medium saucepan of salted water to a boil. Add the haricots verts and cook until just tender, 2 to 3 minutes. With a slotted spoon, transfer to an ice bath to cool, then drain and set aside.

2. Heat 2 tablespoons of the oil in a medium skillet. Add the shallots and garlic and cook, stirring, until fragrant, about 1 minute. Add the mushrooms and ½ teaspoon each salt and pepper and cook, stirring, until the mushrooms are starting to brown, 4 to 5 minutes. Transfer to a bowl and cover to keep warm. Set the skillet aside.

3. Meanwhile, season both sides of the fillets with 1 teaspoon each of the salt and pepper. Heat 2 tablespoons of the oil in a large skillet, or two smaller skillets, over medium-high heat. Add the fish skin side down and cook until golden brown, 2 to 2½ minutes per side. Remove from the heat and transfer to a large plate; cover to keep warm.

4. In the skillet used to cook the mushrooms, heat the remaining 1 tablespoon oil over medium-high heat. Add the gnocchi, haricots verts, and the remaining ¼ teaspoon each salt and pepper and cook, stirring, until warmed through, 1 to 2 minutes. Add the cream sauce and stir well to blend.

5. Divide the gnocchi and haricots verts among four plates. Place the fish fillets in the center of the gnocchi and top with the mushrooms. Garnish each serving with tarragon and Parmesan, and serve.

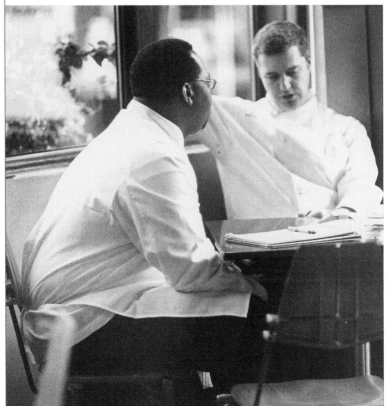

Chefs Dave McCelvey and Bernard Carmouche at Emeril's Orlando

1 large Idaho potato
(12 to 14 ounces)
1 large egg
¼ teaspoon salt
¾ to 1 cup all-purpose flour

Potato Gnocchi

1. Place the potato in a pan of salted water to cover by 1 inch and bring to a boil. Lower the heat and simmer until tender, about 12 minutes. Drain and let cool slightly, then carefully peel the potato and, while it is still hot, pass through a ricer or food mill into a large mixing bowl. Let cool completely.

2. Add the egg and salt to the potato and mix well with a wooden spoon. Add ½ cup of the flour and mix well. Gradually stir in additional flour, 2 to 3 tablespoons, to form a smooth, slightly sticky dough.

3. Bring a large pot of salted water to a rolling boil.

4. Meanwhile, turn the dough out onto a lightly floured surface and briefly knead until smooth but still slightly sticky, incorporating up to 2 tablespoons more flour if needed. Cut the dough into pieces that equal about ¼ cup. One at a time, roll each piece under your palms to form a long rope about ½ inch thick. With a sharp knife, cut into ¾-inch-long pieces. Gently roll in the flour on the work surface and transfer to a parchment-lined baking sheet.

5. As soon as they are all formed, add the gnocchi to the boiling water and cook for 2 to 3 minutes after they have risen to the top. Remove with a slotted spoon to a colander set in a large ice water bath to stop the cooking. Leave in the ice bath until ready to finish cooking, then drain well.

Tarragon-Reggiano Cream Sauce

1 tablespoon olive oil

1 tablespoon finely chopped shallots

1½ teaspoons minced garlic

¼ cup plus 2 tablespoons dry white wine

1 tablespoon chopped fresh tarragon

1 cup heavy cream

1 ounce Parmigiano-Reggiano, grated (about ⅓ cup)

⅛ teaspoon salt

¼ teaspoon freshly ground black pepper

½ pound (2 sticks) cold unsalted butter, cut into pieces

1. Heat the oil in a medium skillet over medium-high heat. Add the shallots and garlic and cook, stirring, until fragrant, about 1 minute. Add the white wine and tarragon and cook until the wine is reduced by half, 2 to 3 minutes. Add the cream and cook until thickened and slightly reduced, 2 to 3 minutes.

2. Add the cheese, stirring to incorporate. Season with the salt and pepper. Whisking constantly, gradually add the butter about 1 tablespoon at a time, adding each new piece before the previous one has been completely incorporated, and removing the pan from the heat periodically to prevent the sauce from getting too hot and breaking. Remove from the heat and cover to keep warm, or keep warm in a double boiler, stirring occasionally.

Executive sous chef Diana Davey at Emeril's New Orleans Fish House

SEAFOOD

191

8 CHICKEN, TURKEY, DUCK, QUAIL, AND RABBIT

Open kitchen at NOLA

Chicken Baked in Aromatic Salt Crust with Parslied New Potatoes

One 3- to 3½-pound chicken, well rinsed and patted dry

½ cup finely chopped yellow onions

¼ cup finely chopped carrots

¼ cup finely chopped celery

½ teaspoon chopped garlic

2 bay leaves

2 slices bacon, finely chopped

2 tablespoons yellow cornmeal

1 recipe Aromatic Salt Crust

1 large egg white, lightly beaten

2 tablespoons all-purpose flour

3 tablespoons water

1 cup Rich Chicken Stock (page 21)

1 recipe Parslied New Potatoes

This is a visually spectacular and delicious dish to serve for a special dinner with family or friends. While eating at Roger Vergé's restaurant in the South of France, Le Moulin de Mougins, Chef Dave was inspired by his technique of cooking poultry or fish in a flavorful salt dough. This is his interpretation of Chef Vergé's classic dish.

The salt crust seals in all of the chicken's juices and flavors, keeping the meat perfectly moist. Bear in mind that the salt dough must be used within 15 minutes of being mixed. Once it's baked, though, the salt crust will keep the chicken hot for 45 minutes while you prepare the rest of the meal!

1. Preheat the oven to 400°F.

2. Remove the giblets from the chicken. Chop and reserve for the sauce.

3. Combine the onions, carrots, celery, garlic, bay leaves, and bacon in a bowl and toss to combine. Stuff the mixture inside the chicken.

4. Lightly sprinkle a baking sheet with the cornmeal. Put the smaller piece of salt crust on the baking sheet and center the chicken in the middle. Drape the larger piece of crust over the chicken and press the edges together with your fingertips. With a small sharp knife, trim any excess dough, leaving a 1½-inch border around the chicken. Crimp the edges with a floured fork to seal. Gather the dough scraps together and shape into a 3 × 1-inch round knob. Place on the top of the crust to make a topknot and press to seal. With a pastry brush, paint the crust with the egg white.

5. Bake until the crust is golden and the chicken is cooked, about 1 hour and 20 minutes. Remove from the oven and let rest for 15 minutes.

6. With a sharp knife, cut through the crust around the base of the chicken. Using the knob, gently lift the top crust from the chicken and set aside. Carefully remove the chicken from the bottom crust and place on a platter or large plate. Pour the cooking juices from the baking sheet into a large bowl. Scoop the vegetables from the chicken cavity into the bowl. Pour any accumulated cooking juices from the chicken into the bowl. Return the bottom crust to the baking sheet, or place on a large platter. Return the chicken to the bottom crust and cover with the top crust. Let rest while you make the sauce.

7. Combine the flour and water in a small bowl, whisking to dissolve the flour.

8. Using a slotted spoon, transfer the vegetables to a medium saucepan and add the chopped giblets. Cook, stirring, over medium-high heat until the giblets are browned, about 5 minutes. Add the accumulated cooking juices and the chicken stock and bring to a boil. Pour the flour mixture through a fine-mesh strainer into the stock and bring to a boil, whisking constantly. Reduce the heat to medium-low and simmer, stirring, for about 5 minutes. Remove from the heat and transfer to a gravy boat or serving bowl.

9. Present the chicken at the table, then remove the top crust and carve. Divide the chicken and potatoes among four dinner plates and pass the gravy.

Aromatic Salt Crust

8 cups all-purpose flour
2½ cups kosher salt
2 tablespoons coarsely
ground black pepper
1 tablespoon chopped fresh
rosemary
1 tablespoon chopped fresh
sage
1 tablespoon chopped fresh
thyme
3 cups water

1. Combine the dry ingredients in a large mixing bowl. With a hand-held mixer on low speed, beat in the water in a steady stream, mixing until the dough comes together. (Or use a stand mixer.) Turn the dough out onto a lightly floured surface and knead it briefly until smooth and only slightly sticky. Shape into a large log.

2. Cut off one-third of the dough, and roll it into an oval a few inches larger than the chicken, about 10 × 12 inches, and ½ inch thick. Transfer to a parchment-lined baking sheet. Roll out the remaining piece of dough into an oval large enough to completely cover the chicken, about 15 × 20 inches. Transfer to a second parchment-lined baking sheet. Refrigerate for up to 15 minutes while preparing the chicken.

MAKES 4 SERVINGS

Parslied New Potatoes

2 pounds small red potatoes
(about 1¼ inches in
diameter)
2 tablespoons unsalted
butter
2 tablespoons chopped fresh
parsley
½ teaspoon salt
¼ teaspoon freshly ground
black pepper

1. Put the potatoes in a medium pot, cover with salted water by 1 inch, and bring to a boil. Cook until the potatoes are tender, 12 to 15 minutes. Drain in a colander and return to the pot.

2. Add the remaining ingredients, cover, and shake to coat the potatoes. Keep covered to keep warm until ready to serve.

Roasted Poussins with Spiced Butternut Squash Purée, Crispy Sage Leaves, and Fresh Huckleberry Syrup

MAKES 4 SERVINGS

Four 1¼-pound poussins, rinsed well and patted dry

2 tablespoons plus 2 teaspoons olive oil

1 teaspoon salt

1 teaspoon freshly ground black pepper

1 cup chopped yellow onions

1 cup chopped celery

1 cup chopped carrots

½ teaspoon minced garlic

½ teaspoon chopped fresh thyme

1 cup dry white wine

½ cup vegetable oil

16 large fresh sage leaves, stems removed

1 recipe Spiced Butternut Squash Purée

1 recipe Huckleberry Syrup

Poussin is a fancy name for a small young chicken. If you can't find any, try this recipe with small Cornish game hens, and adjust the cooking time slightly. If huckleberries are difficult to find, substitute either fresh blackberries or dried currants plumped in warm sweetened water.

1. Preheat the oven to 425°F.

2. Rub ½ teaspoon of the olive oil over each poussin, and lightly season each one inside and out with ¼ teaspoon of the salt and ¼ teaspoon of the pepper. Place breast side up in a large roasting pan.

3. Heat the remaining 2 tablespoons oil in a large skillet over medium-high heat. Add the onions, celery, and carrots and cook, stirring, until soft, about 3 minutes. Add the garlic and thyme and cook, stirring, for 30 seconds. Deglaze the pan with the white wine, stirring to loosen any bits stuck to the bottom, and cook until almost all the wine has evaporated. Remove from the heat and let cool.

4. Stuff each bird with about ½ cup of the vegetable mixture. Roast breast side up for 15 minutes, then lower the heat to 350°F and cook until golden brown and the juices run clear when the thigh is pierced with a thin sharp knife, 35 to 40 minutes longer. Remove from the oven and let rest for 10 minutes.

5. Meanwhile, heat the vegetable oil in a small skillet over medium-high heat until hot but not smoking. Add the sage leaves and cook until crisped, about 20 seconds. With a slotted spoon, transfer to paper towels to drain.

6. To serve, spoon the squash purée onto four serving plates. Cut each poussin in half through the breastbone and backbone, exposing the stuffing, and place on top of the purée. Spoon 3 tablespoons of the huckleberry syrup decoratively around each poussin, and serve.

MAKES 4 CUPS;
4 TO 6 SERVINGS

**1 large butternut squash
(2½ to 3 pounds), cut in
half, seeds and fibers
removed**
**¼ teaspoon ground
cinnamon**
¼ teaspoon grated nutmeg
¼ teaspoon salt
**⅛ teaspoon freshly ground
black pepper**
**8 tablespoons (1 stick)
unsalted butter**

Spiced Butternut Squash Purée

1. Preheat the oven to 400°F.

2. Place the squash halves cut side up on a foil-lined baking sheet. Season with the cinnamon, nutmeg, salt, and pepper, and top each with 4 tablespoons of the butter. Bake until tender, 1 hour to 1 hour and 10 minutes. Let cool.

3. Pour off the butter from the squash and reserve. Scoop the flesh from the shells and transfer to a food processor. Add the reserved butter and process to a purée. Adjust the seasoning to taste.

4. Transfer to a small saucepan, heat gently over low heat, and serve.

MAKES 1¼ CUPS

**2 pints fresh huckleberries
or blackberries, rinsed
and picked over**
1 cup rice wine vinegar
½ cup sugar

Huckleberry Syrup

Combine all the ingredients in a medium heavy saucepan and bring to a boil. Reduce the heat to medium-low and simmer, stirring occasionally, until reduced to a chunky syrup, about 50 minutes. Remove from the heat and let cool to room temperature. (Any leftover syrup can be refrigerated for up to 1 week.)

*Chef Bernard Carmouche at
Emeril's Orlando evening
pre-meal meeting*

Roasted Garlic–Glazed Chicken with Lemon Herb Sauce, Creole Rice Pilaf, and Vegetable Brochettes

Two 3-pound chickens, well rinsed and patted dry

1 tablespoon Emeril's Original Essence or Creole Seasoning (page 28)

2 tablespoons olive oil

4 tablespoons unsalted butter

4 sprigs fresh thyme

1 recipe Roasted Garlic Glaze

1 recipe Creole Rice Pilaf

1 recipe Lemon Herb Sauce

1 recipe Vegetable Brochettes

This dish was created to capture all the best flavors of summer. Prepare the garlic purée a day or two before, and the dish will not seem like such a daunting task. The vegetable brochettes are a good addition to any grilled entrée. Substitute any vegetable you wish and adjust the cooking time appropriately.

1. Preheat the oven to 375°F.

2. Place the chickens on a work surface and, using kitchen shears, cut out and remove the backbones. With a sharp knife, cut each bird in half through the breast. Remove the breast and rib bones. Cut away the wing tip and second joint of each wing bone, leaving the last joint intact. Cut into the thigh and remove the bone.

3. Season the chickens on both sides with the Essence. Heat 1 tablespoon of the oil in each of two large overproof skillets over medium-high heat. Place the chickens skin side down in the hot pans and sear only for 6 minutes.

4. Remove from the heat, add 2 tablespoons of the butter and 2 sprigs of thyme to each pan, and place in the oven. Roast for 16 minutes. Remove from the oven and carefully turn the chicken halves with tongs. Brush the skin side of each chicken with the garlic glaze and roast skin side up until the skin is crisp, about 10 minutes longer. Remove from the oven.

5. Divide the pilaf among four large dinner plates, and arrange the chicken in the middle of the pilaf. Spoon the sauce over the chicken and serve with the vegetable brochettes.

Roasted Garlic Glaze

MAKES ABOUT 1½ CUPS

6 heads garlic
½ cup plus 2 tablespoons
  extra-virgin olive oil
1 teaspoon salt
½ teaspoon freshly ground
  white pepper
2 large egg yolks
2 tablespoons fresh lemon
  juice

1. Preheat the oven to 325°F.

2. Cut off the top third of each head of garlic. Put them on a parchment- or foil-lined baking sheet, drizzle 2 tablespoons of the oil over the tops, and sprinkle with ½ teaspoon of the salt and ¼ teaspoon of the pepper. Turn the garlic cut side down and roast until the cloves are soft and golden brown, about 1 hour. Remove from the oven and let sit until cool enough to handle.

3. Squeeze each head of garlic gently to release the flesh. Combine the garlic, egg yolks, lemon juice, and the remaining ½ teaspoon salt and ¼ teaspoon pepper in a food processor, and purée on high speed. Add the remaining ½ cup oil in a slow, steady stream and process until the glaze is thick and smooth.

4. Transfer to an airtight container and refrigerate until ready to use. (The glaze can be made up to 1 day in advance.)

Creole Rice Pilaf

MAKES 4 CUPS

2 tablespoons vegetable oil
4 ounces andouille sausage,
  removed from casings and
  finely chopped
1 cup chopped yellow onions
½ cup chopped red bell
  peppers
½ cup chopped celery
⅔ cup corn kernels
3 ounces okra, stems
  removed and cut into
  ¼-inch-thick slices
1 teaspoon minced garlic
1½ cups long-grain white
  rice
2 cups Rich Chicken Stock
  (page 21)
¾ cup plus 2 tablespoons
  V-8 juice or tomato juice
1 bay leaf
1¼ teaspoons salt
½ teaspoon freshly ground
  black pepper

1. Heat the oil in a large saucepan over medium-high heat. Add the andouille and cook until lightly browned, about 4 minutes. Add the onions, bell peppers, and celery and cook, stirring, until just soft, about 3 minutes. Add the corn, okra, and garlic and cook until tender, about 4 minutes. Add the rice and cook, stirring, until opaque and lightly toasted, 2 to 3 minutes.

2. Add the chicken stock, V-8 juice, bay leaf, salt, and pepper, and bring to a boil. Reduce the heat to low, cover, and simmer until the rice is tender and all the liquid has been absorbed, 20 minutes. Remove from the heat and let sit for 10 minutes. Remove the bay leaf, fluff the rice with a fork, and serve.

MAKES ABOUT 1¼ CUPS

1 cup Rich Chicken Stock
(page 21)
1 teaspoon Dijon mustard
2 tablespoons fresh lemon
juice
½ cup olive oil
1 tablespoon chopped mixed
fresh herbs, such as basil,
parsley, chives, and
oregano

Lemon Herb Sauce

1. Put the chicken stock in a small saucepan and bring to a simmer. Transfer to a blender or food processor.

2. Add the mustard and process to blend. With the motor running, add the lemon juice, olive oil, and herbs and process until smooth. Serve immediately.

MAKES 4 SERVINGS

1 Japanese eggplant (about
6 ounces), halved
lengthwise and then
crosswise (or 1 globe
eggplant, trimmed to
6 ounces and cut into
4 equal portions)
1 yellow squash, halved
lengthwise and then
crosswise
1 zucchini, halved
lengthwise and then
crosswise
1 portobello mushroom,
stem removed, wiped
clean, and quartered
1 red bell pepper, cored,
seeds and ribs removed,
and cut into 4 pieces
¼ cup olive oil
¼ cup chopped mixed fresh
herbs, such as basil,
parsley, and oregano
2 teaspoons fresh lemon
juice
1 teaspoon salt
½ teaspoon freshly ground
white pepper
½ teaspoon minced garlic

Vegetable Brochettes

1. Thread one piece each of the eggplant, squash, zucchini, mushroom, and bell pepper onto four wooden or flat metal skewers.

2. Combine the oil, herbs, lemon juice, salt, white pepper, and garlic in a large shallow bowl and whisk to blend. Add the brochettes and marinate for 15 minutes, turning twice.

3. Preheat the broiler.

4. Place the brochettes on a baking sheet and broil until charred around the edges, about 3 minutes. Turn with tongs and cook for 3 minutes on the second side. Serve immediately.

CHICKEN, TURKEY, DUCK, QUAIL, AND RABBIT

Caribbean-Style Chicken with Brown Sugar–Peanut Spice Rub, Sweet Potato–Banana Casserole, Guacamole, and Crispy Plantain Strips

½ cup finely ground roasted peanuts
½ cup packed light brown sugar
1 tablespoon plus ⅛ teaspoon kosher salt
2¼ teaspoons cayenne
½ teaspoon ground bay leaf, plus a pinch
½ teaspoon ground cloves, plus a pinch
½ teaspoon grated nutmeg, plus a pinch
½ teaspoon ground cinnamon, plus a pinch
One 3½-pound chicken, rinsed well, patted dry, and cut into 8 pieces
1 cup Rich Chicken Stock (page 21)
1 teaspoon fresh lime juice
1 teaspoon chili powder
One 6-inch corn tortilla, torn into small pieces
1 tablespoon smooth peanut butter
1 recipe Sweet Potato-Banana Casserole
1 recipe Guacamole
1 recipe Crispy Plantain Strips

The ground peanuts combined with a blend of island spices made this dish a favorite on the menu at NOLA for years. Chef Dave tapped the creativity of Pastry Chef Joe Trull to come up with the accompanying sweet potato–banana casserole. This side dish would go well with Thanksgiving dinner!

Green plantains must be used for the crispy food strips, as they have a higher starch content. Make note that plantains cannot be peeled like bananas; the skins must be cut away with a sharp knife.

1. Preheat a grill to medium and preheat the oven to 350°F.

2. Combine the peanuts, brown sugar, 1 tablespoon of the salt, the cayenne, ground bay leaf, cloves, nutmeg, and cinnamon in a small bowl.

3. Place the chicken in a large bowl. Add the spice rub and toss to coat evenly, rubbing the spices into the chicken.

4. Place the chicken skin side down on the grill and cook until grill marks appear, about 3 minutes. Turn and grill for about 3 minutes on the second side. Transfer to a roasting pan or baking sheet lined with aluminum foil, skin side up, and roast until browned and cooked through (the juices should run clear when the thigh is pierced with a fork), about 35 minutes. Transfer to a plate and cover to keep warm.

5. Drain ¼ cup of the pan juices into a small saucepan. Add the chicken stock, lime juice, chili powder, the remaining ⅛ teaspoon salt, and the tortilla pieces and bring to a boil. Reduce the heat and simmer for 5 minutes. Transfer to a blender, add the peanut butter, and blend on high speed until smooth.

6. Divide the chicken among four dinner plates. Serve immediately with the sweet potato casserole, guacamole, and plantains.

1¾ pounds sweet
   potatoes
2 tablespoons unsalted
   butter
1 cup chopped yellow
   onions
1 teaspoon granulated
   sugar
2 large eggs
¼ cup plus 1 tablespoon
   packed light brown
   sugar
¼ cup molasses
2 tablespoons dark rum
1½ teaspoons salt
¾ teaspoon ground
   allspice
¾ teaspoon ground
   cinnamon
¼ teaspoon cayenne
3 bananas, peeled and
   cut crosswise into
   1-inch pieces
⅓ cup chopped pecans

Sweet Potato–Banana Casserole

1. Preheat the oven to 350°F.

2. Place the sweet potatoes on a baking sheet. Bake until tender and starting to ooze sugary syrup, about 1 hour and 20 minutes. Remove from the oven and let sit until cool enough to handle.

3. Cut a slit down each potato and scoop the flesh into a large bowl. Discard the skins.

4. Butter a 9-inch square baking dish with 1 tablespoon of the butter.

5. Melt the remaining 1 tablespoon butter in a large skillet over medium-high heat. Add the onions and cook, stirring, for 3 minutes. Add the granulated sugar and cook, stirring, for 3 minutes. Add to the bowl with the sweet potatoes.

6. Combine the eggs, brown sugar, molasses, rum, salt, allspice, cinnamon, and cayenne in a bowl and whisk to combine. Add to the potatoes and mash to combine. Pour into the prepared dish and smooth with the back of a spoon. Space the bananas evenly in the potatoes, about 2 inches apart, and push down lightly with an index finger. Sprinkle the top with the pecans, and cover with aluminum foil.

7. Bake for 45 minutes. Remove the foil and bake until bubbly and starting to brown, about 15 minutes more. Serve hot.

1 ripe Hass avocado,
   peeled, seeded, and
   diced
2 tablespoons minced
   red onions
1 tablespoon fresh lime
   juice
⅛ teaspoon salt
⅛ teaspoon freshly
   ground white pepper

Guacamole

Combine all the ingredients in a small bowl and mash with a fork to combine. Adjust the seasoning to taste. Transfer to an airtight container and refrigerate until ready to serve, or up to 2 hours.

CHICKEN, TURKEY, DUCK, QUAIL, AND RABBIT

Crispy Plantain Strips

½ *cup sugar*
2 *tablespoons ground*
cinnamon
1 *teaspoon ground allspice*
2 *green plantains*
4 *cups vegetable oil, for*
deep-frying

1. Combine the sugar, cinnamon, and allspice in a small bowl; set aside.

2. With a sharp paring knife, remove the ends of the plantains. Carefully, using a downward stroke, cut the peel from the plantains to expose the banana-like flesh.

3. Cut the plantains crosswise in half. Using a mandoline or other vegetable slicer, or a sharp heavy knife, slice lengthwise as thin as possible.

4. Heat the oil in a medium heavy pot or a deep-fryer to 350°F. Add the plantains, in batches, and fry until golden brown, 1½ to 2 minutes. Remove and drain on paper towels. Immediately sprinkle with the spiced sugar and serve.

Chef Dana D'Anzi in Delmonico Steakhouse kitchen

Funky Chicken Roulade with Parslied Rigatoni

Four 6-ounce boneless, skinless chicken breasts, rinsed and patted dry

10 ounces mild Italian sausage, removed from the casings and crumbled

½ cup fine dry bread crumbs

¼ cup freshly grated Parmigiano-Reggiano

1 tablespoon chopped fresh basil

1 tablespoon chopped fresh parsley

1 teaspoon Worcester-shire sauce

1 teaspoon Emeril's Kick It Up Red Pepper Sauce or other hot pepper sauce

2 teaspoons Emeril's Original Essence or Creole Seasoning (page 28)

2 teaspoons olive oil

½ cup Creole Marinara Sauce (page 242)

1 recipe Parslied Rigatoni

There are a variety of pounded and stuffed chicken breast dishes, from Chicken Cordon Bleu, with its ham and cheese filling, to Chicken Kiev, with its flavored butter. This is my take on that impressive but simple presentation. With my love of pork fat, it's no surprise that these roulades include Italian sausage! Be sure to pound the breasts sufficiently thin, or the chicken will not cook evenly.

1. Preheat the oven to 350°F.

2. One at a time, place the chicken breasts between two sheets of plastic wrap and pound with the flat side of a meat mallet until about ⅛ inch thick. Set aside.

3. Heat a medium skillet over medium-high heat. Add the sausage and cook, stirring, until browned, 8 to 10 minutes. Remove and drain on paper towels.

4. Combine the sausage, bread crumbs, cheese, basil, parsley, Worcestershire sauce, and hot sauce and mix well. Lay each chicken breast flat on a piece of plastic wrap with a short end facing you. Spread one-quarter of the filling over the center of each breast, leaving about ¾ inch uncovered at the top. Starting at the end closest to you, roll the chicken up around the filling, like a jelly roll. Secure each breast with three toothpicks and season with ½ teaspoon Essence. Place in a baking dish and drizzle ½ tea-spoon of oil over each breast.

5. Bake for 12 minutes. Remove from the oven (leave the oven on) and top each roulade with 2 tablespoons of the marinara sauce. Return to the oven and bake until an instant read thermometer inserted in the center of a roulade reads 165°F, 8 to 12 minutes more. Remove from the oven and discard the toothpicks.

6. Cut each roulade into 4 equal pieces and transfer to plates. Serve with the rigatoni.

CHICKEN, TURKEY, DUCK, QUAIL, AND RABBIT

½ *pound rigatoni or penne*
¼ *cup extra-virgin olive oil*
1 *tablespoon chopped fresh*
   parsley
1 *tablespoon chopped fresh*
   basil
¼ *cup freshly grated*
   Pecorino-Romano
1 *teaspoon minced garlic*
¾ *teaspoon kosher salt*
½ *teaspoon freshly ground*
   black pepper

Parslied Rigatoni

1. Bring a large pot of salted water to a boil. Add the pasta and cook until al dente, 10 to 12 minutes. Drain in a colander.

2. Return the pasta to the pot and add the remaining ingredients. Toss to coat evenly. Cover to keep warm until ready to serve.

Young patron at
Emeril's Delmonico

2 quarts apple cider
2 cups packed dark
   brown sugar
2 cups kosher salt
¼ cup black peppercorns
1 tablespoon juniper
   berries
4 bay leaves
Two cinnamon sticks
1 teaspoon whole cloves
4 quarts dark beer
One 8- to 10-pound
   turkey, neck and
   giblets reserved, well
   rinsed and patted dry
3 cups chopped yellow
   onions
1½ cups chopped celery
1½ cups chopped carrots
6 garlic cloves, peeled
   and smashed
8 tablespoons (1 stick)
   plus 1 tablespoon
   unsalted butter
2 tablespoons Emeril's
   Original Essence or
   Creole Seasoning
   (page 28)
4 cups Rich Chicken
   Stock (page 21)
1 tablespoon olive oil
3 tablespoons all-
   purpose flour
½ cup dry white wine
2 tablespoons chopped
   fresh sage

Beer-Brined Turkey with Turkey Giblet Gravy

I'm a big fan of turkey and not only at Thanksgiving. In the early days at Emeril's, I would serve panéed turkey cutlets, turkey loaf, and kicked-up turkey patties. This is a perfect summer recipe to make for a brunch or afternoon gathering. The secret to flavoring this dish is letting the bird marinate for twenty-four hours. We have done many experiments with brining in the test kitchen at Homebase in New Orleans. This unique method makes the turkey hoppy-hoppy and your guests happy-happy! If you don't have enough room in your refrigerator to brine the bird, place the turkey and brine in an ice chest in a cool location and cover it with bags of ice to keep it cold.

1. Combine the apple cider, brown sugar, salt, peppercorns, juniper berries, bay leaves, cinnamon sticks, and cloves in a large pot or bowl. Stir to dissolve the sugar and salt. Combine the mixture with the beer in a 40-quart cooler or large plastic container. Place the turkey in the brine and, if necessary, weight it down with heavy dinner plates to completely submerge it. Cover and refrigerate for 24 hours.

2. Preheat the oven to 400°F.

3. Spread the onions, celery, carrots, and garlic in a large roasting pan. Add the turkey neck.

4. Remove the turkey from the brine and rinse well under cold running water. Pat dry with paper towels and place on top of the vegetables in the roasting pan.

5. Combine 1 stick of the butter and the Essence in a small saucepan and melt over medium heat. Remove from the heat.

6. With a pastry brush, baste the top and sides of the turkey with half of the butter. Roast for 30 minutes.

7. Baste the turkey with the remaining seasoned butter, reduce the oven temperature to 300°F, and roast for 30 minutes.

8. Baste the turkey with ½ cup of the chicken stock. Return to the oven and roast until golden and an instant-read thermometer

CHICKEN, TURKEY, DUCK, QUAIL, AND RABBIT

inserted in the thickest part of the thigh registers 160°F, 1½ to 2 hours longer, basting once with ½ cup of the chicken stock.

9. Remove the turkey from the oven and transfer to a platter or cutting board. Tent with foil and let rest for 15 minutes before carving. Set the roasting pan aside.

10. Melt the remaining 1 tablespoon butter with the olive oil in a medium heavy pot over medium-high heat. Add the reserved giblets and cooked turkey neck and cook, stirring, until browned, 2 to 3 minutes. Add half of the vegetables from the roasting pan and cook, stirring, for 5 minutes. Add the flour and cook, stirring, for 1 minute. Add the white wine and stir to deglaze the pan. Add the remaining 3 cups chicken stock and any juices from the roasting pan and bring to a boil. Reduce the heat, add the sage, and simmer briskly until reduced by half, about 10 minutes. Remove from the heat and discard the neck.

11. In batches, pulse the liquid and solids in a food processor into a thick gravy. Strain through a fine-mesh strainer into a bowl, pressing against the solids with a spoon to extract as much liquid as possible, and transfer to a gravy boat. Adjust the seasoning to taste.

12. To serve, carve the turkey and serve with the gravy.

Citrus-and-Tea-Glazed Duck with Savory Wild Mushroom Bread Pudding

MAKES 4 SERVINGS

4 quarts brewed tea
4 quarts water
2¾ cups kosher salt
1½ cups packed light brown sugar
1 ancho chile or ½ guajillo chile
6 lemons, cut in half
6 limes, cut in half
1 tablespoon fennel seeds
1 teaspoon black peppercorns
1 teaspoon red pepper flakes
Two 4- to 5-pound ducks, well rinsed and patted dry, giblets and necks reserved
1 recipe Tea Glaze
1 recipe Savory Wild Mushroom Bread Pudding

Soaking the duck in a tea-flavored brine, drying it overnight, and then roasting it gives it a fragrant, herbal flavor. While the brining process may seem a little involved, it is definitely worth the effort. Chef Chris brews Lipton tea for the duck brining liquid and tea glaze, but feel free to experiment with different-flavored teas to come up with your own dish!

If you have any tea glaze left over, drizzle some over the duck before serving it. Or keep it refrigerated in an airtight container and use it as a glaze for barbecued ribs or chicken. Bring it to room temperature before using it so that it can be spread.

1. To make the brining liquid, combine the tea, water, salt, sugar, chile, lemons, limes, fennel seeds, peppercorns, and red pepper in a large heavy pot and bring to a boil. Remove from the heat and let cool completely (or chill in an ice water bath until cool).

2. Add the ducks to the brine and weight with a small plate to submerge them. Refrigerate for at least 24 hours, or up to 48 hours, turning the ducks occasionally.

3. Bring a large pot of water to a rolling boil. Remove the ducks from the brine. Add one at a time to the boiling water and poach for 3 minutes. Remove with tongs and place on a wire rack set on a baking sheet. Pat dry with paper towels. Pour ¼ cup of the glaze onto the top of each duck, rubbing to coat evenly. Refrigerate, uncovered, for 24 hours; during this time, spread ¼ cup glaze on each duck three times, every 6 to 8 hours.

4. Preheat the oven to 500°F.

5. Remove the ducks from the refrigerator and let come to room temperature.

6. Spread about ¼ cup of the glaze over each duck, rubbing to coat evenly. Set on a rack in a roasting pan. Roast until deep golden brown, 15 to 18 minutes. Reduce the temperature to 375°F and roast until the skin is a deep mahogany color and the juices run clear, 1 hour and 45 minutes to 2 hours; add 1 cup water to the

CHICKEN, TURKEY, DUCK, QUAIL, AND RABBIT

roasting pan every 30 minutes to prevent the dripping glaze from burning. Remove from the oven and let rest for 15 minutes before carving.

7. With poultry shears, cut along either side of the backbone of each duck and remove. With a sharp knife, cut through the breast and remove the rib cage.

8. Divide the bread pudding among four large dinner plates. Place one duck half on top of each portion, drizzle with any remaining tea glaze, if desired, and serve.

Tea Glaze

MAKES ABOUT 2½ CUPS

2 cups light corn syrup
1 cup dark corn syrup
1 cup white distilled vinegar
½ cup sugar
½ cup fresh orange juice
¼ cup fresh lime juice
¼ cup plus 2 tablespoons honey
2 tablespoons fresh lemon juice
One 2-inch piece cinnamon stick
2 teaspoons coriander seeds
½ teaspoon fennel seeds
3 tea bags

1. Combine all the ingredients except the tea bags in a large heavy saucepan and bring to a boil. Reduce the heat to medium-low and simmer until reduced to a thick syrup, about 1 hour and 10 minutes.

2. Add the tea bags and simmer for 5 minutes. Remove from the heat and remove and discard the tea bags. Strain into a clean container and let cool before using. (The glaze keeps for up to 1 month, refrigerated, in an airtight container.)

Savory Wild Mushroom Bread Pudding

2 teaspoons vegetable oil

1 cup sliced yellow onions

10 ounces mixed wild mushrooms, such as oyster, shiitake, chanterelle, wood ear, and/or porcini, stems trimmed (discard stems if using shiitakes), wiped clean, and sliced

1 teaspoon minced garlic

1 tablespoon Emeril's Original Essence or Creole Seasoning (page 28)

1½ teaspoons salt

1 teaspoon freshly ground black pepper

¼ cup lager beer

5 large eggs

3 cups heavy cream

¼ cup molasses

1½ teaspoons Worcestershire sauce

1 teaspoon minced fresh thyme

¾ cup grated Gouda

¾ cup grated white Cheddar

¾ pound stale white bread, cut into 1-inch cubes, about 10 cups

1 teaspoon unsalted butter

1 tablespoon fine dry bread crumbs

Bread puddings in South Louisiana are traditionally sweet, such as the Cane Syrup–Pecan Bread Pudding (page 310). But, through the years, I've adapted the pudding and made a variety of savory ones at each of the restaurants. This wild mushroom bread pudding is a great use of stale bread (particularly French bread) and makes an ideal pairing for game, meats, and poultry. Or, serve it on its own with a big green salad for a lighter meal.

If you have any leftovers, this bread pudding will keep for several days refrigerated. Reheat before serving.

1. Heat the oil in a large deep skillet over high heat. Add the onions and cook until golden brown and tender, about 5 minutes. Add the mushrooms, ½ teaspoon of the garlic, 1½ teaspoons of the Essence, 1 teaspoon of the salt, and ¾ teaspoon of the pepper and cook, stirring, until the mushrooms have given off their liquid and are tender, about 5 minutes. Add the beer and cook, stirring, to deglaze the pan, then cook until the mixture is almost dry, 1 to 2 minutes. Remove from the heat and let cool.

2. In a large bowl, combine the eggs, cream, molasses, Worcestershire, thyme, and the remaining 1½ teaspoons Essence, ½ teaspoon salt, and ¼ teaspoon pepper and whisk well to blend. Add the cheeses and stir well. Add the bread cubes and let sit, stirring occasionally, until the bread has absorbed the liquid, about 2 hours.

3. Preheat the oven to 350°F.

4. Butter a 9 × 13-inch baking dish with the butter. Add the bread crumbs, shaking to cover the bottom evenly. Pour the bread pudding mixture into the pan and cover with aluminum foil. Bake for 1 hour, uncover, and continue baking until the pudding rises, is set in the center, and is golden brown, 20 to 30 minutes. Let cool slightly before serving.

CHICKEN, TURKEY, DUCK, QUAIL, AND RABBIT

NOLA

Cumin-Rubbed Duck Breast with Cilantro Sticky Rice, Smoky Black Beans, and Rock Shrimp Salsa Fresca

1 cup dried black beans, rinsed and picked over

Four 6-ounce boneless skin-on duck breast halves, rinsed and patted dry

2 tablespoons ground cumin

1 teaspoon salt

1/2 teaspoon freshly ground black pepper

2 strips bacon, chopped

1/2 cup finely chopped red onions

1 tablespoon minced garlic

3 1/2 cups Rich Chicken Stock (page 21)

1 bay leaf

1 recipe Cilantro Sticky Rice

1 recipe Rock Shrimp Salsa Fresca

1/2 cup chopped fresh cilantro, for garnish

This is one of my favorite lunch items at NOLA where the duck is cleverly paired with rice and black beans, a play on a Cuban dish called congris. *Cooking the duck breast skin side down renders a lot of the fat and lightens the dish.*

1. Place the beans in a pot and cover with water by 2 inches. Let soak overnight. Discard any beans that have floated to the surface, and drain the beans.

2. Place the duck breasts in a baking dish and season with the cumin, salt, and pepper. Cover with plastic wrap and refrigerate for at least 6 hours, or overnight.

3. Cook the bacon in a medium saucepan over medium-high heat, stirring, until slightly crisp, about 4 minutes. Add the onions and cook, stirring, for 3 minutes. Add the garlic and cook, stirring for 30 seconds. Add the black beans, chicken stock, and bay leaf and bring to a boil. Reduce the heat to medium-low and simmer, partially covered, stirring occasionally, until the beans are tender, 2 to 2 1/2 hours, adding more liquid as needed to keep the beans moist. Remove from the heat. Discard the bay leaf and adjust the seasoning to taste. Cover to keep warm until ready to serve.

4. Heat a large heavy skillet over medium-high heat. Add the duck breasts skin side down and sear for 5 minutes per side for medium-rare. Transfer to a cutting board to rest for 3 minutes, then slice into 1/2-inch slices.

5. To serve, place the rice in the center of four large dinner plates. Top with the duck breasts, and spoon the black beans around the rice. Top with the shrimp salsa and garnish with the cilantro. Serve immediately.

Cilantro Sticky Rice

MAKES ABOUT 3 CUPS

1 cup short-grain Japanese sushi rice
1½ cups water
½ teaspoon salt
3 tablespoons olive oil
2 tablespoons chopped fresh cilantro
1 tablespoon minced garlic

1. Place the rice in a colander and rinse under cool running water until the water runs clear; drain.

2. Transfer to a heavy medium saucepan, add the water and salt, and bring to a boil. Reduce the heat to low, cover, and simmer until the rice is tender and all the water is absorbed, about 20 minutes. Remove from the heat and let stand, covered, for 10 minutes.

3. Fluff the rice with a fork. Stir in the olive oil, cilantro, and garlic. Adjust the seasoning to taste, and serve.

Rock Shrimp Salsa Fresca

MAKES 2 CUPS

6 ounces peeled and deveined rock shrimp
1 teaspoon Emeril's Original Essence or Creole Seasoning (page 28)
2 teaspoons olive oil
1 cup peeled, seeded, and chopped tomatoes
¼ cup finely chopped red onions
¼ cup fresh lime juice
1 tablespoon chopped fresh cilantro
1½ teaspoons minced, seeded jalapeño
½ teaspoon minced garlic
¼ teaspoon salt
⅛ teaspoon freshly ground black pepper
2 teaspoons extra-virgin olive oil

1. Season the shrimp with the Essence. Heat the olive oil in a medium skillet over medium-high heat. Add the shrimp and cook until firm and pink, 2 to 3 minutes. Remove from the heat and let cool completely.

2. In a medium nonreactive bowl, combine the tomatoes, onions, lime juice, cilantro, jalapeño, and garlic and mix well. Add the shrimp, salt, pepper, and extra-virgin olive oil and mix well. Let sit for 15 minutes before serving.

Pan-Roasted Quail with Creamy Cheese Grits, Spicy Beef Grillades, Crispy Red Onion Rings, and Creole Tomato Glaze

MAKES 6 SERVINGS

12 boneless quail (about 3½ ounces each), rinsed and patted dry
1 tablespoon salt
¾ teaspoon freshly ground black pepper
3 tablespoons vegetable oil
1 recipe Creamy Cheese Grits
1 recipe Spicy Beef Grillades
¼ cup Creole Tomato Glaze (page 128)
1 recipe Crispy Red Onion Rings

At Delmonico, they put a spin on the classic Creole brunch dish, grillades and grits, by substituting filet mignon trimmings for the usual veal medallions. And, I'll tell you what, pan-roasted quail have never tasted so good! Although they braise filet mignon in the restaurant to make the rich sauce, we've substituted beef stew meat here to make the dish a little more affordable for the home cook. Either way, it's delicious—and if you feel like kicking it up with the more expensive meat, go ahead. If you prepare the grillades one day in advance, you'll find this meal comes together easily. Have your butcher bone the quail so they are split down the back.

1. Preheat the oven to 375°F.

2. Season each quail with ¼ teaspoon of the salt and a pinch of pepper.

3. Heat 1 tablespoon of the oil in each of three large ovenproof skillets over medium-high heat (or use one pan and brown the quail in batches, then transfer to a roasting pan). Add 4 quail to each pan and cook for 3 minutes. Turn and cook for 2 minutes on the second side.

4. Transfer the quail to the oven and roast until cooked through and tender, 6 minutes. Remove from the oven.

5. To serve, divide the grits among six large deep bowls. Spoon the grillades over the grits and top with the quail. Drizzle each portion with 1 tablespoon of the tomato glaze, and garnish with the onion rings.

4¹/₂ cups whole milk
1 cup regular grits
    (not instant)
2 teaspoons salt
1 teaspoon freshly
    ground white pepper
1¹/₂ cups grated smoked
    Cheddar cheese

Creamy Cheese Grits

1. Bring the milk to a boil in a large heavy pot. Slowly add the grits, salt, and pepper, whisking constantly, and return to the boil. Reduce the heat to low and simmer, stirring occasionally, until thickened, about 20 minutes.

2. Remove from the heat and adjust the seasoning to taste. Cover to keep warm until ready to serve, then stir in the cheese before serving.

2 pounds beef stew
    meat, such as
    shoulder, fat and
    sinew trimmed, and
    cut into 2-inch cubes
1 tablespoon Emeril's
    Original Essence or
    Creole Seasoning
    (page 28)
¹/₂ teaspoon salt
2 tablespoons vegetable
    oil
1 cup chopped yellow
    onions
¹/₂ cup chopped celery
¹/₂ cup chopped green
    bell peppers
1 teaspoon minced garlic
1¹/₂ cups peeled, seeded,
    and diced tomatoes
1 teaspoon tomato paste
1 bay leaf
6 cups Reduced Veal
    Stock (page 25)

Spicy Beef Grillades

1. Season the meat on both sides with 2 teaspoons of the Essence and the salt.

2. Heat the vegetable oil in a large heavy skillet over medium-high heat. Add the meat and cook, turning often, until browned, about 10 minutes. Add the onions, celery, and bell peppers and cook, stirring, until soft, about 3 minutes. Add the garlic and cook, stirring, for 30 seconds. Add the tomatoes, tomato paste, bay leaf, and the remaining 1 teaspoon Essence and cook, stirring, for 3 minutes. Add the veal stock and bring to a low simmer. Cover the pan and cook over medium-low heat, stirring occasionally, until the meat is very tender and starting to shred, about 2 hours.

3. Remove from the heat and discard the bay leaf. Remove the meat with a slotted spoon and place in a bowl. Stir hard until the meat falls apart into shreds. Skim the fat from the cooking liquid, and return the meat to the pan. Cover to keep hot until ready to serve. Or, cool, then cover and refrigerate for up to 48 hours. Reheat before serving.

CHICKEN, TURKEY, DUCK, QUAIL, AND RABBIT

Crispy Red Onion Rings

4 cups vegetable oil, for deep-frying
½ cup Emeril's Kick It Up Red Pepper Sauce or other hot pepper sauce
1 cup all-purpose flour
1 tablespoon Emeril's Original Essence or Creole Seasoning (page 28), plus more for dusting
1 large red onion, peeled and cut into thin rings

1. Preheat the oil in a large heavy pot or deep-fryer to 350°F.

2. Place the hot sauce in a medium bowl. Combine the flour and Essence in a shallow dish. Add the onions to the hot sauce, tossing to coat, then dredge in the flour, in batches, shaking to remove any excess.

3. Add the onions to the hot oil, in batches, and fry, turning occasionally, until golden brown, about 2 minutes. Remove with a slotted spoon and drain on paper towels. Sprinkle lightly with Essence, and serve hot.

Chef Chris Wilson working the line at Emeril's New Orleans

**8 boneless quail (about
3½ ounces each),
rinsed and patted dry**
**1 recipe Tasso and Corn-
bread Stuffing**
**3 tablespoons unsalted
butter, melted**
**1 tablespoon plus
1 teaspoon Emeril's
Original Essence or
Creole Seasoning
(page 28)**
1 recipe Fig Glaze
**1 recipe Southern
Cooked Greens
(page 227)**

Tasso-and-Cornbread–Stuffed Quail with Fig Glaze

Cornbread stuffing is always best if the cornbread is made the day before and allowed to go stale overnight. But sometimes, when I just want a simple Creole dish like this, I realize I haven't planned ahead and don't have the cornbread on hand. For that reason, whenever you've got cornbread left over from another meal, put it in an airtight bag and stick it in the freezer. When the mood strikes, you can take it out and make this stuffing. You'll find it goes well with any poultry, or simply on its own. Southern Cooked Greens (page 227) or roasted beets are perfect accompaniments to the country-style quail. And the fig glaze is a breath of summer any time of year.

1. Preheat the oven to 400°F.

2. Place the quail breast side down on a baking sheet. Divide the stuffing into 8 equal portions and form into firm balls. Insert one ball in the cavity of each quail and bring the meat and skin up and around to cover completely. Turn breast side up, on the baking sheet.

3. In a small bowl, combine the melted butter and the Essence. With a pastry brush, brush the butter over the tops and sides of the quail. Roast for 10 minutes.

4. Remove the quail from the oven and spread about 2 teaspoons of the fig glaze over each bird. Return to the oven and roast until golden brown and cooked through, about 10 minutes.

5. To serve, place 2 birds in a V-shape on each of four large serving plates, and arrange the greens in the center. Serve immediately.

CHICKEN, TURKEY, DUCK, QUAIL, AND RABBIT

2 tablespoons olive oil
2 ounces tasso, finely
chopped
½ cup chopped yellow
onions
¼ cup chopped green bell
peppers
¼ cup chopped celery
½ tablespoon minced garlic
3 cups crumbled Cornbread
(page 35)
1 tablespoon chopped fresh
parsley
1 teaspoon chopped
fresh sage
½ teaspoon chopped fresh
thyme
1 cup Rich Chicken Stock
(page 21)
1 teaspoon Worcestershire
sauce
1 teaspoon salt
¼ teaspoon freshly ground
white pepper

Tasso and Cornbread Stuffing

1. Heat the oil in a large skillet over medium-high heat. Add the tasso and cook until browned, about 3 minutes. Add the onions, bell peppers, and celery and cook, stirring, until soft, about 3 minutes. Add the garlic and cook for 30 seconds. Add the cornbread, parsley, sage, and thyme and stir well to blend. Add the chicken stock, stir well and cook for 1 minute.

2. Remove from the heat, add the Worcestershire, salt, and pepper, and mix well. Let cool for about 10 minutes before using.

½ cup fig preserves
¼ cup Rich Chicken Stock
(page 21)
1 tablespoon apple cider
vinegar
¼ teaspoon salt
⅛ teaspoon freshly ground
black pepper

Fig Glaze

Combine all the ingredients in a small skillet. Bring to a boil and cook, stirring constantly, until reduced to a thick glaze, 3 to 4 minutes. Remove from the heat and use warm. (Leftover glaze will keep in an airtight container in the refrigerator for up to 1 week.)

Mushroom-Stuffed Quail with Celery Root–Braised Cabbage, and Natural Jus

8 boneless quail (each about 3½ ounces), bones reserved for Natural Jus, quail rinsed and patted dry

2 tablespoons Emeril's Original Essence or Creole Seasoning (page 28)

1 recipe Mushroom Stuffing

4 tablespoons unsalted butter, melted

1 recipe Celery Root– Braised Cabbage

1 recipe Natural Jus

Celery root is just what the name implies, the root of a special celery plant; its texture is like that of a turnip and it tastes like a cross between celery and parsley. You'll find this braised cabbage goes well with many other dishes and that its flavor improves if allowed to sit overnight (refrigerated).

1. Preheat the oven to 400°F.

2. Lay the quail skin side down on a baking sheet and season with 1 tablespoon of the Essence. Divide the stuffing into 8 equal portions and form into firm balls. Insert one ball into the cavity of each quail and bring the meat and skin up and around to cover completely. Turn the quail breast side up, brush with the butter, and season with the remaining tablespoon Essence.

3. Roast until the birds are golden brown and cooked through, about 20 minutes.

4. To serve, place ½ cup of the braised cabbage in the center of each of four large plates. Arrange 2 quail on either side of the cabbage, drizzle with the jus, and serve.

CHICKEN, TURKEY, DUCK, QUAIL, AND RABBIT

2 tablespoons olive oil
1/4 cup minced shallots
1 tablespoon minced garlic
2 pounds mixed mushrooms,
    such as button, shiitake,
    wood ear, and
    chanterelle, stems
    trimmed (removed if using
    shiitakes), wiped clean
    and coarsely chopped
1 1/4 teaspoons salt
1/2 teaspoon freshly ground
    black pepper
1/2 cup dry white wine
1/2 cup freshly grated
    Parmigiano-Reggiano
1/4 cup fine dry bread crumbs
1 tablespoon chopped fresh
    parsley
1 tablespoon chopped fresh
    basil
1 tablespoon chopped fresh
    oregano

Mushroom Stuffing

1. Heat the oil in a large heavy skillet over medium-high heat. Add the shallots and garlic and cook, stirring, for 30 seconds. Add the mushrooms, salt, and pepper and cook, stirring, until the mushrooms are wilted and beginning to brown, 5 to 7 minutes. Deglaze the pan with the wine, stirring to loosen any browned bits in the bottom of the pan, and cook until almost all the liquid has evaporated, 5 to 8 minutes. Remove from the heat.

2. Transfer the mushrooms to a food processor. Add the cheese, bread crumbs, parsley, basil, and oregano and process to a thick paste. Transfer to a bowl, cover, and set aside until ready to use.

1/2 pound bacon, chopped
1 cup chopped yellow onions
1 teaspoon minced garlic
2 1/2 cups chopped green
    cabbage
1 teaspoon salt
1/2 teaspoon freshly ground
    black pepper
2 cups Rich Chicken Stock
    (page 21)
3/4 cup lager beer
4 ounces celery root, peeled
    and thinly sliced (heaping
    1/2 cup)

Celery Root–Braised Cabbage

Cook the bacon in a large heavy skillet over medium-high heat until crisp and golden, about 5 minutes. Add the onions and cook, stirring, for 3 minutes. Add the garlic and cook, stirring, for 30 seconds. Add the cabbage, salt, and pepper and cook, stirring, for 3 minutes. Add the chicken stock and beer and bring to a boil. Reduce the heat and simmer for 20 minutes, stirring occasionally, or until the cabbage is tender. Add the celery root and cook until tender, 2 to 3 minutes. Remove from the heat and serve.

**Reserved bones from
  8 quail (page 219)**
**½ cup chopped yellow
  onions**
¼ cup chopped celery
¼ cup chopped carrots
1 tablespoon olive oil
½ teaspoon salt
**¼ teaspoon freshly
  ground black pepper**
½ cup dry red wine
**3 cups Rich Chicken
  Stock (page 21)**

Natural Jus

1. Preheat the oven to 400°F.

2. Combine the quail bones, onions, celery, carrots, oil, salt, and pepper in a roasting pan, tossing to mix. Roast until the bones are deeply colored, about 45 minutes.

3. Transfer the bones and vegetables to a medium heavy pot. Place the roasting pan on two burners over medium-high heat, add the wine, and stir with a wooden spoon to deglaze the pan. Pour the wine and pan juices into the pot with the bones, add the stock, and bring to a boil. Reduce the heat to medium-low and simmer, uncovered, until reduced to 1 cup, about 30 minutes.

4. Remove from the heat and strain through a fine-mesh strainer into a saucepan. Cover to keep warm, or gently reheat when ready to serve.

*Chef Neal Swidler at Emeril's
Delmonico evening pre-meal
meeting*

Emeril's
HOMEBASE

Rabbit Braised with Tasso, Wild Mushrooms, and Marsala, Served over Almond Rice with Sweet Pea Tendrils

Two 2½-pound rabbits, each cut into 6 serving pieces (front legs, hind legs, and loins), giblets reserved

1 tablespoon salt

1 tablespoon cracked black pepper

1 cup all-purpose flour

¼ cup olive oil

3 ounces tasso or ham, diced (about ½ cup)

1 cup chopped yellow onions

½ cup chopped celery

½ cup chopped carrots

1 tablespoon chopped garlic

1 pound wild mushrooms, such as oyster, shiitake, or chanterelle, stems trimmed (removed if using shiitakes), wiped clean, and sliced ⅛ inch thick

1 cup dry Marsala wine or dry Madeira

2 bay leaves

1 teaspoon chopped fresh thyme

4 cups Rich Chicken Stock (page 21)

1 cup peeled, chopped, and seeded tomatoes

1 recipe Almond Rice

½ pound fresh pea tendrils or watercress

Emeril's Delmonico is equipped with beautiful copper pots in which we serve certain dishes. When Chef Dave was the chef there, he wanted to come up with an impressive tableside dish, and here is his creation.

While cutting up a rabbit isn't difficult, you might not want to do it at home; instead, have your butcher cut the two rabbits into serving portions. Note that you'll have the two carcasses left over, which can be used to make gumbo or another soup. Or, if you have the time, make a rich rabbit stock for the almond rice that is served with the braised rabbits: Roast the bones for 1 hour at 400°F, then simmer with chicken stock for an hour; strain and use. This rabbit is so delicious and tender that the meat falls right off the bone.

1. Season both sides of the rabbits with 1 teaspoon each of the salt and pepper. In a bowl, combine the flour with 1 teaspoon each of the salt and pepper. Dredge the rabbit in the flour, shaking to remove any excess.

2. Heat the oil in a large Dutch oven or other large heavy pot over medium heat. Add the rabbit leg portions and cook until golden, about 15 minutes on the first side and 12 minutes on the second side. Remove from the pan and drain on paper towels. Add the loins to the fat remaining in the pan and cook until golden, about 3 minutes per side. Remove and drain on paper towels.

3. Add the tasso to the pot and cook, stirring, for 1 minute. Add the onions, celery, carrots, and the remaining 1 teaspoon each salt and black pepper and cook, stirring, for 1 minute. Add the garlic and cook, stirring, for 30 seconds. Add the mushrooms and cook, stirring, until soft, about 5 minutes. Add the Marsala and cook, stirring, to deglaze the pan. Add the bay leaves and thyme, return the rabbit legs to the pan, add the chicken stock, and bring to a boil. Cover with the lid slightly ajar, reduce the heat to medium-low, and simmer for 1 hour.

4. Add the rabbit loins, partially cover again, and cook for 15 minutes.

5. Meanwhile, chop the reserved giblets.

6. Add the giblets and tomatoes to the pot, and stir well to incorporate. Cover tightly and cook until the meat is fork-tender, about 15 minutes. Remove from the heat and adjust the seasoning to taste.

7. To serve, spoon the almond rice into the center of four deep large plates. Arrange the rabbit pieces on the rice, top with the pan gravy, and arrange the pea tendrils around the rims of the plates. Serve immediately.

Almond Rice

MAKES ABOUT 4 CUPS

1½ cups Rich Chicken Stock (page 21)
½ teaspoon salt
¼ teaspoon freshly ground white pepper
1 bay leaf
¾ cup long-grain white rice
¼ cup toasted almonds
¼ cup currants
1 tablespoon chopped fresh mint

1. Bring the chicken stock to a boil in a medium saucepan. Add the salt, pepper, bay leaf, and rice, stir, and return to a boil. Reduce the heat to low, cover tightly, and cook until the rice is tender and all the liquid is absorbed, about 20 minutes. Remove from the heat and let stand, covered, for 10 minutes.

2. Remove the bay leaf and fluff the rice with a fork. Stir in the almonds, currants, and mint and serve.

2 teaspoons salt

½ teaspoon freshly ground
black pepper

¼ teaspoon freshly ground
white pepper

¼ teaspoon cayenne

Two 2½-pound rabbits, each
cut into 6 serving pieces
(front legs, hind legs, and
loins), giblets reserved

1 cup buttermilk

1 cup all-purpose flour

4 cups vegetable oil, for
deep-frying

¼ cup chopped yellow
onions

1 teaspoon minced garlic

2½ cups whole milk

1 tablespoon Emeril's Kick It
Up Red Pepper Sauce or
other hot pepper sauce

Country-Fried Rabbit
with White Pan Gravy

A simple preparation is best for fresh rabbit. This is a very Southern way to serve rabbit, with a milk pan gravy. And, hey, if it's got lumps, all the better! When preparing the rabbit, the front and back legs are fairly easy to remove. To remove the loins, cut along the backbone from one end to the other and gently pull away.

1. Combine the salt, black pepper, white pepper, and cayenne in a small bowl.

2. Put the rabbit in a large bowl and season on both sides with half of the seasoning mix. Add the buttermilk, and marinate for 2 hours in the refrigerator.

3. Chop the rabbit giblets; set aside.

4. Combine the remaining seasoning mixture with the flour in a large plastic storage bag. One at a time, remove the rabbit pieces from the milk, place in the bag, and shake to coat evenly with the flour. Place on a baking sheet. Reserve the flour for the gravy.

5. Heat the oil to 300°F in a large deep skillet. Add the rabbit, several pieces at a time, and fry, turning once, until golden and cooked through, 5 minutes per side for the front legs and loin pieces, 8 minutes per side for the hind legs. Remove and drain on paper towels.

6. Carefully drain off all but 2 tablespoons of the hot oil from the pan. Add the giblets, onions, and garlic and cook, stirring, for 2 minutes. Add the flour and cook, stirring, for 1 minute. Add the milk and hot sauce and cook, whisking, for 5 minutes. Remove from the heat.

7. Divide the rabbit among four plates and spoon the sauce on top. Serve immediately.

ORLANDO

Roasted Rabbit Tenderloins with Creole Mustard Spaetzle, Southern Cooked Greens, and Ham Hock Gravy

½ cup whole milk

1 large egg

½ cup all-purpose flour

1 tablespoon plus 1 teaspoon Emeril's Original Essence or Creole Seasoning (page 28)

½ cup fine dry bread crumbs

Four 4-ounce rabbit tenderloins

3 tablespoons vegetable oil

1 recipe Ham Hock Gravy

1 recipe Creole Mustard Spaetzle

1 recipe Southern Cooked Greens

The rich flavor and gelatinous quality of veal stock make it a key ingredient of the ham hock gravy. Although you can substitute another stock, be warned that you won't achieve the same intensity. The cooked greens, which go well with any Southern dish, also pair well with the German and Alsatian notes of this dish. For an authentic touch, open a nice bottle of dry German Riesling to go with this.

1. Preheat the oven to 375°F.

2. In a shallow bowl, combine the milk and egg and whisk well. In another shallow dish, combine the flour and 1½ teaspoons of the Essence. In a third shallow dish, combine the bread crumbs with 1½ teaspoons of the Essence.

3. Season the rabbit tenderloins with the remaining 1 teaspoon Essence. Dredge the tenderloins in the flour, then in the egg, and then in the seasoned bread crumbs, shaking to remove any excess.

4. Heat the oil in a large ovenproof nonstick skillet over medium heat. Add the tenderloins and cook until golden brown, 1 to 2 minutes per side.

5. Transfer to the oven and roast until cooked through, 6 to 8 minutes. Remove from the oven and let rest for 5 minutes.

6. To serve, spoon ¼ cup ham hock gravy over one-third of each of four large serving plates. Place the spaetzle and greens alongside the gravy. Slice each tenderloin into 6 pieces and place atop the gravy. Serve immediately, drizzling with additional gravy as desired.

Ham Hock Gravy

3 tablespoons olive oil
1 cup chopped yellow onions
1 cup chopped green bell
   peppers
½ cup chopped celery
1 teaspoon minced garlic
1 tablespoon tomato paste
1 cup dry red wine
2 medium ham hocks
   (about 1½ pounds)
6 cups Reduced Veal Stock
   (page 25)
2 tablespoons unsalted
   butter
2 tablespoons all-purpose
   flour
Salt and freshly ground black
   pepper to taste

1. Heat the oil in a Dutch oven or other large heavy pot over medium-high heat. Add the onions, bell peppers, and celery and cook, stirring, until they begin to caramelize, about 5 minutes. Add the garlic and cook, stirring, for 30 seconds. Add the tomato paste, stirring well to combine, and cook until it begins to brown, about 1½ minutes.

2. Add the red wine and stir to deglaze the pot, loosening any browned bits clinging to the bottom. Add the ham hocks and veal stock and bring to a boil. Reduce the heat to medium and simmer until the liquid is reduced by half, about 2 hours and 45 minutes. Remove from the heat.

3. Remove the ham hocks from the gravy and set aside to cool. Remove the fat and skin from the ham hocks and discard. Remove the meat from the bone and finely chop.

4. Meanwhile, melt the butter in a small saucepan over medium heat. Add the flour, whisking constantly until a smooth, thick roux forms, about 2 minutes. Continue to cook, stirring constantly, until the roux has a nutty aroma and is a light peanut butter color, about 3 minutes longer. Remove from the heat and let cool.

5. Whisk the cooled roux into the hot gravy and bring to a boil. Reduce the heat to medium-low and simmer for 5 minutes or until thickened.

6. Return the ham hock meat to the gravy, add salt and pepper to taste, and serve or cover to keep warm until ready to serve.

Creole Mustard Spaetzle

1 cup plus 2 tablespoons
all-purpose flour
1¾ teaspoons salt
3 large eggs, lightly
beaten
⅓ cup whole milk
¼ cup plus 1 tablespoon
Creole mustard or
other whole-grain
mustard
1 teaspoon vegetable oil
1 tablespoon unsalted
butter
1 tablespoon chopped
fresh parsley
½ teaspoon fresh lemon
juice

1. Combine the flour and ¾ teaspoon of the salt in a large bowl. In another bowl, whisk together the eggs and milk, then add to the flour, whisking until smooth. Add ¼ cup of the mustard and the oil and mix well.

2. Prepare an ice bath in a large bowl; set aside.

3. Bring 4 quarts water and the remaining 1 teaspoon salt to a rolling boil in a large Dutch oven or other large heavy pot. Pour half of the batter into a spaetzle maker or a medium colander and, with a rubber spatula, force the batter through the holes into the water. (The water will rise and foam.) Cook, stirring, until the dumplings rise to the surface, about 5 minutes. Transfer with a long-handled slotted spoon or strainer to the ice bath. Repeat with the remaining batter. Drain and place in a large bowl. (The spaetzle can be prepared up to 2 hours in advance, drained, and kept tightly covered in a bowl the refrigerator.)

4. Melt the butter in a large nonstick skillet over medium-high heat. When the butter is foamy, add the remaining 1 tablespoon mustard and swirl to blend. Add the spaetzle, parsley, and lemon juice and stir to mix. Cook until the spaetzle is warmed through and the flavors are well blended, about 2 minutes. Serve immediately.

Southern Cooked Greens

MAKES 4 SERVINGS

¼ pound bacon, diced
1 cup sliced yellow onions
1 teaspoon minced garlic
2 tablespoons dark
brown sugar
2 pounds greens:
mustard, kale, or
collard, tough stems
removed and rinsed
¼ cup beer
1 tablespoon molasses
1½ teaspoons rice wine
vinegar
1 teaspoon freshly
ground black pepper
⅛ teaspoon salt
⅛ teaspoon red pepper
flakes

1. Cook the bacon in a medium pot over medium-high heat until crisp, about 5 minutes. Add the onions and cook, stirring, until soft, about 3 minutes. Add the garlic and cook, stirring, for 30 seconds. Add the sugar and cook, stirring, until dissolved.

2. Add the greens and all the remaining ingredients, and cook, stirring occasionally, until starting to wilt, 5 to 8 minutes. Lower the heat to medium and cook, stirring occasionally, until wilted, 45 minutes to 1 hour. Remove from the heat and adjust the seasoning to taste. Cover to keep warm until ready to serve.

CHICKEN, TURKEY, DUCK, QUAIL, AND RABBIT

9 | BEEF, VEAL, PORK, AND LAMB

Chef Christian Czerwonka at Delmonico Steakhouse

Dry-Aged Rib-Eyes with Emeril's Maître d'Hôtel Butter and Mashed Potatoes

½ cup vegetable oil
½ cup Emeril's Original Essence or Creole Seasoning (page 28)
Four 20- to 22-ounce bone-in dry-aged rib-eye steaks
Four ½-inch-thick slices Emeril's Maître d'Hôtel Butter
1 recipe Mashed Potatoes
1 tablespoon finely chopped fresh parsley, for garnish

Here's my advice on dry-aging beef: Don't try this at home! My restaurants have specially equipped walk-in coolers that control temperature and humidity levels according to exacting specifications. See the Source Guide (page 333) for a purveyor who sells dry-aged beef through mail order and online. At the restaurants, we cut our own steaks and leave the bone in for a spectacular presentation. Have your butcher cut these to your specifications.

1. Combine the oil and Essence in a small bowl and mix well. Spread over both sides of the steaks. Place in a shallow dish, cover tightly with plastic wrap, and refrigerate for at least 4 hours, or up to 24 hours.

2. About 30 minutes before grilling, remove the steaks from the refrigerator and bring to room temperature.

3. Preheat the grill to medium-high and preheat the oven to 450°F.

4. Place the steaks on the hot grill and cook for 4 to 6 minutes on each side for medium-rare. (Alternatively, use a grill pan or large skillet over medium-high heat.)

5. Transfer the steaks to a large ovenproof skillet or baking sheet and roast in the oven for 3 to 5 minutes for medium-rare, or until the meat reaches an internal temperature of 140°F. Remove from the oven and increase the temperature to broil.

6. Place a slice of butter on each steak and broil until just starting to melt, 20 to 30 seconds. Transfer the rib-eyes to four dinner plates. Spoon the potatoes next to the steaks, garnish with the parsley, and serve.

MAKES ½ POUND

½ pound (2 sticks)
unsalted butter, at
room temperature
¼ cup minced fresh
parsley
1 tablespoon plus
1 teaspoon fresh
lemon juice
½ teaspoon salt
¼ teaspoon freshly
ground black pepper

Emeril's Maître d'Hôtel Butter

1. Combine all the ingredients in a food processor and mix well. (Alternatively, place the butter in a medium bowl and cream with a wooden spoon or rubber spatula. Add the remaining ingredients and mix well.)

2. Spoon the butter mixture into the center of a large sheet of plastic wrap or wax paper, forming a log about 1½ inches in diameter. Fold the wrap over the butter and gently push in and under to form a smooth cylinder. Twist the ends to seal. Refrigerate until firm, about 1 hour. (Refrigerate for up to 1 week or freeze for up to 1 month.)

MAKES 4 CUPS

3 pounds Idaho
potatoes, peeled and
cut into 1-inch pieces
1¾ teaspoons salt
8 tablespoons (1 stick)
unsalted butter, cut
into pieces
½ cup heavy cream
¼ teaspoon freshly
ground white pepper

Mashed Potatoes

1. Place the potatoes and 1 teaspoon of salt in a heavy medium pot, cover with water by 1 inch, and bring to a boil. Reduce the heat to a simmer and cook until the potatoes are fork-tender, 20 to 25 minutes. Drain in a colander.

2. Return the potatoes to the pot, set over low heat, and add the butter. Using a potato masher, mash the butter into the potatoes. Add the cream, the remaining ¾ teaspoon salt, and the pepper and mash with the potato masher over medium-low heat to incorporate the ingredients and achieve a light texture, 4 to 5 minutes. (If preferred, leave the potatoes slightly lumpy.) Serve immediately.

BEEF, VEAL, PORK, AND LAMB

Seared Beef Tournedos with Herb-Roasted Potatoes and Sauce au Poivre

MAKES 2 SERVINGS

Six 3-ounce beef tournedos
1 teaspoon salt
1 teaspoon cracked black
pepper
1 tablespoon plus
1 teaspoon vegetable oil
1 recipe Sauce au Poivre
1 recipe Herb-Roasted
Potatoes (page 263)

Tournedos are nothing more than medallions of filet mignon cut from the center of the tenderloin, or the Châteaubriand, to be fancy. The tournedos can be grilled or pan-seared, and the sauce au poivre works well with any kind of steak. Use this recipe as a launching pad for your own steak invention!

1. Season the tournedos on both sides with the salt and pepper. Heat the oil in a heavy ovenproof nonstick skillet over medium-high heat. Add the meat and sear for 2½ minutes on each side for medium-rare. (Note: Depending upon the thickness of the meat, the steaks may need to cook slightly longer.)

2. Place 3 tournedos on each serving plate. Drizzle with the sauce and serve with the herb-roasted potatoes.

MAKES 1 CUP

1 tablespoon coarsely
ground black pepper
1 tablespoon vegetable oil
1 tablespoon chopped
shallots
1 tablespoon drained,
rinsed, and crushed
canned green
peppercorns
½ cup brandy
1½ teaspoons Dijon mustard
2 cups Reduced Veal Stock
(page 25)
⅛ teaspoon salt

Sauce au Poivre

1. Place the black pepper in a dry small saucepan and toast over medium-high heat until fragrant, 1 to 2 minutes. Add the oil and stir to combine. Add the shallots and green peppercorns and cook, stirring, for 30 seconds. Add the brandy and simmer until reduced by three-quarters.

2. Add the mustard and stir to combine, then add the veal stock and bring to a boil. Reduce the heat to medium-low and simmer until reduced by half, 10 to 12 minutes. Remove from the heat and add the salt. Serve hot.

Braised Beef Short Ribs with Cheddar Polenta and Coleslaw

MAKES 4 SERVINGS AS A MAIN
COURSE, 8 AS AN APPETIZER

1 rack beef short ribs
   (about 2½ pounds),
   cut into eight 5-ounce
   portions
1 tablespoon Emeril's
   Original Essence or
   Creole Seasoning
   (page 28)
2 quarts water
2 cups sliced yellow
   onions
5 garlic cloves, peeled
   and smashed
1 cup Worcestershire
   sauce
1 cup packed light brown
   sugar
⅓ cup kosher salt
3 tablespoons soy sauce
2 ancho chile peppers
1 teaspoon red pepper
   flakes
1 recipe Cheddar Polenta
1 recipe Coleslaw

At Emeril's we serve this as an appetizer, but you might want to serve it instead as a main course. After cooking for hours, the meat shreds right off the bone, just like a pot roast. The long cooking time also enriches the pan juices, yielding a divine sauce for the polenta. Just let it all run together, with the slaw's touch of sweetness, and you've got one satisfying dinner!

1. Place the ribs in a baking pan and season on both sides with the Essence. Wrap tightly in plastic wrap and refrigerate for at least 6 hours, or overnight.

2. Preheat the oven to 350°F.

3. Combine the water, onions, garlic, Worcestershire, sugar, salt, soy sauce, chiles, and red pepper flakes in a large heavy roasting pan or large heavy pot and bring to a simmer over medium-high heat. Adjust the seasoning to taste.

4. Remove the plastic wrap from the ribs and add the ribs to the pot. Cover, transfer to the oven, and cook until the ribs are tender and the meat is falling from the bones, 4 to 4½ hours. Remove from the oven.

5. To serve, divide the polenta among four large bowls. Place the ribs on top of the polenta and top with the cooking liquid. Spoon coleslaw over each portion, and serve immediately.

BEEF, VEAL, PORK, AND LAMB

Cheddar Polenta

4 cups water
2½ cups milk
2 teaspoons minced garlic
2 teaspoons chopped fresh
    thyme
1 bay leaf
1½ teaspoons salt
½ teaspoon freshly ground
    black pepper
1½ cups polenta or yellow
    cornmeal
4 tablespoons unsalted
    butter, cut into pieces
1 cup grated Cheddar
2 tablespoons freshly grated
    Parmigiano-Reggiano

1. Combine the water, milk, garlic, thyme, bay leaf, salt, and pepper in a large heavy saucepan and bring to a boil. Gradually whisk in the polenta. Reduce the heat to low and cook, stirring often with a large wooden spoon, until smooth and creamy, 35 to 40 minutes.

2. Add the butter, Cheddar, and Parmesan and stir until melted. Remove from the heat and discard the bay leaf. Adjust the seasoning to taste and serve hot.

Coleslaw

3 cups shredded green
    cabbage
1 cup finely sliced red onions
¾ cup finely sliced carrots
1 tablespoon rice wine
    vinegar
½ teaspoon sugar
½ teaspoon salt
¼ teaspoon freshly ground
    white pepper
¼ cup Mayonnaise
    (page 31) or store-bought

1. Combine all the ingredients except the mayonnaise in a large bowl and toss well to mix. Let sit for 15 minutes.

2. Add the mayonnaise and stir well. Serve immediately, or refrigerate in an airtight container for up to 1 day.

Châteaubriand à la Bouquetière with Marchand de Vin Sauce

MAKES 2 SERVINGS

1 large carrot, peeled
and cut into 1-inch
pieces

1 large turnip, peeled
and cut into 1-inch
pieces

10 pearl onions, peeled
and trimmed

1 small zucchini,
trimmed and cut into
1-inch pieces

1 small yellow squash,
trimmed and cut into
1-inch pieces

1 tablespoon
vegetable oil

¼ teaspoon salt

½ teaspoon freshly
ground black pepper

1 tablespoon olive oil

One 1¼-pound center-
cut beef fillet roast

1½ teaspoons freshly
cracked black pepper

1 teaspoon kosher salt

3 tablespoons chopped
fresh parsley

1½ teaspoons chopped
fresh thyme

1½ teaspoons chopped
fresh rosemary

1 recipe Marchand de
Vin Sauce

Châteaubriand may not be on your menu every Sunday night, but when you really want to kick it up for a special occasion, the Steakhouse's version will certainly do the trick. The Châteaubriand is the center section of the tenderloin, with none of the side meat, or "chain," attached. Special order your meat and have the butcher prepare it for you. A variety of sauces are offered on the menu at Delmonico Steakhouse. Try your Châteaubriand with Béarnaise Sauce (page 125) or Sauce au Poivre (page 232), instead of the Marchand de Vin Sauce, if you like.

1. Preheat the oven to 350°F.

2. Combine the vegetables with the vegetable oil, salt, and pepper in a baking dish and toss to coat evenly. Roast, stirring occasionally, until the vegetables are tender, about 45 minutes. Remove from the oven and cover to keep warm. Increase the oven temperature to 425°F.

3. Rub the olive oil evenly over the meat and season with the cracked black pepper and kosher salt. Coat the meat evenly with the herbs, pressing them firmly onto the meat to adhere.

4. Heat a large skillet over medium heat. Add the meat and sear on all sides, 6 to 7 minutes. Transfer to a roasting pan and roast to the desired doneness, 20 to 22 minutes for medium-rare (140°F on an instant-read thermometer). Remove from the oven and let rest for 5 minutes before serving.

5. To serve, cut into four thick slices and place 2 slices on each plate. Arrange the vegetables around the meat, and serve with the sauce.

Marchand de Vin Sauce

½ *pound meat from beef*
shanks or oxtails, cut into
½-inch cubes
1 *teaspoon salt*
1 *teaspoon freshly ground*
black pepper
1 *teaspoon olive oil*
¼ *cup coarsely chopped*
shallots
½ *teaspoon chopped garlic*
1 *cup dry red wine*
1 *bay leaf*
1 *sprig fresh thyme*
4 *cups Reduced Veal Stock*
(page 25)
1 *tablespoon cold unsalted*
butter, cut into pieces

1. Season the meat with ½ teaspoon each of the salt and pepper.

2. Heat the oil in a medium heavy pot over medium-high heat. Add the meat and cook, stirring, until evenly browned, about 6 minutes. Add the shallots and garlic and cook, stirring, until soft, about 1 minute. Add the red wine and stir to deglaze the pan. Bring to a boil, add the bay leaf and the remaining ½ teaspoon each salt and pepper, and cook until reduced to ¼ cup, about 10 minutes.

3. Add the veal stock and bring to a boil. Reduce the heat to medium-low and simmer, stirring occasionally, until the sauce is reduced by half and coats the back of a spoon, about 1 hour.

4. Strain the sauce through a fine-mesh strainer into a saucepan (reserve the meat for another use). Over low heat, add the butter, one piece at a time, whisking constantly to incorporate. Remove from the heat and adjust the seasoning to taste. Serve immediately.

Delmonico Steakhouse staff

Pan-Roasted Filet Mignons with Potato-Walnut Confit, Port Wine Reduction, Stilton Cheese, and Shallot Rings

MAKES 4 SERVINGS

1½ pounds small red
   potatoes, scrubbed
   and cut lengthwise
   into 8 wedges each
1 tablespoon extra-virgin
   olive oil
1 teaspoon dried thyme
2½ teaspoons salt
¼ teaspoon freshly
   ground black pepper
3 ounces bacon, chopped
½ cup walnut pieces
2 tablespoons chopped
   shallots
1 teaspoon chopped
   garlic
½ cup ruby Port
1 cup Reduced Veal
   Stock (page 25)
8 tablespoons (1 stick)
   cold unsalted butter,
   cut into pieces, plus
   2 tablespoons butter
Four 8-ounce filet
   mignon steaks
2 teaspoons cracked
   black pepper
2 tablespoons olive oil
1 cup crumbled Stilton,
   or other high-quality
   blue cheese
1 recipe Shallot Rings
1 tablespoon chopped
   fresh parsley

Here's a dish that's been on the menu at NOLA since 1993, and it's so popular that I haven't been able to take it off. And while it might sound like there's too much going on, trust me, the first bite will prove that everything here was meant to go together. This is one of those dishes that I recommend preparing exactly as the recipe states—and while you might want to substitute another cheese, English Stilton is the king of blue cheeses, and it is available at most grocery store cheese counters.

1. Preheat the oven to 400°F. Line a baking sheet with parchment paper.

2. In a medium bowl, toss the potatoes with the extra-virgin olive oil, thyme, ½ teaspoon of the salt, and the pepper. Spread on the prepared baking sheet and roast until golden brown, 25 to 30 minutes. Remove from the oven and transfer to a large bowl. Leave the oven on.

3. Heat a large skillet over medium-high heat. Add the bacon and cook, stirring, until just starting to turn golden, about 2 minutes. Add the walnuts and cook, stirring, for 2 minutes. Transfer with a slotted spoon to the bowl with the potatoes. Cover tightly to keep warm.

4. Add the shallots and garlic to the same skillet and cook, stirring, for 30 seconds. Add the Port and stir to deglaze, loosening any browned bits in the pan, then cook until reduced by half, about 2 minutes. Add the veal stock and cook, stirring, until reduced by half, 8 to 9 minutes. Add 8 tablespoons of the butter 1 tablespoon at a time, whisking constantly and adding each piece before the previous one has been completely incorporated, removing the pan from the heat periodically to prevent the sauce from getting too hot and breaking; the sauce should be thick enough to coat the back of a spoon. Remove from the heat and cover to keep warm.

5. Season each filet on both sides with ½ teaspoon each of the remaining salt and the cracked pepper.

6. Melt the remaining 2 tablespoons butter with the oil in a large ovenproof skillet over high heat. Add the filets and cook for 3 minutes on each side. Place 2 tablespoons of the cheese on top of each filet, transfer to the oven, and roast until medium-rare (140°F on an instant-read thermometer), 8 to 10 minutes. Remove from the oven.

7. To serve, mound the potatoes in the center of four plates. Lay the filets on top of the potatoes and top with the sauce. Garnish with the remaining ½ cup Stilton, the fried shallots, and the parsley.

Shallot Rings

MAKES 4 SERVINGS
AS A GARNISH

1½ cups thinly sliced shallot
rings
2 tablespoons Emeril's Kick
It Up Red Pepper Sauce or
other hot pepper sauce
4 cups vegetable oil, for
deep-frying
½ cup all-purpose flour
½ teaspoon salt
⅛ teaspoon freshly ground
black pepper

1. In a bowl, toss the shallots with the pepper sauce. Let marinate for 30 minutes.

2. Heat the vegetable oil in a deep heavy saucepan or deep-fryer to 360°F. Put the flour in a shallow bowl and season with the salt and pepper. Dredge the shallot rings in the flour to coat evenly, tapping off the excess. Fry until golden brown, about 2 minutes.

3. Remove with a slotted spoon and drain on paper towels. Season with salt to taste, and serve hot.

MAKES 4 SERVINGS

Four 5-ounce veal sirloin medallions
1 teaspoon salt
½ teaspoon freshly ground black pepper
½ cup all-purpose flour
1½ teaspoons Emeril's Original Essence or Creole Seasoning (page 28)
¼ cup olive oil
1 recipe Tasso Creamed Spinach
1 recipe Homemade Ricotta Ravioli
1 recipe Creole Marinara Sauce

Panéed Veal with Tasso Creamed Spinach, Homemade Ricotta Ravioli, and Creole Marinara Sauce

If you're not up to making your own ravioli, good store-bought cheese tortellini will certainly do. Everything else in this dish will come together quickly. Before cooking, be sure to pound the veal thin, or it may be tough. And the spinach? Perfectly addictive!

1. One at a time, place the veal medallions between two sheets of plastic wrap and pound with the flat side of a meat mallet until about ¼ inch thick. Season the veal on both sides with the salt and pepper.

2. Combine the flour and Essence in a shallow dish. One at a time, dredge the veal medallions in the flour and shake to remove any excess.

3. Heat 2 tablespoons of the oil in a large skillet over medium-high heat. Add 2 of the medallions and cook until golden, about 2 minutes per side. Transfer to a platter and cover to keep warm. Add the remaining 2 tablespoons oil and cook the remaining medallions.

4. To serve, spoon a dollop of spinach onto each of four dinner plates. Overlap the spinach with 4 ravioli and place a veal medallion at the bottom of each plate. Spoon the sauce over the veal and ravioli and serve.

Tasso Creamed Spinach

1¼ pounds spinach, tough
stems removed, and well
rinsed
1 teaspoon vegetable oil
½ cup minced tasso
(about 2 ounces)
1½ teaspoons unsalted
butter
2 tablespoons minced yellow
onions
⅛ teaspoon minced garlic
1 tablespoon all-purpose
flour
1 cup whole milk
½ cup grated Gouda
½ teaspoon salt
¼ teaspoon Emeril's Original
Essence or Creole
Seasoning (page 28)

1. Bring a medium pot of salted water to a boil. Add the spinach and cook until wilted, about 1 minute. Remove with a slotted spoon and cool in an ice water bath. Drain and squeeze out the excess water. Chop, and set aside.

2. Heat the oil in a medium saucepan over medium heat. Add the tasso and fry until golden brown, about 2 minutes. Add the butter. When it is melted, add the onions and garlic, and cook, stirring, until wilted, about 1 minute. Add the flour, reduce the heat to low, and cook, stirring constantly with a wooden spoon, until a light roux forms, 2 to 3 minutes. Add the milk in a steady stream and cook, whisking constantly, until thickened, about 4 minutes. Add the chopped spinach and stir well. Remove from the heat and fold in the cheese, salt, and Essence. Serve hot.

In the kitchen at
Emeril's Orlando

**1 tablespoon unsalted
butter**
**1½ cups finely chopped
yellow squash**
**1 recipe Homemade
Ricotta**
**1 cup grated white
Cheddar**
**¼ cup freshly grated
Parmigiano-Reggiano**
**2 tablespoons minced
shallots**
**1 tablespoon extra-virgin
olive oil**
**1½ teaspoons chopped
fresh basil**
**1½ teaspoons chopped
fresh oregano**
½ teaspoon salt
**½ teaspoon freshly
ground black pepper**
**1 large egg, beaten with
2 teaspoons water,
for eggwash**
**4 fresh pasta sheets
(measuring about
9 × 15 inches)**

Homemade Ricotta Ravioli

Yes, this calls for making your own ricotta cheese, which is really easy. The secret to making the cheese is to cook the milk mixture over very low heat and never let it reach a simmer. You must watch carefully and remove the pot from the heat when the liquid begins to separate into small solid masses. While the liquid's initial cooking temperature is 112°F, as it cooks, it may reach as high as 160°F before the curds and whey separate.

1. Melt the butter in a small skillet over medium heat. Add the squash and cook, stirring, until tender, about 8 minutes. Remove from the heat and let cool completely.

2. In a large bowl, combine the squash with the remaining ingredients (except the pasta) and mix well.

3. Place 1 pasta sheet on a work surface. Scoop heaping tablespoonfuls of the squash filling evenly down the pasta sheet, about 4 inches apart in two rows of 4. Using a pastry brush, lightly coat the areas around the filling with eggwash. Place another pasta sheet on top and press down around each mound of filling to squeeze out the air pockets and seal. With a 4-inch round cutter, cut into individual ravioli. Repeat with the remaining pasta and filling.

4. Bring a large pot of salted water to a boil. Add the ravioli and cook until tender, 4 to 5 minutes. Remove with a slotted spoon and serve hot.

2 quarts whole milk
2 cups buttermilk
**1 tablespoon fresh
lemon juice**

Homemade Ricotta

1. Combine all the ingredients in a medium pot and bring to 112°F (use an instant-read thermometer) over low heat. Cook, without simmering, until the liquid separates into solid curds and whey, 45 to 50 minutes. Remove from the heat.

2. Using a slotted spoon, transfer the solids to a fine-mesh strainer or a colander lined with cheesecloth placed over a bowl. Let drain in the refrigerator until the ricotta is thick and the excess liquid has drained away, about 30 minutes. Remove the cheese from the cheesecloth, wrap in plastic wrap, and refrigerate until ready to use. (The liquid may be discarded or used in another recipe, such as homemade bread.)

BEEF, VEAL, PORK, AND LAMB

1 veal shank bone
1 tablespoon vegetable oil
1 cup finely chopped yellow
    onions
1 cup grated carrots
1 tablespoon minced garlic
6 cups peeled, seeded, and
    diced ripe tomatoes
    (about 8 tomatoes)
One 14-ounce can whole
    Roma (plum) tomatoes,
    with their juice
¼ cup dry red wine
1 teaspoon balsamic vinegar
1⅛ teaspoons salt
1⅛ teaspoons freshly
    ground black pepper
1 tablespoon chopped fresh
    basil
1 tablespoon chopped fresh
    oregano
1 tablespoon chopped fresh
    parsley

Creole Marinara Sauce

1. Preheat the oven to 375°F.

2. Place the veal shank bone in a roasting pan. Roast, turning occasionally, until golden brown, about 1 hour. Remove from the oven.

3. Heat the oil in a medium heavy pot over medium-high heat. Add the onions, carrots, and garlic and cook, stirring, until soft, about 4 minutes. Add the roasted bone, the tomatoes, canned tomatoes with their juice, the red wine, vinegar, salt, and pepper and bring to a boil. Reduce the heat to medium-low and simmer, uncovered, stirring occasionally, until thick, about 1½ hours.

4. Add ¾ cup water, stir well, and continue to simmer for 30 minutes. Remove from the heat, and remove and discard the bone. Add the chopped herbs and adjust the seasoning to taste.

5. Transfer half of the sauce to a food processor or blender and purée. Return the puréed sauce to the pot and stir to blend. Cover to keep warm until ready to serve.

MAKES 4 SERVINGS

Twelve 1½-ounce veal
medallions
1¼ teaspoons salt
1⅛ teaspoons freshly
ground white pepper
⅔ cup all-purpose flour
About ½ cup vegetable
oil
2 tablespoons plus
1 teaspoon unsalted
butter
1 pound white button
mushrooms,
stemmed, wiped
clean, and sliced
½ cup finely chopped
green onions (green
parts only)
1 pound jumbo lump
crabmeat, picked over
for shells and
cartilage
16 spears Blanched
Asparagus (page 14)
1 cup Hollandaise Sauce
(page 29)

Veal Marcelle

When we opened Emeril's Delmonico in 1998, I wanted to pay homage to Marcelle Bienvenu, my good friend and food guru who's assisted me on all of my cookbooks. This dish is both rich and pleasant, just like Marcelle. Make sure to get fresh crabmeat and carefully pick out any shells, since they make for an unwelcome surprise.

1. One at a time, place the veal medallions between two sheets of plastic wrap and pound with the flat side of a meat mallet until ⅛ inch thick. Season the veal on both sides with 1 teaspoon each of the salt and pepper. Place the flour in a shallow dish. One at a time, dredge the veal medallions in the flour, and shake to remove any excess.

2. Heat 3 tablespoons of the oil in a large skillet over medium-high heat. Add 3 or 4 of the medallions and cook until golden, about 1 minute per side. Remove from the pan. Cook the remaining medallions, adding more oil as needed.

3. Discard any oil remaining in the pan, and melt 2 tablespoons of the butter over medium-high heat. Add the mushrooms and green onions and cook, stirring, until wilted, 3 to 5 minutes. Add the crabmeat and the remaining ¼ teaspoon salt and ⅛ teaspoon of pepper. Cook, stirring gently, until warmed through, about 1 minute.

4. Meanwhile, in a large skillet, melt the remaining 1 teaspoon butter over medium-high heat. Add the asparagus and toss until heated through, about 1 minute.

5. To serve, shingle 3 medallions alternately with the crabmeat mixture on each of four plates. Top each serving with 4 asparagus spears and drizzle with the hollandaise sauce. Serve immediately.

BEEF, VEAL, PORK, AND LAMB

Emeril's ORLANDO

Grilled Veal Chops with Herb Cheese, Wild Mushroom–Tomato Bordelaise, and Prosciutto-Wrapped Asparagus

Four 14-ounce bone-in veal chops
4 teaspoons Emeril's Original Essence or Creole Seasoning (page 28)
20 spears Blanched Asparagus (page 14)
4 thin slices prosciutto (about 3 ounces)
¼ cup Herb Cheese, cut into 4 slices
1 recipe Wild Mushroom– Tomato Bordelaise

Chef Bernard has a way of taking a family of flavors and throwing a big party on one plate! If you can't find milk-fed veal, the redder grain-fed veal will do just fine; just make sure the chops weigh at least 12 ounces each. For simplicity's sake, the sauce can be made a day or two ahead of time and kept refrigerated, then reheated gently before serving.

If you like, the Herb Cheese makes a great dip or spread for croutons, crackers, or crudités.

1. Preheat the grill to medium-high and preheat the oven to 400°F.

2. Season each chop on both sides with 1 teaspoon of the Essence. Place on the grill and cook for 2 minutes. Turn each chop one-quarter turn to make grill marks, and cook for an additional 2 minutes. Turn and cook on the second side for 4 minutes.

3. Transfer to a baking sheet. Roast the chops until cooked to medium, 8 to 10 minutes. Remove from the oven.

4. Meanwhile, divide the asparagus into bundles of 5 and wrap each in a slice of prosciutto.

5. Place the veal chops on four large plates and top each with a slice of the herb cheese. Arrange the asparagus next to the chops and spoon the bordelaise around the chops. Serve immediately.

Herb Cheese

½ cup whole milk ricotta
½ cup cream cheese, softened
1 tablespoon unsalted butter, softened
1½ teaspoons finely chopped fresh chives
1½ teaspoons finely chopped fresh parsley
1 teaspoon finely chopped shallots
¾ teaspoon sherry vinegar
½ teaspoon finely chopped fresh tarragon leaves
½ teaspoon minced garlic
¼ teaspoon salt
⅛ teaspoon ground white pepper

1. Place the ricotta in a fine-mesh strainer set over a bowl. Press down with the back of a spoon to extract as much liquid as possible. Refrigerate until well drained, about 2 hours. Place in a food processor and process until smooth, about 30 seconds. Add the remaining ingredients and pulse to blend, being careful not to overprocess.

2. Spoon the mixture into the center of a large sheet of plastic wrap or wax paper, forming a log about 1 inch in diameter. Fold the wrap over the mixture and gently push in and under to form a smooth cylinder. Twist the ends to seal. Refrigerate until firm, about 2 hours. (Alternatively, spoon the cheese into a small decorative bowl, smoothing the top, to serve as a dip.) The cheese will keep, refrigerated, for up to 5 days.

Chef Jean Paul Labadie in Emeril's New Orleans Fish House kitchen

BEEF, VEAL, PORK, AND LAMB

Wild Mushroom–Tomato Bordelaise

I doubt you'll have any sauce left over, but if you do, this is great on fettuccine!

¼ cup olive oil
½ cup chopped yellow
  onions
¼ cup chopped carrots
¼ cup chopped celery
1 teaspoon minced garlic
½ pound portobello
  mushrooms, stems
  removed, wiped clean,
  and chopped
½ pound oyster mushrooms,
  stems trimmed, wiped
  clean, and thinly sliced
½ pound shiitake
  mushrooms, stems
  removed, wiped clean,
  and thinly sliced
½ teaspoon salt
½ teaspoon freshly ground
  black pepper
½ cup peeled, seeded, and
  chopped tomatoes
1 cup dry red wine
4 cups Reduced Veal Stock
  (page 25)

1. Heat the oil in a Dutch oven or other large heavy pot over medium-high heat. Add the onions, carrots, and celery and cook, stirring, until soft, about 3 minutes. Add the garlic and cook, stirring, for 30 seconds. Add the mushrooms and cook, stirring occasionally, until they give off their liquid, 4 to 5 minutes. Add the salt and pepper and stir to mix well, then add the tomatoes and cook, stirring, for 1 minute. Add the wine and stir to deglaze, loosening any bits on the bottom of the pan, then cook until the wine is reduced by half.

2. Add the veal stock and bring to a boil. Reduce the heat to medium-low and simmer until reduced by half, about 1 hour and 20 minutes. Remove from the heat and adjust the seasoning to taste. Cover and keep warm until ready to serve.

Rack of Lamb with Creole Mustard Crust, Emeril's New Orleans

Panéed Veal Medallions with Lump Crabmeat Ravioli, Red Pepper Cream Sauce, and Asparagus

Eight 2½-ounce veal cutlets cut from the top round

2 teaspoons Emeril's Original Essence or Creole Seasoning (page 28)

1 cup Clarified Butter (page 15) or vegetable oil, or more as needed

1 recipe Red Pepper Cream Sauce

16 spears Blanched Asparagus (page 14)

1 recipe Lump Crabmeat Ravioli

3 tablespoons freshly grated Parmigiano-Reggiano, for serving

1 tablespoon plus 1 teaspoon finely sliced fresh basil leaves, for garnish

This is a dish you'll want to prepare in stages: make the sauce two days in advance, the ravioli filling and pasta dough the day before, and everything else just before "showtime." You'll find your efforts rewarded by a memorable meal. Something to think about as you're working through the various steps—Chef Dave used to sell sixty of these a night at NOLA when he was chef there!

We don't strain our sauce after puréeing it. However, if you'd prefer a smoother sauce, go ahead and strain it.

---

1. One at a time, place the veal cutlets between two sheets of plastic wrap and pound with the flat side of a meat mallet until ⅛ inch thick and 5 inches in diameter. Season both sides of each cutlet with ⅛ teaspoon of the Essence.

2. Heat the clarified butter in a large skillet over medium-high heat. Add half of the veal and cook until golden brown, 1 to 2 minutes per side. Drain on paper towels. Repeat with the remaining veal and butter.

3. To serve, spoon ¼ cup of sauce onto each of four large plates. Top each with a veal cutlet, 4 asparagus spears, 4 ravioli, and another ¼ cup of the sauce. Sprinkle cheese over each serving, and top with the basil. Serve immediately.

Red Pepper Cream Sauce

2 red bell peppers (about ¾ pound), cored, seeded, and chopped

2 cups heavy cream

1 teaspoon paprika

1 teaspoon fresh lemon juice

¾ teaspoon salt

⅛ teaspoon freshly ground white pepper

Pinch of cayenne

1. Combine the bell peppers and cream in a medium heavy pot and bring to a boil. Reduce the heat to medium-low and simmer, stirring occasionally, until the cream is reduced by half, about 35 minutes. Remove from the heat.

2. Add the paprika, lemon juice, salt, white pepper, and cayenne. With a hand-held immersion blender, or in batches in a food processor, purée the sauce until smooth. Serve hot.

BEEF, VEAL, PORK, AND LAMB

Lump Crabmeat Ravioli

½ pound chilled, peeled,
and deveined shrimp
1 large egg white, chilled
1½ teaspoons chopped
fresh parsley
1½ teaspoons chopped
fresh basil
1 teaspoon fresh lemon juice
1 teaspoon minced garlic
½ teaspoon salt
¼ teaspoon freshly ground
white pepper
¼ cup cold heavy cream
6 ounces lump crabmeat,
picked over for shells and
cartilage
¼ cup freshly grated
Parmigiano-Reggiano
2 tablespoons chopped
shallots
1 large egg, beaten with
2 teaspoons water,
for eggwash
4 fresh pasta sheets
(measuring about 9 × 15
inches)

To achieve the right consistency, make sure the shrimp and egg white are very cold, and chill the food processor bowl and blade in the refrigerator for 20 minutes before beginning.

1. Combine the shrimp, egg white, parsley, basil, lemon juice, garlic, salt, and white pepper in a food processor and pulse for 5 seconds. Scrape down the sides and pulse for 5 seconds. With the machine running, add the cream in a steady stream. Transfer to a bowl and fold in the crabmeat, cheese, and shallots.

2. Place a pasta sheet on a work surface. Scoop heaping table-spoonfuls of the crabmeat filling evenly down the sheet, about 4 inches apart in two rows of 4. Using a pastry brush, lightly coat the areas around the filling with eggwash. Place another pasta sheet on top and press down around each mound of filling to squeeze out the air pockets and seal. With a 4-inch round cutter, cut into individual ravioli. Repeat with the remaining pasta and filling.

3. Bring a large pot of salted water to a boil. Add the ravioli and cook until tender, 4 to 5 minutes. Remove with a slotted spoon and serve hot.

Root Beer–Glazed Pork Chops with Bourbon-Mashed Sweet Potatoes and Caramelized Onions

MAKES 4 SERVINGS

2 cups root beer
2 cups Reduced Veal Stock (page 25)
Four 16-ounce double-cut bone-in pork chops
4 teaspoons Emeril's Original Essence or Creole Seasoning (page 28)
4 teaspoons olive oil
1 recipe Bourbon-Mashed Sweet Potatoes
1 recipe Caramelized Onions (page 271)

One of Chef Bernard's many strengths is his ability to spontaneously create a dish for a special customer. This invention came about during one lunch, in 1994, when some guests at the food bar were looking for something different. One of the pot washers gave Bernard a can of root beer and he reduced it with veal stock to a rich syrup. While it's unconventional, I think you'll love this dish as much as those first folks did then!

1. To make the glaze, combine the root beer and stock in a medium heavy saucepan. Bring to a boil over medium-high heat. Reduce the heat to medium-low and simmer until reduced to a thick syrup (about 1 cup), 50 minutes to 1 hour. Remove from the heat.

2. Preheat the grill to medium-high, and preheat the oven to 425°F.

3. Season each chop on both sides with 1 teaspoon of the Essence. Place on the grill and cook for 3 minutes. Turn each chop one quarter turn to make grill marks, and cook an additional 2 minutes. Turn and cook on the second side for 5 minutes.

4. Transfer to a baking sheet. Drizzle 1 teaspoon of the oil over each chop. Roast until cooked through and an internal thermometer inserted into the center reaches 150°F, 12 to 15 minutes.

5. Place the chops on four serving plates and drizzle with the glaze. Spoon the sweet potatoes and caramelized onions onto the plates, and serve.

Bourbon-Mashed Sweet Potatoes

*1¾ to 2 pounds sweet
  potatoes*
½ cup heavy cream
¼ cup bourbon whiskey
*3 tablespoons light brown
  sugar*
2 tablespoons molasses
⅛ teaspoon salt

1. Preheat the oven to 350°F.

2. Place the potatoes on a foil-lined baking sheet. Bake until tender and starting to ooze sugary syrup, about 1 hour and 15 minutes, depending upon their size. Remove from the oven and let sit until cool enough to handle.

3. Cut a slit down each potato and scoop the flesh into a large bowl. Discard the skins. Add the cream, bourbon, brown sugar, molasses, and salt and beat on high speed with an electric mixer until smooth. Cover to keep warm, or gently reheat before serving.

*Chef Chris Wilson outside
Emeril's New Orleans*

Grilled Honey-Cured Pork Chops with Creole Mustard Reduction, Fried Oysters, and Hoppin' John

14 cups water

3 cups honey

2 cups kosher salt

2 tablespoons chopped fresh thyme

2 tablespoons freshly ground black pepper

1 tablespoon ground cloves

Four 12-ounce bone-in pork chops

1 recipe Creole Mustard Reduction

1 recipe Hoppin' John (page 266)

1 recipe Fried Oysters (page 52)

When Chef Christian told me he wanted to serve these pork chops at Delmonico Steakhouse, I told him they'd better be pretty darn good to stand up to our dry-aged beef. These won't disappoint you—trust me. Keep in mind that the honey cure must be made 4 hours in advance, even though the actual meat brining takes only 2 hours.

1. Combine the water, honey, and salt in a large saucepan and bring to a simmer. Stir to dissolve the honey and salt. Remove from the heat. Add the thyme, pepper, and cloves and refrigerate until well chilled, about 2 hours.

2. Once it is cool, submerge the pork chops in the brining liquid. Marinate for 2 hours, refrigerated.

3. Preheat the oven to 400°F.

4. Heat a large heavy nonstick grill pan or nonstick skillet over medium-high heat. Remove the chops from the brine and pat dry with paper towels. Add the chops to the pan, in batches if necessary, and cook for 2 minutes. Turn the chops one-quarter turn to make grill marks, if using a grill pan, and cook for 1 additional minute. Turn the chops and cook on the second side for 30 seconds, then turn one quarter turn and cook for 30 seconds more.

5. Transfer the chops to a roasting pan or baking sheet and roast until cooked through and an internal thermometer inserted into the center reaches 150°F, 18 to 20 minutes. Remove from the oven and let rest for 5 minutes.

6. To serve, spoon the mustard reduction onto four large serving plates. Top with the Hoppin' John and the pork chops. Arrange the fried oysters around the edges of the plates, and serve immediately.

BEEF, VEAL, PORK, AND LAMB

Creole Mustard Reduction

1 tablespoon olive oil
1 tablespoon minced
    shallots
½ teaspoon chopped garlic
1 cup dry red wine
2 cups Reduced Veal Stock
    (page 25) or Rich Chicken
    Stock (page 21)
¼ cup Creole mustard or
    other whole-grain
    mustard

1. Heat the oil in a medium heavy saucepan over medium-high heat. Add the shallots and garlic and cook, stirring, until fragrant, 1 minute. Add the wine, stir, and bring to a boil. Reduce the heat to medium-low and simmer until the wine is reduced to a thick glaze, 18 to 20 minutes.

2. Add the veal stock and Creole mustard, stir well, and bring to a simmer. Simmer for 10 minutes to allow the flavors to blend. Remove from the heat and cover to keep warm until ready to serve.

Chef Emeril Lagasse

1½ teaspoons unsalted
   butter
1 pork tenderloin
   (about 1½ pounds)
1 tablespoon Emeril's
   Original Essence or
   Creole Seasoning
   (page 28)
3 tablespoons vegetable
   oil
1 sheet frozen puff
   pastry (one-half
   17¼-ounce package),
   thawed
All-purpose flour, for
   dusting
¼ cup Creole mustard or
   other spicy whole-
   grain mustard
1 recipe Mushroom
   Stuffing (page 220)
1 large egg, beaten with
   2 teaspoons water,
   for egg wash

Pork Tenderloin en Croûte

This is my take on that classic dish, Beef Wellington. It's an elegant main course for small dinner parties and much easier to assemble than the original. If you want to kick this up to notches unknown, pair it with the Béarnaise Sauce (page 125) that accompanies Delmonico restaurant's Poached Eggs Erato.

1. Preheat the oven to 400°F. Line a large baking sheet with aluminum foil and grease the center with the butter.

2. Season the pork tenderloin on all sides with the Essence. Heat the oil in a large skillet or Dutch oven over medium-high heat. Add the tenderloin, reduce the heat to medium, and brown evenly on all sides. Then cook, turning frequently, until the meat reaches an internal temperature of 110°F, 16 to 18 minutes. Remove from the pan and let cool for 10 minutes.

3. On a lightly floured work surface, roll out the pastry to a 12 × 18-inch rectangle. If necessary, turn the dough so a long side is facing you.

4. Coat the tenderloin evenly on all sides with the mustard. Pack the mushroom stuffing mixture onto the top and sides of the pork tenderloin. Place the coated meat across the bottom third of the pastry. Brush a ½-inch border of egg wash on the pastry around the meat. Gently lift the remaining pastry over the meat to completely enclose it, and press gently to seal the seams. With a small knife, cut away the excess pastry to make an even border. Crimp the pastry edges with a fork dipped in flour.

5. Carefully transfer the tenderloin to the prepared baking sheet. Brush the top and sides of the pastry evenly with egg wash. With a small knife, make a decorative crosshatch pattern across the top, being careful not to cut through the pastry.

6. Bake for 10 minutes, then turn the baking sheet around. Bake until golden brown and an instant-read thermometer inserted in the center reads 150°F, 10 to 12 minutes. Remove from the oven and let rest for 5 minutes before serving.

BEEF, VEAL, PORK, AND LAMB

Braised Lamb Shank with Gorgonzola Crust and Sweet Corn–Tomato Risotto

Four 1-pound lamb shanks
1 tablespoon kosher salt
2¼ teaspoons freshly ground black pepper
¼ cup all-purpose flour
2 tablespoons olive oil
1 cup chopped yellow onions
½ cup chopped carrots
½ cup chopped celery
1 tablespoon chopped garlic
2 cups dry red wine
6 cups Rich Chicken Stock (page 21) or Reduced Veal Stock (page 25)
2 bay leaves
1 tablespoon chopped fresh rosemary
1½ cups fine dry bread crumbs
2 ounces Gorgonzola, crumbled
1 large egg
1 teaspoon chopped fresh thyme
¼ teaspoon salt
½ cup Dijon mustard
1 recipe Sweet Corn–Tomato Risotto

To simplify making this dish, you can braise the shanks the day before you want to serve them and refrigerate them overnight. Then coat them with the mustard and the Gorgonzola crust, and roast them until the crust is golden, about 35 minutes. You'll also find that the shanks are quite delicious simply braised without the crust.

1. Season the shanks on all sides with the kosher salt and 2 teaspoons of the pepper. Put the flour on a large plate. Dredge the shanks in the flour and shake to remove any excess.

2. Heat the oil in a Dutch oven or other large heavy pot over high heat. Add the shanks and sear, turning occasionally, until well browned on all sides, about 8 minutes. Transfer the shanks to a platter. Add the onions, carrots, and celery to the pot and cook, stirring, for 4 minutes. Add the garlic and cook, stirring, for 1 minute. Add the wine and stir to deglaze the pan, loosening any browned bits on the bottom and sides, then cook until slightly reduced, about 5 minutes.

3. Return the shanks to the pot. Add the stock, bay leaves, and rosemary and bring to a boil. Reduce the heat to medium-low, partially cover, and simmer until the shanks are tender, 1 hour and 45 minutes to 2 hours, skimming occasionally to remove any foam that rises to the surface.

4. Remove from the heat and remove the bay leaves. Transfer the shanks to a large plate and let rest until cool enough to handle. Bring the braising liquid and vegetables to a boil, reduce the heat to medium-low, and simmer until reduced by one-third, about 30 minutes, skimming occasionally to remove any foam that rises to the surface. Remove from the heat.

5. Preheat the oven to 375°F. Line a large baking dish with foil.

6. To make the crust, combine the bread crumbs, Gorgonzola, egg, thyme, salt, and the remaining ¼ teaspoon pepper in a food processor. Pulse several times, until the mixture resembles wet sand. Transfer to a medium bowl.

7. When the shanks are cool, coat each one evenly with 2 tablespoons of the Dijon mustard. Dredge one at a time in the Gorgonzola mixture, pressing down so it adheres, using about ⅓ cup per shank. Reserve the remaining crust mixture.

8. Place the shanks in the prepared baking dish and bake until golden brown, 20 to 25 minutes. Remove from the oven.

9. Meanwhile, add the remaining crust mixture to the reduced braising liquid and simmer over medium heat for 6 minutes. Remove from the heat. With a hand-held immersion blender, or in batches in a food processor, purée the mixture. Cover to keep warm until ready to serve, then transfer to a gravy boat or decorative bowl.

10. To serve, place a portion of the risotto in the middle of each of four large plates and top with a lamb shank. Drizzle with some of the sauce, and pass the remaining sauce at the table. Serve immediately.

Sauté station on Delmonico Steakhouse line

Sweet Corn–Tomato Risotto

5 cups Rich Chicken Stock
(page 21)
1 teaspoon salt
½ teaspoon freshly ground
black pepper
1 tablespoon extra-virgin
olive oil
1 tablespoon unsalted butter
2 tablespoons minced
shallots
1 teaspoon minced garlic
1¼ cups corn kernels (from
about 2 ears of corn)
1 cup Arborio rice
1 cup peeled, seeded, and
chopped tomatoes
1 tablespoon chopped fresh
chives
1 tablespoon chopped fresh
parsley
½ cup freshly grated
Parmigiano-Reggiano

This risotto could easily serve 6, or could be halved for smaller side dish portions.

1. Combine the stock, salt, and pepper in a small saucepan and bring to a low simmer over medium heat. Reduce the heat to low and cover to keep warm.

2. Heat the olive oil in a medium pot over medium-high heat. Add the butter, and when it is foamy, add the shallots and garlic and cook, stirring, for 1 minute. Add the corn and rice and cook, stirring, for 3 minutes. Reduce the heat to medium, add ½ cup of the hot stock and cook, stirring constantly, until it has been absorbed. Continue to cook, adding more stock ½ cup at a time, stirring, until the previous amount is nearly absorbed before adding more until all the stock has been added and the rice is tender, 15 to 18 minutes. Add the tomatoes, chives, and parsley and cook, stirring, for 1 minute.

3. Remove from the heat. Add the cheese and stir well. Adjust the seasoning to taste and serve immediately.

Bar at NOLA

Rack of Lamb with Creole Mustard Crust, Rosemary Creamed Potatoes, and Rosemary Jus

MAKES 4 SERVINGS

½ cup fine dry bread crumbs

3 tablespoons olive oil

1 tablespoon chopped fresh basil

1 teaspoon chopped fresh rosemary

1 teaspoon chopped fresh thyme

5 teaspoons Emeril's Original Essence or Creole Seasoning (page 28)

2 racks of lamb (8 bones each), trimmed and Frenched (have the butcher do this)

¼ cup Creole mustard or other whole-grain mustard

1 recipe Rosemary Creamed Potatoes

1 recipe Rosemary Jus

Many a line cook in my restaurants can attest to the popularity of this dish. Try to get domestic lamb from Colorado or elsewhere in the States. I find the flavor of New Zealand lamb a little too grassy for this dish. If you can't find Creole mustard, try a coarse-grain or stone-ground mustard from France or elsewhere that's not overly spicy.

1. Combine the bread crumbs, oil, basil, rosemary, thyme, and 1 teaspoon of the Essence in a shallow bowl and mix well.

2. Cut the racks of lamb crosswise in half. Season each half-rack on both sides with 1 teaspoon of the remaining Essence.

3. Preheat the oven to 400°F.

4. Heat a large skillet over medium-high heat for 1 minute. Add 2 half-racks of lamb fat side down and sear for 1 minute on each side, including both ends. Remove and repeat with the remaining racks. Let cool for 10 minutes.

5. Completely coat the meat of each half-rack with 1 tablespoon of the mustard. Dredge in the herbed bread crumb mixture to coat evenly, using your hands to pack the crust onto the meat. Place the lamb fat side up on a large rimmed baking sheet.

6. Roast for 20 to 25 minutes, or until the lamb reaches an internal temperature of 135° on an instant-read thermometer for medium-rare. Remove from the oven and let rest for 5 minutes.

7. To serve, spoon the creamed potatoes into the center of four plates. Cut each half-rack into chops and arrange on top of the potatoes. Spoon ¼ cup of the jus onto each serving, and serve.

BEEF, VEAL, PORK, AND LAMB

2½ *pounds Idaho potatoes,
peeled and cut into
1-inch chunks*
1 *cup heavy cream*
8 *tablespoons (1 stick)
unsalted butter, cut into
pieces*
1½ *tablespoons minced
fresh rosemary*
½ *teaspoon salt*
¼ *teaspoon freshly ground
white pepper*

Rosemary Creamed Potatoes

1. Place the potatoes in a heavy medium pot with salted water to cover by 1 inch, and bring to a boil. Cook until the potatoes are just fork-tender, 10 to 12 minutes.

2. Drain in a colander and return to the pot over medium-low heat to dry, about 2 minutes.

3. Add the remaining ingredients and increase the heat to medium. With a potato masher, mash until creamy and well blended. Serve hot.

2 teaspoons olive oil

2 tablespoons minced shallots

1 tablespoon minced garlic

1 tablespoon chopped fresh rosemary

½ teaspoon salt

¼ teaspoon freshly ground black pepper

1½ cups Reduced Veal Stock (page 25) or Rich Chicken Stock (page 21)

Rosemary Jus

Heat the oil in a small saucepan over medium-high heat. Add the shallots, garlic, rosemary, salt, and pepper and cook, stirring, for 1 minute. Add the stock and bring to a boil. Reduce the heat to medium-low and simmer until reduced to 1 cup, 20 to 25 minutes. Strain the jus through a fine-mesh strainer into a small bowl. Serve immediately, or cover to keep warm until ready to serve.

Chef Dave McCelvey testing recipes at Emeril's Homebase

BEEF, VEAL, PORK, AND LAMB

10 SIDES

*Plates being prepped on the dinner line
at Emeril's Orlando*

1 teaspoon unsalted butter
4 cups heavy cream, or more
    as needed
2 teaspoons salt
1 teaspoon freshly ground
    black pepper
3 to 3¼ pounds Idaho
    potatoes, peeled and cut
    into ¼-inch slices
8 ounces Swiss cheese,
    grated

Scalloped Potatoes

These could very well be the richest potatoes you have ever put in your mouth! Dress up roasted chicken or any other simple main course with this great side dish. You also can make these potatoes in individual ramekins.

1. Preheat the oven to 400°F. Lightly grease a 2-quart baking dish with the butter.

2. Bring the cream to a simmer in a large saucepan over medium-high heat. Add the salt and pepper and stir well. Add the potatoes, adding more cream as necessary to completely cover them. Lower the heat to medium-low and simmer until the potatoes are barely fork-tender, 10 to 12 minutes. Remove from the heat.

3. With a large spoon, transfer one-third of the potatoes, with some of the cream, to the prepared dish, making an even layer. Top with one-third of the cheese, and continue layering the potatoes and cheese, ending with cheese.

4. Place the dish on a baking sheet and roast until golden brown and bubbly, about 30 minutes. Remove from the oven and let sit for 5 minutes. Serve hot.

Delmonico Steakhouse

MAKES 6 SERVINGS

2½ pounds small red potatoes, scrubbed and quartered
¼ cup chopped mixed fresh herbs, such as parsley, basil, thyme, rosemary, and chives
¼ cup extra-virgin olive oil
1 teaspoon salt
½ teaspoon freshly ground black pepper

Herb-Roasted Potatoes

If you're looking for a straightforward but flavorful potato dish that lets the main course shine, this is the one for you!

1. Preheat the oven to 400°F.

2. Combine all the ingredients in a large bowl and toss to mix well. Transfer to a roasting pan and roast until the potatoes are fork-tender, 30 to 40 minutes. Serve immediately.

Delmonico Steakhouse

MAKES 4 SERVINGS

2 pounds small red potatoes, scrubbed and patted dry
6 cups vegetable oil, for deep-frying
¼ cup freshly grated Parmigiano-Reggiano
1 tablespoon truffle oil
1½ teaspoons salt
1½ teaspoons freshly ground black pepper

Truffled Potato Chips

1. Using a mandoline or very sharp heavy knife, slice the potatoes into rounds as thin as possible. Place in a large bowl of water to prevent discoloration.

2. Heat the oil in a large heavy pot to between 325° and 350°F.

3. Drain the potatoes and pat dry completely. Add to the oil, in batches, and cook, stirring with a long-handled spoon so the potatoes cook evenly, until golden brown, about 2 minutes. Drain briefly on paper towels.

4. Place the potato chips in a large bowl. Toss with the cheese, truffle oil, salt, and pepper. Serve immediately.

SIDES

MAKES 4 TO 6 SERVINGS

5 tablespoons unsalted butter, cut into pieces
1 quart whole milk
¾ teaspoon salt
¼ teaspoon freshly ground white pepper
⅛ teaspoon grated nutmeg
1¾ cups 00-grade semolina flour
3 large eggs
½ cup freshly grated Parmigiano-Reggiano

Baked Semolina Gnocchi

This isn't the potato gnocchi commonly found on Italian restaurant menus. Instead, it's a recipe typical of Italy's Emilia-Romagna region, also referred to, oddly enough, as Parisian gnocchi. We use coarse-grain 00-grade semolina flour to make the gnocchi. And though this may not look like much, one bite will tell you it's a special dish.

1. Preheat the oven to 425°F. Grease a 10 × 15-inch baking sheet with 1 teaspoon of the butter; butter a piece of parchment paper the same size as the baking sheet with 1 teaspoon of the butter, and set aside. Butter a 9-inch square baking pan with 1 teaspoon of the butter and set aside.

2. Combine the milk, salt, pepper, and nutmeg in a medium heavy pot and bring to a boil. Add ¼ cup of the semolina and whisk constantly until the mixture begins to thicken. Lower the heat to medium-low and add the remaining semolina flour ¼ cup at a time, stirring constantly with a wooden spoon. Continue to cook until the mixture is very stiff and thick, about 12 minutes. Remove from the heat and let rest for 5 minutes.

3. Beat the eggs in a large bowl. Add ½ cup of the semolina mixture and whisk well to incorporate. Add to the remaining semolina mixture and stir as hard as possible to blend. Add ¼ cup of the cheese and stir well to blend. Turn the mixture out onto the prepared baking sheet and, using an offset metal icing spatula or rubber spatula, spread across the bottom of the pan. Place the buttered parchment paper on the batter. With an outward motion, spread the batter evenly across the pan and smooth the top. Refrigerate until completely cooled, 20 to 25 minutes.

4. With a knife, cut the semolina mixture into 24 pieces, about 1½ inches square, dipping the knife in hot water as needed to cut cleanly. Lay the pieces in 4 rows in the prepared 9-inch pan, shingling them to fit. Dot the top with the remaining 4 tablespoons butter and sprinkle with the remaining ¼ cup cheese.

5. Bake until the top begins to brown and the gnocchi are puffed, about 25 minutes. Remove from the oven before serving.

**1 bunch green onions
(green parts only)**
**2 tablespoons extra-
virgin olive oil**
2 cups whole milk
2 cups water
2 teaspoons salt
**½ teaspoon freshly
ground white pepper**
**⅛ teaspoon freshly
ground black pepper**
**1 cup old-fashioned
white grits
(not instant)**
**¼ pound white Cheddar,
grated**
**4 tablespoons unsalted
butter**

Green Onion Grits

The green onion purée makes these grits bright green. But don't be put off by the color—this is absolutely delicious! It would make a terrific accompaniment to roasted or stewed meats, or even grilled chicken.

1. Bring a medium pot of salted water to a boil. Add the green onions and blanch for 20 seconds. Remove with a slotted spoon and cool in an ice bath. Drain and dry on paper towels.

2. Thinly slice the green onions and purée in a blender with the olive oil.

3. Combine the milk, water, salt, and black and white peppers in a medium heavy pot and bring to a boil. Add the grits in a steady stream, whisking constantly, and return to a boil. Reduce the heat to low and cook, stirring occasionally with a wooden spoon, until the grits are tender and creamy, about 25 minutes.

4. Add the cheese, butter, and green onion purée and stir until the cheese melts completely. Remove from the heat and serve.

MAKES 4 SERVINGS

½ **pound dried black-eyed peas, rinsed and picked over**

About 7½ **cups Rich Chicken Stock (page 21)**

½ **pound bacon, chopped**

2 **tablespoons minced shallots**

1 **tablespoon minced garlic**

1 **cup long-grain white rice**

¼ **teaspoon salt**

⅛ **teaspoon freshly ground black pepper**

2 **tablespoons chopped green onions (green parts only)**

Hoppin' John

Hoppin' John is a traditional Southern dish of black-eyed peas cooked with bacon or salt pork, usually served over rice. It's a real grass-roots dish that we find goes well with pork chops and other meat dishes. This side is on the menu at the Fish House, and it also is served at the Steakhouse as an accompaniment to the Grilled Honey-Cured Pork Chops (page 251). Talk about an all-around Las Vegas favorite!

---

1. In a large saucepan, combine the black-eyed peas and 6 cups of the stock and bring to a boil. Reduce the heat to medium-low and simmer until tender, about 30 minutes. Drain in a colander set over a large bowl, reserving the cooking liquid.

2. In a medium heavy pot, cook the bacon over medium-high heat until brown and crisp, about 5 minutes. Add the shallots and garlic and cook, stirring, until fragrant, 1 minute. Add the rice, salt, and pepper and cook, stirring, for 1 minute. Measure the reserved cooking liquid and add enough additional stock if necessary to make 2 cups, then add to the pot, stir well, and bring to a simmer. Cover, lower the heat to medium-low, and cook, without stirring, until the liquid is absorbed and the rice is tender, about 20 minutes.

3. Remove from the heat and let sit, covered, for 10 minutes. Fluff the rice with a fork, and add the black-eyed peas, stirring to mix. Garnish with the green onions and serve hot.

Emeril's HOMEBASE

Andouille Crowder Peas

MAKES 7 CUPS; 6 SERVINGS

1 tablespoon vegetable
   oil
8 ounces andouille
   sausage or other spicy
   smoked sausage, cut
   into ½-inch slices
1 cup chopped yellow
   onions
½ cup chopped celery
½ cup chopped green
   bell peppers
1 teaspoon minced garlic
2 bay leaves
1 teaspoon salt
½ teaspoon cayenne
1 pound dried crowder
   peas, rinsed and
   picked over
6 cups Rich Chicken
   Stock (page 21)
1 teaspoon chopped
   fresh parsley
½ teaspoon chopped
   fresh thyme

Also called field peas, crowder peas are dried after harvest. You'll find that they taste very much like black-eyed peas. They don't need to be soaked prior to cooking, so they cook quickly, and they're creamy once cooked. Be careful not to overcook them, though, or they'll be mushy.

1. Heat the oil in a large pot over medium-high heat. Add the sausage and cook, stirring, for 2 minutes. Add the onions, celery, and bell peppers and cook, stirring, until soft, about 3 minutes. Add the garlic, bay leaves, salt, and cayenne and cook, stirring, for 30 seconds. Add the peas and chicken stock, stir, and bring to a boil. Reduce the heat to medium-low and simmer, uncovered, stirring occasionally, until the peas are tender, 1 hour and 15 minutes to 1 hour and 30 minutes.

2. Remove from the heat and remove the bay leaves. Add the parsley and thyme, and serve hot.

Chef Christian Czerwonka in Delmonico Steakhouse kitchen

SIDES

White Bean and Goat Cheese Purée

MAKES 3 CUPS; 4 SERVINGS AS A
SIDE DISH, MORE AS A SNACK

*1/2 pound dried Great
    Northern beans, rinsed
    and picked over*
*2 tablespoons extra-virgin
    olive oil*
1 cup chopped yellow onions
1/3 cup finely chopped celery
*3 garlic cloves, smashed and
    peeled*
*1/4 teaspoon freshly ground
    white pepper*
1 1/2 teaspoons salt
*3 ounces goat cheese, cut
    into pieces*
*1/2 teaspoon chopped fresh
    thyme*
*1/2 teaspoon chopped fresh
    rosemary*

This super-rich concoction can be served as an accompaniment to roasted or grilled lamb or roasted pork, or as a snack with crackers or croutons.

1. Put the beans in a medium heavy pot, cover with water by 2 inches, and bring to a boil. Remove from the heat and let sit, covered, for 1 hour. Drain and discard the cooking liquid.

2. Heat 1 tablespoon of the oil in a medium heavy pot. Add the onions and celery and cook, stirring, until soft, about 3 minutes. Add the garlic and white pepper and cook, stirring, for 2 minutes. Add the beans and 2 1/2 cups water and bring to a boil. Cover, reduce the heat to medium-low, and simmer, stirring occasionally, for 30 minutes.

3. Add the salt, stir well, and cook for 30 minutes longer. Remove from the heat. Drain the beans in a colander set over a bowl and reserve the cooking liquid.

4. Combine the beans, goat cheese, thyme, rosemary, and the remaining tablespoon of olive oil in a food processor and process until very smooth, about 2 minutes. If the mixture is too tight, add some of the reserved cooking liquid, 1 tablespoon at a time, to reach the desired consistency. Serve warm.

MAKES 4 SERVINGS

*2 pounds spinach, tough
stems removed and
washed*
¼ cup heavy cream
*4 tablespoons unsalted
butter*
*1 tablespoon finely
chopped shallots*
1 teaspoon minced garlic
*¼ cup plus 2 table-
spoons all-purpose
flour*
1¾ cups whole milk
1 teaspoon salt
*¼ teaspoon freshly
ground white pepper*
*¼ teaspoon grated
nutmeg*
*¼ cup grated Swiss
cheese*
*¼ cup freshly grated
Parmigiano-Reggiano*

Creamed Spinach

To kick up this version of creamed spinach even more, place it in a gratin dish, top it with an additional ¼ cup each of both cheeses, and run it under the broiler for a few minutes until it's hot and bubbly.

1. Bring a large pot of salted water to a boil. Add the spinach and cook for 2 minutes. Drain in a fine-mesh strainer, pressing with a large spoon to release as much water as possible. Let cool slightly, then finely chop and set aside.

2. Bring the cream to a low boil in a small saucepan. Remove from the heat.

3. Melt the butter in a medium heavy saucepan over medium-high heat. Add the shallots and garlic and cook, stirring, until soft, about 1 minute. Add the flour, reduce the heat to low, and cook, stirring constantly with a heavy wooden spoon, until a light blond roux forms, 2 to 3 minutes. Add the milk in a steady stream, whisking constantly, and cook, whisking, until thick and smooth, 1 to 2 minutes. Add the salt, white pepper, and nutmeg and simmer until thickened, 3 to 5 minutes. Add the hot cream, whisking constantly, and cook for 1 minute. Fold in the Swiss and Parmesan cheeses and mix until smooth.

4. Add the spinach, mix well, and cook until completely warmed through, 1 to 2 minutes. Remove from the heat and adjust the seasoning to taste. Serve hot.

Garlic Mushrooms

1 tablespoon olive oil
1 tablespoon chopped
   shallots
1 teaspoon chopped garlic
1¼ pounds mixed
   mushrooms, such as
   oyster, shiitake, button,
   and portobello, stems
   removed, wiped clean,
   and halved
1 teaspoon salt
1 teaspoon freshly ground
   black pepper
1 tablespoon unsalted butter

*Looking for something other than a sauce to top your steak?
Here you go—these simple mushrooms add an elegant touch.*

1. Heat the oil in a large skillet over medium-high heat. Add the
shallots and garlic and cook, stirring, until fragrant, about 1
minute. Add the mushrooms, salt, and pepper and cook, stirring, until the mushrooms are tender and have released their
liquid, 5 to 6 minutes. Add the butter and cook, stirring, for
1 minute.

2. Serve immediately.

Emeril's
NEW ORLEANS

Bacon-Smothered Haricots Verts

1½ pounds haricots verts or
   small, thin green beans,
   ends trimmed
½ pound bacon, chopped
1 tablespoon minced
   shallots
1 teaspoon minced garlic
1 tablespoon all-purpose
   flour
1 cup Rich Chicken Stock
   (page 21)
1 teaspoon salt
½ teaspoon freshly ground
   black pepper
½ teaspoon sherry vinegar

*These small French green beans have been given a Southern
twist by cooking them with shallots and a healthy dose of
bacon. Serve them with just about any roasted meat or fowl.*

1. Bring a large pot of salted water to a boil. Add the beans and
cook until tender, 2 to 3 minutes. Drain in a colander and transfer to an ice bath to cool. Drain well.

2. Cook the bacon in a large skillet over medium-high heat, stirring, until crisp and golden, about 5 minutes. Add the shallots
and garlic and cook, stirring, for 1 minute. Add the flour and
cook, stirring constantly, for 2 minutes. Add the stock, salt,
pepper, and vinegar and cook, stirring, until thickened, 4 to 5
minutes. Add the green beans and cook until warmed through,
about 2 minutes. Remove from the heat and serve.

ORLANDO

**8 tablespoons (1 stick)
unsalted butter**

**2 pounds yellow onions,
peeled and very thinly
sliced**

Caramelized Onions

*We serve these as an accompaniment to both the Bacon Pancakes
(page 120) and the Root Beer–Glazed Pork Chops (page 249).*

Melt the butter in a large skillet over medium-high heat. Add the
onions, reduce the heat to medium-low, and cook slowly, stirring
occasionally, until golden brown and caramelized, 45 minutes to 1
hour. Remove from the heat and serve hot.

*General manager Tony Lott
in the kitchen of Emeril's
New Orleans*

SIDES

Caponata

MAKES 8 CUPS

*2 very ripe tomatoes,
quartered*

*1 small eggplant, trimmed
and cut lengthwise into
¹/₂-inch-thick slices*

*1 large zucchini, trimmed
and cut lengthwise into
¹/₂-inch-thick slices*

*1 large yellow squash,
trimmed and cut
lengthwise into ¹/₂-inch-
thick slices*

*1 small red onion, peeled
and sliced into ¹/₂-inch-
thick rings*

*1 medium red bell pepper,
cored, seeds and ribs
removed, and cut in half*

*1 medium yellow bell
pepper, cored, seeds and
ribs removed, and cut in
half*

3 tablespoons olive oil

2 teaspoons salt

*1¹/₂ teaspoons freshly
ground black pepper*

2 tablespoons minced garlic

*¹/₄ cup pine nuts, lightly
toasted*

¹/₄ cup balsamic vinegar

¹/₄ cup sherry vinegar

¹/₄ cup extra-virgin olive oil

4 anchovy fillets, chopped

*2 tablespoons capers,
drained*

*2 tablespoons minced fresh
basil*

*2 tablespoons minced fresh
parsley*

This caponata varies from the classic Sicilian dish in that the vegetables are grilled before being sautéed. It's a full-flavored variation we like to serve with roasted meats such as lamb.

1. Preheat the oven to 400°F, and preheat the grill to very high heat.

2. Place the tomatoes on a baking sheet and roast until tender, 25 to 30 minutes. Let cool, then dice into ¹/₂-inch pieces.

3. Meanwhile, place the eggplant, zucchini, yellow squash, onions, and bell peppers in a large bowl and toss with 2 table-spoons of the oil, 1 teaspoon of the salt, and ¹/₂ teaspoon of the pepper. Grill until marked by the grill, about 1 minute per side. Remove with tongs and let cool. (Alternatively, arrange the vegetables in one layer on two baking sheets. Preheat the oven to broil. Broil until beginning to char, 2 to 3 minutes per side. Let cool.)

4. Dice all the vegetables into ¹/₂-inch pieces. Heat the remaining tablespoon of olive oil in a large heavy pot over high heat. Add the vegetables and cook, stirring, for 1 minute. Add the garlic and the remaining 1 teaspoon each salt and pepper and cook, stirring, for 2 minutes. Remove from the heat, add the remaining ingredients, and stir well. Let cool to room temperature. Add the diced tomatoes, cover, and refrigerate for at least 6 hours, or overnight, to allow the flavors to develop.

5. Serve at room temperature.

HOMEBASE

1½ pounds parsnips, peeled and chopped
6 tablespoons unsalted butter
1 tablespoon light brown sugar
¼ teaspoon ground cinnamon
⅛ teaspoon ground allspice
4 ripe d'Anjou pears, peeled, cored, and cut into 1-inch pieces
2 tablespoons Frangelico or other nut-flavored liqueur, such as Nocello
½ cup sour cream
½ teaspoon salt
½ teaspoon freshly ground white pepper

Pear and Parsnip Purée

This looks like grown-up baby food, but the flavor is just awesome. Trust me! This would make a great Thanksgiving side dish, and it goes well with roasted pork or grilled pork chops instead of the usual applesauce.

1. Preheat the oven to 325°F.

2. Combine the parsnips, 2 tablespoons of the butter, the brown sugar, cinnamon, and allspice in a baking dish and cover tightly with aluminum foil. Bake until the parsnips are tender, about 45 minutes. Remove from the oven, uncover, and set aside.

3. Melt 1 tablespoon of the butter in a large skillet over medium heat. Add the pears and cook, stirring, for 3 minutes. Add the liqueur and carefully tilt the pan to ignite it. (Alternatively, remove from the heat and light with a match, then return to the heat.) Cook until the flames die down, about 2 minutes. Transfer to a food processor.

4. Melt the remaining 3 tablespoons butter in the same skillet over medium heat. Cook, swirling the pan, until the butter is golden brown and has a nutty aroma. Add the butter and baked parsnips, with their cooking liquid, to the food processor. Purée for 30 seconds. Add the sour cream, salt, and pepper and process until smooth. Serve immediately.

ORLANDO

6 medium red onions (each
    about ½ pound)
2½ tablespoons olive oil
1¼ teaspoons salt
½ teaspoon freshly ground
    black pepper
½ pound mascarpone
    cheese, at room
    temperature
2 teaspoons chopped fresh
    thyme
1 teaspoon minced garlic
1 teaspoon minced shallots
6 sprigs fresh thyme

Roasted Red Onions Stuffed with Thyme-Mascarpone Mousse

These onions make an amazing side dish for any kind of meat dish, from grilled steaks to roasted pork and veal.

1. Preheat the oven to 400°F. Line a baking sheet with aluminum foil and set aside.

2. Peel the onions. Trim the root ends so they will stand upright, and remove ½ inch from the tops. Rub 1¼ teaspoons of the oil over each onion and season with ⅛ teaspoon of the salt and a pinch of the pepper. Place on the baking sheet and roast until tender and caramelized around the edges, about 45 minutes. Remove from the oven and let cool slightly. Leave the oven on.

3. When the onions are cool enough to handle, push out the centers, leaving a shell. Return a piece of the center to each to form a bottom. Chop the remaining centers.

4. In a bowl, combine the mascarpone, thyme, garlic, shallots, and the remaining ½ teaspoon salt and ¼ teaspoon pepper and mix until blended. Stuff the onions in the baking dish with the cheese mixture.

5. Bake until the onions are warmed through and the cheese has melted completely, 5 to 6 minutes. Remove from the oven and transfer to serving plates. Place 1 thyme sprig in the center of each onion, and serve immediately, with a spoonful of the onion pieces alongside.

Roasted Portobello Mushrooms

4 large portobello
   mushroom caps
2 tablespoons extra-
   virgin olive oil
½ teaspoon salt
¼ teaspoon freshly
   ground black pepper

These make a flavorful vegetarian burger. Place one roasted cap on a bun that's been spread with homemade mayonnaise (page 31), top it with a fat onion slice and some tomatoes, and you've got a meal! These are also delicious served on the side of risotto, or chopped and tossed with pasta.

1. Preheat the oven to 400°F.

2. Rub both sides of the mushroom caps with the oil, and season with the salt and pepper. Place gill side down on a baking sheet and roast until tender and fragrant, about 25 minutes. Let cool slightly on the baking sheet, and serve warm.

General manager Ed Tuohy (left) with assistant general manager Chuck Binette (center) and Kevin Czak, former assistant general manager, at Emeril's New Orleans Fish House

SIDES

11 | DESSERTS

Pies and tarts from Emeril's Orlando pastry kitchen

NOLA

1 recipe Flourless Chocolate
   Cake
1 cup chocolate cookie
   crumbs
2 tablespoons unsalted
   butter, melted
1 recipe Chocolate Mousse
1 ounce white chocolate,
   finely chopped
1 recipe Chocolate Ganache
1 recipe Apricot Sauce

Chocolate Buzz Bomb with Apricot Sauce

Why "Buzz Bomb"? One bite will tell you why—this is an intensely rich, intensely chocolate frozen dessert that will pump you up for hours to come! To make the chocolate cookie crumbs at NOLA, we pulverize Oreo cookies in a food processor after removing the cream centers, but you can use the chocolate wafers available in many supermarkets.

1. Place the chocolate cake in a 9-inch springform pan.

2. Combine the cookie crumbs and butter in a small bowl. Using an offset metal icing spatula, spread in an even layer on the top of the cake. Top with the chocolate mousse, spreading it evenly out to the edges of the pan. Cover with plastic wrap, pressing it directly against the mousse, and refrigerate until the mousse is firm, at least 3 hours, or overnight.

3. To assemble the cake, melt the white chocolate in the top of a double boiler or in a small stainless steel bowl set over a pot of simmering water, stirring until smooth. Cut one 6-inch square of parchment paper. Roll into a small cone and tuck in one edge to secure. Pour the melted white chocolate into the cone and snip off the tip. Set aside.

4. Remove the cake from the refrigerator and remove the sides of the pan. Smooth the sides of the cake with a metal icing spatula so the mousse is even with the edges of the cake. Place the cake on a wire rack set over a baking sheet lined with parchment paper. Ladle the liquid chocolate ganache over the top and sides of the cake, letting it run evenly over the surface. While the chocolate is still wet, pipe small swirls of melted white chocolate onto the top. Transfer the cake to a cake plate or stand, and refrigerate until the chocolate is set, about 3 hours.

5. To serve, spoon the apricot sauce onto the dessert plates and top with wedges of the cake.

Flourless Chocolate Cake

11 tablespoons unsalted
  butter
2 cups chopped bitter-
  sweet chocolate
  (10½ ounces)
½ cup sugar
5 large eggs
⅓ cup dark rum
⅔ cup diced dried
  apricots

1. Position a rack in the middle of the oven and preheat the oven to 325°F. Lightly grease a 9-inch springform pan with 1 teaspoon of the butter. Line with parchment paper and butter the paper with ½ teaspoon of the butter. Wrap the outside of the pan with aluminum foil. Set aside.

2. Combine the remaining butter, the chocolate, and sugar in the top of a double boiler or a stainless steel bowl set over a pot of simmering water. Heat gently, stirring occasionally, until the sugar is dissolved and the chocolate is melted. Remove from the heat and let cool slightly, stirring often. Whisk in the eggs one at a time, beating well after each addition. Fold in the rum and apricots.

3. Pour the batter into the prepared pan and place in a roasting pan. Place in the oven and pour enough hot water into the roasting pan to come halfway up the sides of the cake pan. Bake until a toothpick inserted into the center of the cake comes out clean, 25 to 35 minutes.

4. Remove the sides of the pan and invert the cake onto a wire rack. Remove the pan bottom and the parchment paper. Let cool.

Chocolate Mousse

1 cup chopped bitter-
  sweet chocolate
  (5¼ ounces)
4 tablespoons unsalted
  butter, at room
  temperature
2 large eggs, separated
1 tablespoon dark rum
⅛ teaspoon salt
3 tablespoons sugar
⅔ cup heavy cream

1. Melt the chocolate in the top of a double boiler or in a stainless steel bowl set over a pot of simmering water, stirring occasionally until smooth. Remove from the heat and whisk in the butter. Add the egg yolks and rum and whisk well until smooth.

2. In a large bowl, beat the egg whites and salt until frothy. Gradually add the sugar, beating until stiff peaks form. In another large bowl, whip the cream until stiff. Fold the cream into the egg whites.

3. Fold one-third of the egg white mixture into the chocolate mixture to lighten it. Fold the chocolate mixture into the remaining egg white mixture, being careful not to overwork it and deflate the egg whites. (The mousse is easier to spread at room temperature and should be used as soon as possible for this dessert, instead of being held in the refrigerator.)

DESSERTS

1 cup heavy cream
8 ounces bittersweet
   chocolate, chopped

Chocolate Ganache

1. Scald the cream in a small saucepan over medium heat. Remove from the heat.

2. Place the chocolate in a heatproof bowl. Add the hot cream and let sit for 2 minutes, then whisk until smooth. Use the ganache as soon as possible for this dessert.

2 cups chopped dried
   apricots
3½ cups water
1 cup sugar
¼ cup dark rum
2 tablespoons fresh lemon
   juice

Apricot Sauce

1. Combine the apricots, water, and sugar in a medium saucepan and bring to a boil. Reduce the heat to medium-low and simmer, uncovered, for 20 minutes.

2. In batches, transfer to a blender or food processor and purée. Strain through a fine-mesh strainer, pressing down on the solids with a rubber spatula to extract as much liquid as possible. Add the rum and lemon juice, and stir to combine. Serve slightly chilled with this dessert. (This sauce can be stored in an airtight container in the refrigerator for up to 3 days.)

*Young patron with friend
at Emeril's Orlando*

ORLANDO

White Chocolate Buttermilk Cake with Strawberry Sauce

MAKES ONE 10-INCH CAKE;
8 TO 10 SERVINGS

12 tablespoons
(1½ sticks) plus
1 teaspoon unsalted
butter, at room
temperature
¾ cup heavy cream
6 ounces good-quality
white chocolate,
chopped
1½ cups sugar
5 large eggs
1½ teaspoons pure
vanilla extract
3 cups all-purpose flour
1½ teaspoons baking
soda
¼ teaspoon salt
1 cup buttermilk
Double recipe (6 cups)
Strawberry Sauce
(page 286)

As you may know, white chocolate is really not chocolate at all because it contains only cocoa butter, milk, and sugar—no chocolate liquor—but it does add flavor to this buttermilk cake. The strawberry sauce is just the right complement to it.

1. Preheat the oven to 350°F. Butter a 10 × 3-inch springform pan with ½ teaspoon of the butter. Line with parchment paper, butter the paper with ½ teaspoon of the butter, and set aside.

2. Scald the cream in a small saucepan over medium heat. Remove from the heat. Place the white chocolate in a heatproof bowl. Add the hot cream and let sit for 2 minutes, then whisk until smooth.

3. With an electric mixer, in a large bowl, cream the remaining 1½ sticks of butter and the sugar until pale and fluffy. Add 4 of the eggs, one at a time, beating well after each addition. Beat the remaining egg in a small bowl, and add 2 tablespoons of the egg to the batter (discard the remainder). Add the melted white chocolate and vanilla and beat well, scraping down the sides of the bowl as needed.

4. Sift together the flour, baking soda, and salt. Add the dry ingredients and the buttermilk alternately to the batter, beating well after each addition and ending with the flour mixture. Pour into the prepared pan.

5. Bake until golden brown and a cake tester inserted into the center comes out clean, about 1 hour and 15 minutes. Let cool on a wire rack for 1 hour, then remove the sides of the pan and turn the cake out onto the wire rack to finish cooling.

6. To serve, cut the cake into wedges. Spoon the strawberry sauce onto the dessert plates and stand a wedge of cake in each pool of sauce. Serve.

DESSERTS

MAKES ONE 9-INCH CAKE

2 teaspoons unsalted butter
4 large eggs, separated
2/3 cup sugar
Grated zest of 1 lemon
1/2 teaspoon pure vanilla
extract
1/2 cup all-purpose flour
1/2 cup cornstarch
1 recipe Citron Syrup
1 recipe Lemon Curd
1 recipe Meringue Icing
1 recipe Citron-Blueberry
Ice Cream

Lemon Meringue Layer Cake

You might think this is complicated, but once all the components are put together, you'll see that it's all worth it. It's a lemon lover's dream! Just remember to make the lemon curd ahead of time to allow it to chill thoroughly, and refrigerate the assembled cake for about 4 hours in order for it to firm up before icing. Serve right after icing.

1. Preheat the oven to 350°F. Lightly grease the bottom of a 9-inch springform pan with 1 teaspoon of the butter. Line with parchment paper, butter the paper with the remaining 1 teaspoon butter, and set aside.

2. In a large bowl, beat the egg yolks, 1/3 cup of the sugar, the lemon zest and vanilla with an electric mixer on medium speed until thick and almost doubled in volume. (The yolks should form dissolving ribbons when the beaters are lifted out.)

3. In another large bowl, whip the egg whites with clean beaters on medium speed until frothy. Gradually add the remaining 1/3 cup sugar and whip on high speed until stiff peaks form. Fold the egg whites into the egg yolk mixture, being careful not to overmix. Sift half of the flour and cornstarch into the egg mixture, and gently fold to blend. Repeat with the remaining flour and cornstarch. Pour the batter into the prepared pan.

4. Bake the cake for 20 minutes. Turn the cake around and bake until a tester comes out clean and the cake starts to pull away from the sides of the pan, about 10 minutes longer. Remove from the oven and release the sides of the pan. Let cool completely on a wire rack.

5. To assemble the cake, slice the cooled cake horizontally into 2 layers. Place 1 layer on a cake plate and brush with half of the citron syrup. Spread with half of the lemon curd and smooth evenly. Repeat with the remaining cake, citron syrup, and lemon curd. Cover with plastic wrap and refrigerate for 4 hours.

6. Remove the cake from the refrigerator. With a palette knife, spread a thin even layer of the icing over the sides and top of the cake. Put the remaining icing in a pastry bag fitted with a star tip and pipe rosettes decoratively on top and around the bottom of the cake.

7. Brown the meringue lightly with a household blowtorch. Serve immediately, with scoops of the ice cream on the side.

Lemon Curd

MAKES ABOUT 1½ CUPS

6 large egg yolks
½ cup sugar
½ cup fresh lemon juice
8 tablespoons (1 stick)
*   unsalted butter, cut*
*   into pieces*

1. In the top of a double boiler or in a stainless steel bowl, whisk together the yolks, sugar, and lemon juice. Place over simmering water and whisk until the mixture is thickened and forms a ribbon when the whisk is lifted.

2. Remove from the heat and whisk in the butter until melted and blended.

3. Cover with plastic wrap, pressing it directly against the surface to prevent a skin from forming. Refrigerate until cold, at least 3 hours, or overnight.

Citron Syrup

½ cup sugar
½ cup Absolut Citron or
*   other lemon-flavored*
*   vodka or liqueur (such*
*   as limoncello)*

Combine the sugar and vodka in a small heavy saucepan and gently heat over medium heat, stirring occasionally, until the sugar dissolves. Remove from the heat and let cool before using.

Meringue Icing

1 ½ cups sugar
2 tablespoons light corn
*   syrup*
⅓ cup cold water
3 large egg whites
½ teaspoon cream of
*   tartar*
Pinch of salt
1½ teaspoons pure
*   vanilla extract*
1 tablespoon fresh
*   lemon juice*
1 tablespoon hot water

1. Combine the sugar, corn syrup, and cold water in a small heavy saucepan. Bring to a boil, stirring until the sugar dissolves. Boil, uncovered, until the syrup reaches the soft-ball stage (240°F on a candy thermometer). Remove from the heat.

2. Meanwhile, in a large bowl (or the bowl of a stand mixer) beat the egg whites, cream of tartar, and salt with an electric mixer until frothy. Beating constantly, slowly pour the hot syrup down the side of the bowl into the whites (being careful not to pour the syrup onto the beaters). When all the syrup has been added, add the vanilla and continue beating until the icing is cooled and fluffy, about 3 minutes. Beat in the lemon juice and water. Use as soon as possible.

DESSERTS

Citron-Blueberry Ice Cream

The combination of blueberries and lemon is a natural, and the colors make the presentation beautiful! We find that this is a refreshing dessert to serve after a seafood dinner, but, hey, you decide.

1 cup sugar
¼ cup water
2 cups fresh blueberries, rinsed and picked over
2 cups whole milk
1 cup heavy cream
2 teaspoons grated lemon zest
6 large egg yolks
¼ cup fresh lemon juice
¼ cup Absolut Citron or other lemon-flavored vodka or liqueur (such as limoncello)

1. Combine ¼ cup of the sugar and the water in a medium heavy saucepan and bring to a boil over high heat. Reduce the heat to medium-low and simmer until the sugar dissolves, about 2 minutes. Add the blueberries and cook, stirring occasionally, until the berries burst and the syrup thickens, about 5 minutes.

2. Transfer to a blender or food processor, and purée. Strain through a fine-mesh strainer, pressing down on the solids with a rubber spatula to extract as much purée as possible. Let cool slightly. (The purée can be stored in an airtight container in the refrigerator for up to 3 days.)

3. Combine the milk, cream, the remaining ¾ cup sugar, and the lemon zest in a medium heavy saucepan and bring to a gentle boil over medium heat. Remove from the heat.

4. In a medium bowl, beat the egg yolks until frothy and lemon colored, about 2 minutes. Whisk in 1 cup of the hot milk in a slow, steady stream. Gradually add the egg mixture to the hot milk, whisking constantly. Cook over medium-low heat, stirring occasionally, until the mixture thickens enough to coat the back of a spoon, about 5 minutes.

5. Remove from the heat and strain through a fine-mesh strainer into a clean bowl. Whisk in the blueberry purée, lemon juice, and vodka. Cover with plastic wrap, pressing it directly against the surface to prevent a skin from forming. Refrigerate until well chilled, about 2 hours.

6. Pour the mixture into an ice cream maker and freeze according to the manufacturer's instructions. Transfer to an airtight container, and freeze until ready to serve.

NEW ORLEANS FISH HOUSE

Lemon Pudding Cakes with Strawberry Sauce

MAKES 6 SERVINGS

1½ tablespoons plus
   2 teaspoons unsalted
   butter, at room
   temperature
3 large eggs, separated
1½ cups whole milk
1 tablespoon grated
   lemon zest
⅓ cup fresh lemon juice
¾ cup granulated sugar
¼ cup all-purpose flour
⅛ teaspoon salt
Confectioners' sugar, for
   garnish
1 recipe Strawberry
   Sauce
6 large mint leaves, cut
   into thin strips

These individual cakes are ideal for summer luncheons or dinner parties. The refreshing taste of lemon coupled with the strawberry sauce is a perfect note on which to end a meal.

1. Preheat the oven to 350°F. Lightly grease six ¾-cup ramekins or custard cups with 2 teaspoons of the butter. Place in a large roasting pan.

2. Combine the egg yolks, milk, lemon zest, and juice in a large bowl and beat with an electric mixer until frothy, about 2 minutes. Add the remaining 1½ tablespoons butter, the granulated sugar, flour, and salt and beat until smooth.

3. In a separate large bowl, beat the egg whites with clean beaters until stiff peaks form. Gently fold into the yolk mixture, being very careful not to overmix.

4. Divide the batter among the prepared ramekins. Pour enough warm water into the roasting pan to come halfway up the sides of the ramekins. Bake until the cakes are puffed and lightly firm to the touch, 25 to 30 minutes. Remove from the oven, transfer the ramekins to six dessert plates, and let cool slightly.

5. Sift confectioners' sugar over each pudding cake and top with ½ cup of the strawberry sauce. Garnish with the mint and serve warm.

Strawberry Sauce

6 cups fresh strawberries, rinsed and hulled
⅓ cup honey

Summer is, of course, the best time of year to make this, as berries are at their ripest and sweetest. Depending upon the sweetness of the berries, you might want to add more honey to taste.

1. In a food processor or blender, purée 2 cups of the strawberries. Transfer to a large bowl.

2. Quarter the remaining strawberries and add to the purée. Add the honey and mix to combine. Let stand at room temperature for at least 30 minutes. (The sauce can be made up to 6 hours ahead and refrigerated; let come to room temperature before serving.)

Chef Joel Morgan at NOLA evening pre-meal meeting

Emeril's
NEW ORLEANS FISH HOUSE

Molasses Cake with Sweet Potato Ice Cream and Praline Sauce

MAKES ONE 10-INCH CAKE;
8 TO 10 SERVINGS

4 tablespoons plus ¾ teaspoon unsalted butter

1 cup molasses

½ cup buttermilk

½ cup packed light brown sugar

2 large eggs

2 cups all-purpose flour

1½ teaspoons ground ginger

1 teaspoon baking soda

1 recipe Sweet Potato Ice Cream

1 recipe Praline Sauce

Molasses, the result of refining sugarcane or sugar beets, has long been used in the United States, and particularly the South, as a plentiful sweetener for everything from candies, cakes, cookies, and pies to rum. Here in Louisiana, a favorite molasses is made by the Steen's refinery in Abbeville.

This cake is a rather sweet, old-fashioned dessert that's ideally offset by the subtly flavored sweet potato ice cream. And, if you have a sweet tooth, the praline sauce will be perfect for you. It also would be good served on Vanilla Ice Cream (page 319).

1. Preheat the oven to 325°F. Butter a 10-inch round cake pan with ½ teaspoon of the butter. Line the bottom of the pan with parchment paper, and butter the parchment with ¼ teaspoon of the butter. Set aside.

2. Melt the remaining 4 tablespoons butter in a medium heavy saucepan over low heat. Remove from the heat and stir in the molasses. Add the buttermilk, brown sugar, and eggs and whisk until well blended, breaking up any lumps of sugar by pressing against the sides of the pan.

3. Sift together the flour, ginger, and baking soda into a large bowl. Add the molasses mixture, stirring well to blend. Pour the batter into the prepared pan.

4. Bake for 40 to 45 minutes, or until a cake tester inserted into the center comes out clean. (The cake will sink slightly in the center.) Remove from the oven and let cool in the pan on a wire rack for about 1 hour.

5. To serve, unmold the cake onto a serving plate. Cut into portions and serve with the ice cream on the side and the warm sauce drizzled over the cake and ice cream.

DESSERTS

One 8-ounce sweet potato
2 cups heavy cream
1 cup whole milk
6 large egg yolks
¾ cup sugar

Sweet Potato Ice Cream

Now don't turn up your nose at this. The taste and color of the sweet potatoes really kick up this ice cream to notches unknown! Trust me.

1. Preheat the oven to 350°F.

2. Place the sweet potato on a baking sheet. Bake until tender and starting to ooze sugary syrup, about 1 hour and 15 minutes. Remove from the oven and let sit until cool enough to handle. Cut a slit down the potato and scoop the flesh into a bowl. Discard the skin.

3. Combine the cream and milk in a medium heavy saucepan and bring to a gentle boil over medium heat. Remove from the heat.

4. Beat the egg yolks and sugar in a medium bowl until frothy and lemon colored, about 2 minutes. Whisk 1 cup of the hot cream into the egg yolks. Gradually add the egg mixture to the hot cream, whisking constantly. Cook over medium-low heat, stirring occasionally, until the mixture thickens enough to coat the back of a spoon, about 5 minutes. Add the sweet potato and whisk over low heat until well blended.

5. Remove from the heat and strain through a fine-mesh strainer into a clean bowl. Cover with plastic wrap, pressing it directly against the surface to prevent a skin from forming. Refrigerate until well chilled, about 2 hours.

6. Pour the mixture into an ice cream maker and freeze according to the manufacturer's instructions. Transfer to an airtight container and freeze until ready to serve.

4 tablespoons unsalted
*   butter*
¾ cup all-purpose flour
1¼ cups packed light brown
*   sugar*
¾ cup light corn syrup
¾ cup evaporated milk
1¼ cups coarsely chopped
*   pecans*

Praline Sauce

Melt the butter in a medium heavy saucepan over medium heat. Add the flour, whisking to prevent lumps from forming. Add the brown sugar and corn syrup and bring to a boil, stirring constantly. Reduce the heat to medium-low and simmer for 5 minutes. Remove from the heat and gradually stir in the evaporated milk and pecans. Serve immediately.

Sour Cream Toffee Fudge Cake

MAKES ONE 10-INCH CAKE;
8 TO 10 SERVINGS

1 pound plus 3½
   teaspoons unsalted
   butter
2 cups unsweetened
   cocoa powder
2 cups hot brewed
   coffee
1 cup sour cream
1½ tablespoons pure
   vanilla extract
2½ cups all-purpose
   flour
1½ teaspoons baking
   soda
1 teaspoon baking
   powder
3½ cups sugar
4 large eggs
1 recipe Chocolate Icing
1 recipe Butter Toffee

Be careful when making the toffee, as the hot sugar can burn. Also, because breaking the toffee can be a bit difficult, it is best done in two steps—break it first into large pieces, then into smaller pieces inside a deep pot to prevent the pieces from flying around.

1. Preheat the oven to 350°F. Grease three 10-inch round cake pans with 2 teaspoons of the butter. Line each with parchment paper and butter each round of paper with ½ teaspoon butter. Set aside.

2. Place the cocoa in a medium bowl and slowly add the hot coffee, whisking until smooth. Set aside to cool.

3. In a large bowl, whisk together the sour cream and vanilla. Whisk in the cooled coffee mixture.

4. Sift the flour, baking soda, and baking powder together onto a sheet of wax paper or into a bowl.

5. In a large bowl, with an electric mixer, cream the remaining pound butter and the sugar. Add the eggs one at a time, beating well after each addition. On low speed, add the flour mixture alternately with the coffee–sour cream mixture. Beat until glossy.

6. Divide the batter among the three prepared pans. Bake until a cake tester comes out clean, 30 to 35 minutes. Let cool completely in the pans on a wire rack.

7. Remove the cakes from the pans and peel off the parchment paper. Using a long serrated knife, trim off the rounded top from each to make a flat surface. Place the first layer on a cake plate or stand. Spread about 1½ cups of the chocolate icing over the top and out to the edges of the cake, and sprinkle with about ¾ cup crushed toffee. Repeat with the second layer and another 1½ cups icing and ¾ cup crushed toffee. Place the third layer upside down on top. Frost the top and sides of the cake with the remaining icing and press the remaining crushed toffee onto the sides and top of the cake. Serve.

DESSERTS

Chocolate Icing

4½ cups heavy cream
¾ pound (3 sticks) unsalted butter
½ cup plus 2 tablespoons unsweetened cocoa powder
½ cup light corn syrup
2 pounds semisweet chocolate, chopped into pieces
1 tablespoon pure vanilla extract
1 teaspoon pure almond extract

1. Combine the cream, butter, cocoa, and corn syrup in a large saucepan and bring to a simmer over medium heat. Remove from the heat.

2. Put the chopped chocolate in a large bowl. Add the hot cream mixture and let sit for 2 minutes, then whisk until the chocolate is melted and smooth. Add the vanilla and almond extracts and whisk to blend. Cover and refrigerate until needed. (The icing will keep refrigerated for up to 3 days.)

Butter Toffee

8 tablespoons (1 stick) unsalted butter
1½ cups granulated sugar
1 cup packed light brown sugar
¾ cup plus 2 tablespoons heavy cream
½ teaspoon pure vanilla extract

1. Line a baking sheet with parchment or wax paper.

2. Combine the butter, granulated sugar, brown sugar, and cream in a medium heavy saucepan and cook over low heat, stirring occasionally, until the sugar dissolves. Continue to cook until the mixture reaches 300°F, the hard-crack stage (a drop of boiling syrup immersed in cold water crackles); be very careful not to allow the mixture to boil. Remove from the heat, add the vanilla, and stir. Pour onto the prepared baking sheet and let cool completely.

3. Crack the toffee into large shards with a rolling pin. Place the pieces in a large deep pot and break into smaller pieces with the end of the rolling pin. Store in an airtight container until ready to use.

Espresso-Hazelnut Cheesecakes with Orange-Hazelnut Biscotti and Clear Orange Caramel Sauce

MAKES 8 SERVINGS

Vegetable cooking spray
1 recipe Biscotti Crust
**1 pound cream cheese,
    at room temperature**
1 cup sugar
2 tablespoons cornstarch
2 large eggs
2 large egg yolks
**2 teaspoons pure vanilla
    extract**
3 cups sour cream
**2 tablespoons finely
    ground toasted
    hazelnuts**
**2 tablespoons Frangelico
    liqueur**
**2 tablespoons unsweet-
    ened espresso
    concentrate or strong
    brewed espresso or
    coffee**
**1 recipe Clear Orange
    Caramel Sauce**
**1 recipe Orange-Hazelnut
    Biscotti (reserve 6
    biscotti for the crust)**

At Emeril's Delmonico, these individual cheesecakes are made in 10-ounce paper coffee cups. (Yes, you read that correctly.) The crust is packed into the bottom and baked, then the two cheesecake fillings and sour cream topping are poured on top. To serve the desserts, the cups are cut away with scissors and the cheesecakes are unmolded onto plates. If you're a biscotti lover, these cookies are a delicious treat on their own or with ice cream.

1. Preheat the oven to 350°F.

2. Spray eight 10-ounce paper coffee cups with vegetable cooking spray. Divide the biscotti crust mixture among the cups. Press down to make a thick bottom crust.

3. Place on a baking sheet and bake until set, about 10 minutes. Remove from the oven and let cool completely. Lower the oven temperature to 225°F.

4. With an electric mixer fitted with a paddle attachment, beat the cream cheese on high speed until smooth. Combine ¾ cup of the sugar and the cornstarch in a bowl, then add to the cream cheese and beat until smooth.

5. Beat the eggs, egg yolks, and vanilla together in a small bowl. Add to the cream cheese mixture in four additions, scraping down the sides of the bowl after each addition. Add 1 cup of the sour cream and beat to blend. Pour half of the batter into another bowl. Add the hazelnuts and Frangelico to one bowl and beat to blend. Add the espresso to the remaining batter and beat to blend.

6. Pour ¼ cup of the hazelnut mixture into each prepared biscotti crust cup, and top with ¼ cup of the espresso mixture. Bake until the filling is set, about 50 minutes. Meanwhile, to make the sour cream topping, whisk the remaining 2 cups sour cream and ¼ cup sugar together in a medium bowl. Set aside.

7. Remove the baked cheesecakes from the oven and top each one with ¼ cup of the sour cream topping. Return to the oven and bake for 15 minutes longer.

DESSERTS

8. Remove from the oven and let cool for 30 minutes on a wire rack. Refrigerate until cold, at least 4 hours, or overnight.

9. To serve, run a small sharp knife under hot running water, then carefully run the knife around the inside of each cup to loosen the cheesecakes. With kitchen shears, cut away the cups, and place the cheesecakes crust side down on dessert plates. Spoon the caramel sauce around the cheesecakes and serve with the biscotti.

Biscotti Crust

MAKES ABOUT 1½ CUPS

6 Orange-Hazelnut Biscotti
⅓ cup fine dry bread crumbs
¼ cup packed light brown sugar
2 teaspoons finely ground toasted hazelnuts
4 tablespoons unsalted butter, melted

1. Process the biscotti in a food processor to make fine crumbs.

2. Combine the cookie crumbs, bread crumbs, sugar, and hazelnuts in a medium bowl. Add the butter and stir with a fork to blend. Set aside until ready to use.

Clear Orange Caramel Sauce

MAKES 1¾ CUPS

1½ cups sugar
½ cup water
1 tablespoon grated orange zest
1 tablespoon fresh lemon juice
¾ cup fresh orange juice

1. Combine the sugar, water, orange zest, and lemon juice in a medium heavy saucepan and cook over medium-high heat, stirring constantly, until the sugar dissolves. Stop stirring and continue to cook until the mixture thickens and turns golden, 10 to 15 minutes.

2. Remove from the heat and add the orange juice (the mixture will bubble up). Return to medium-high heat and cook, stirring constantly, for 1 minute. Remove from the heat and let cool slightly.

3. Strain the sauce through a fine-mesh strainer into a bowl and let cool to room temperature before serving.

1⅓ cups bread flour
*1½ teaspoons baking
 powder*
*4 ounces hazelnuts
 toasted (heaping
 ¾ cup)*
*½ cup fine dry bread
 crumbs*
*⅓ cup plus 1 tablespoon
 sugar*
*2 tablespoons grated
 orange zest*
*2 teaspoons lightly
 toasted fennel seeds*
2 large eggs
*3 tablespoons fresh
 orange juice*
*1 teaspoon Grand
 Marnier liqueur*

Orange-Hazelnut Biscotti

1. Preheat the oven to 350°F. Line a large baking sheet with parchment paper and set aside.

2. Sift the flour and baking powder together into a large bowl. Add the hazelnuts, bread crumbs, sugar, zest, and fennel seeds and stir to mix.

3. In a medium bowl, beat the eggs, orange juice, and Grand Marnier with an electric mixer on low speed. Slowly add the egg mixture to the dry ingredients, mixing on low speed just until the mixture comes together into a thick dough. Turn out onto a lightly floured work surface and form into a cylinder. Using your hands, roll into a log about 14 inches long and 2 inches in diameter. Place on the prepared baking sheet. With the palm of your hand, press down lightly to flatten the log slightly.

4. Bake until golden brown and firm in the center, about 30 minutes. Remove from the oven and let cool completely on a wire rack. Reduce the oven temperature to 300°F.

5. Transfer the cooled biscotti to a cutting board. With a sharp heavy knife, cut on the bias into ¾-inch-thick diagonal slices. Return to the baking sheet and bake for 15 minutes. Turn the cookies with a spatula and bake until dry and crisp, about 15 minutes longer. Cool on a wire rack. (The biscotti can be stored in an airtight container at room temperature for up to 5 days.)

Emeril's ORLANDO

Caramelized Apple Cheesecake with Spiced Crème Anglaise and Butterscotch Sauce

MAKES ONE 10-INCH CHEESECAKE;
8 TO 10 SERVINGS

**4 tablespoons plus
1 teaspoon unsalted
butter**

**1 cup shortbread crumbs
(about 5½ ounces
cookies)**

**½ cup plus 2 tablespoons
granulated sugar**

**2 tablespoons unsalted
butter, melted**

2 tablespoons water

**1 cup peeled, cored, and
thinly sliced Granny Smith
apples (about 2 apples)**

**1½ pounds cream cheese,
at room temperature**

**¾ cup packed light brown
sugar**

3 large eggs

1 teaspoon fresh lemon juice

**¼ teaspoon ground
cinnamon**

⅛ teaspoon grated nutmeg

**1 recipe Spiced Crème
Anglaise**

1 recipe Butterscotch Sauce

You'll find that this cheesecake is a bit thinner than the usual cheesecake, but don't let that worry you. It has a terrific, intense flavor from the caramelized apples that will more than make up for the slighter appearance. We make our shortbread crumbs by grinding regular store-bought cookies in the food processor. You might wonder if the Spiced Crème Anglaise is a necessary accompaniment—yes!

1. Grease a 10-inch springform pan with 1 teaspoon of the butter.

2. Combine the crumbs, 2 tablespoons of the sugar, and the melted butter in a food processor and mix on low speed until well blended. Transfer to the springform pan and press evenly across the bottom. Chill in the refrigerator for 1 hour.

3. Preheat the oven to 325°F.

4. Combine the remaining ½ cup sugar and the water in a medium heavy saucepan, and bring to a boil. Reduce the heat to medium and cook, stirring occasionally, until the sugar is dissolved. Continue cooking, swirling the pan occasionally, until the caramel is amber in color, 5 to 7 minutes. Add the remaining 4 tablespoons butter, stir, and cook over low heat until the butter is melted and blended, about 1 minute. Add the apples and stir to coat with the caramel. Cook, stirring, over medium heat until the apples are tender, about 5 minutes. Remove from the heat and let cool.

5. Combine the cream cheese and brown sugar in a large bowl and beat with an electric mixer until smooth. Add the eggs one at a time, beating well after each addition and scraping down the sides of the bowl as necessary. Add the lemon juice, cinnamon, and nutmeg and mix well. Fold in the apple-caramel mixture. Pour the batter into the prepared pan. Bake, rotating the pan a quarter turn every 30 minutes, until golden brown and firm around the edges but still slightly loose in the center, 1 hour and 20 minutes to 1 hour and 30 minutes. Remove from the oven and let cool for 2 hours.

6. Cover the cheesecake and refrigerate for at least 4 hours, or overnight.

7. To serve, spoon a portion of the crème anglaise onto each serving plate, top with a slice of the cheesecake, and drizzle with the butterscotch sauce.

Spiced Crème Anglaise

2 cups heavy cream
½ teaspoon grated orange zest
¼ teaspoon ground cinnamon
⅛ teaspoon grated nutmeg
3 large egg yolks
¼ cup sugar

1. Combine 1 cup of the cream, the zest, cinnamon, and nutmeg in a medium saucepan and bring to a simmer over medium heat. Remove from the heat.

2. In a medium bowl, beat the egg yolks and sugar until pale and thick, about 2 minutes. Slowly drizzle in the hot cream, whisking constantly. Return the mixture to the pan and cook over medium heat, stirring constantly, until the sauce thickens and coats the back of a spoon. Remove from the heat and add the remaining cream. Place in an ice bath and stir until cool.

3. Cover with plastic wrap, pressing it directly against the surface to prevent a skin from forming, and refrigerate until well chilled, about 2 hours. Serve cold.

Butterscotch Sauce

1½ *cups sugar*
¼ *cup water*
1 *teaspoon fresh lemon juice*
6 *tablespoons unsalted*
   butter, cut into pieces
1 *cup heavy cream*
¼ *to* ½ *cup whole milk*

1. Combine the sugar, water, and lemon juice in a medium heavy saucepan and cook over medium-high heat, stirring, until the sugar dissolves. Let boil without stirring until the mixture becomes a deep amber color, 3 to 4 minutes, watching closely so it doesn't burn.

2. Remove the pan from the heat, add the butter, and swirl the pan to melt it, about 1 minute. Return to the heat and bring to a boil. Add the cream, whisk to combine, and remove from the heat. Add ¼ cup of the milk, then add up to ¼ cup more, until the desired consistency is reached. Let cool until just warm before serving. (The sauce will thicken as it cools.)

Finishing desserts at
Delmonico Steakhouse

Emeril's NEW ORLEANS

MAKES ONE 9-INCH PIE;
10 SERVINGS

4 cups heavy cream
1½ cups whole milk
1½ cups plus 2
    teaspoons
    granulated sugar
1 vanilla bean, split
    lengthwise in half and
    seeds scraped out,
    seeds and bean
    reserved
2 large eggs
3 large egg yolks
½ cup cornstarch
1 recipe Graham Cracker
    Crust
3 pounds (about 9) ripe
    but firm bananas,
    peeled and cut
    crosswise into
    ½-inch-thick slices
½ teaspoon pure vanilla
    extract
1 recipe Caramel Sauce
1 recipe Chocolate Sauce
Shaved chocolate, for
    garnish
Confectioners' sugar, for
    garnish

Banana Cream Pie with Caramel Drizzles and Chocolate Sauce

There're a few secrets to making this pie (which, incidentally, has been on the menu at Emeril's since Day One, and continues to be one of our most requested desserts). First, the bananas, while ripe, need to be firm, so that they hold their shape when pushed into place. Second, the pastry cream needs to be very stiff, so that the pie will not crumble or slide when sliced. It's also important to cover the bananas completely with the last layer of pastry cream to prevent them from discoloring. And while Mr. Lou (the original pastry chef at Emeril's) piped the whipped cream over each individual slice before serving, feel free to spread your whipped cream over the whole pie, if you'd prefer.

1. Combine 2 cups of the cream, the milk, ½ cup of the sugar, the vanilla bean, and the vanilla seeds in a large heavy saucepan and bring to a gentle boil over medium heat, whisking to dissolve the sugar. Remove from the heat.

2. Combine the eggs, egg yolks, cornstarch, and 1 cup of the sugar in a medium bowl and whisk until pale yellow. Slowly add 1 cup of the hot cream into the egg yolk mixture, whisking constantly until smooth. Gradually add the egg mixture to the hot cream and whisk well to combine. Bring to a simmer, stirring constantly with a heavy wooden spoon, and cook until the mixture thickens, about 5 minutes. (The pastry cream may separate slightly; if so, remove from the heat and beat with an electric mixer until thick and smooth.) Strain through a fine-mesh strainer into a clean bowl. Cover with plastic wrap, pressing it directly against the surface to prevent a skin from forming. Refrigerate until well chilled, about 4 hours.

3. To assemble, spread ½ cup of the pastry cream over the bottom of the prepared crust, smoothing it with the back of a large spoon or rubber spatula. Arrange enough banana slices (not quite one-third) in a tight tiled pattern over the custard, pressing them down with your hands to pack them firmly. Repeat to build a second layer, using another ¾ cup of the pastry cream and enough bananas to cover it. For the third layer, spread ¾ cup pastry cream over the bananas and top with the remaining bananas, starting 1 inch from the outer edge and working toward the center. Spread

DESSERTS

the remaining pastry cream evenly over the bananas, covering them completely to prevent discoloration. Cover with plastic wrap and chill for at least 4 hours, or overnight.

4. In a medium bowl, whip the remaining 2 cups cream until soft peaks form. Add the remaining 2 teaspoons sugar and the vanilla extract and whip until stiff peaks form.

5. With a sharp knife dipped in hot water, cut the pie into 10 slices. Transfer the slices to dessert plates. Fill a pastry bag with the whipped cream and pipe some onto each slice. (Alternatively, spread the whipped cream evenly over the pie before cutting.) Drizzle each slice with caramel sauce and chocolate sauce, sprinkle with chocolate shavings and confectioners' sugar, and serve.

Graham Cracker Crust

MAKES ONE 9-INCH CRUST

1¼ cups graham cracker crumbs
¼ cup sugar
4 tablespoons unsalted butter, melted

1. Preheat the oven to 350°F.

2. Combine the graham cracker crumbs and sugar in a medium bowl and mix well. Add the butter and mix well. Press the mixture into the bottom and up the sides of a 9-inch pie pan. Top with a second pie pan and, with a circular motion, use it to press the crust firmly into the pan; remove the top pan.

3. Bake the crust until browned, about 25 minutes. Let cool completely.

¾ *cup sugar*
2 *tablespoons water*
½ *teaspoon fresh lemon juice*
½ *cup heavy cream*
2 *tablespoons to* ¼ *cup whole milk*

Caramel Sauce

1. Combine the sugar, water, and lemon juice in a medium heavy saucepan and cook over medium-high heat, stirring, until the sugar dissolves. Let boil without stirring until the mixture becomes a deep amber color, 2 to 3 minutes, watching closely so it doesn't burn. Add the cream (be careful—it will bubble up), whisk to combine, and remove from the heat.

2. Add 2 tablespoons of the milk, then add up to 2 more tablespoons, until the desired consistency is reached. Let cool until just warm before serving. (The sauce will thicken as it cools.)

¾ *cup half-and-half*
1 *tablespoon unsalted butter*
½ *pound semisweet chocolate chips (1⅓ cups)*
¼ *teaspoon pure vanilla extract*

Chocolate Sauce

1. Scald the half-and-half with the butter in a small heavy saucepan over medium heat. Remove from the heat.

2. Place the chocolate and vanilla in a medium heatproof bowl. Add the hot half-and-half and let sit for 2 minutes, then whisk until smooth. Serve slightly warm. (The sauce can be kept refrigerated in an airtight container for up to 3 days; rewarm slightly before serving.)

DESSERTS

10 tablespoons plus
  2 teaspoons unsalted
  butter, at room
  temperature
2 cups mashed ripe bananas
  (about 6 medium
  bananas)
1 cup sour cream
4 large eggs
1 tablespoon pure vanilla
  extract
4 cups cake flour
2 teaspoons baking soda
1½ teaspoons baking
  powder
1 teaspoon salt
1¾ cups sugar
1 recipe Pastry Cream
1 recipe Chocolate Ganache

Banana Boston Cream Pie

It's not really a pie, but rather a two-layered sponge cake. It differs a bit from the original Boston cream pie in that mashed bananas are used to make the batter for an even richer cake. Here's a quick clean-up tip: when assembling the cake, place a baking sheet under the wire rack to catch the drips as you pour on the chocolate. Drizzling on the chocolate can get very messy!

1. Preheat the oven to 350°F. Lightly grease two 10-inch round cake pans with 1 teaspoon of the butter. Line the bottoms with parchment paper, and butter the parchment with 1 teaspoon of the butter. Set aside.

2. Purée the bananas with the sour cream, eggs, and vanilla in a food processor.

3. Sift the cake flour, baking soda, baking powder, and salt into a large bowl. In the bowl of an electric mixer, cream together the remaining 10 tablespoons butter and the sugar. On medium speed, add the dry ingredients in 3 additions, alternating with the wet, scraping the sides of the bowl and beating well after the addition of each.

4. Pour the batter into the prepared pans. Bake until the cake is lightly browned and bounces back when touched with your fingers, about 25 minutes. Let cool for 10 minutes before turning out onto a wire rack to cool completely. Peel off the parchment paper.

5. To assemble the cake, using a long serrated knife, trim off the rounded top of each cake layer to make them flat. Place the bottom layer on a wire rack set over a baking sheet lined with parchment paper. Spread the pastry cream evenly over the top. Place the second cake layer upside down on the first. Wrap the sides of the cake with a double layer of plastic wrap to keep the pastry cream from oozing out, and gently press down on the top layer. Remove the plastic wrap and scrape off any excess pastry cream.

6. Slowly pour 1 to 1½ cups of the ganache onto the top of the cake, letting it run down the sides. Let sit for 5 minutes, then, in several applications, slowly pour on the remaining ganache, until the cake is completely covered. Refrigerate until ready to serve.

**2 cups plus 2 tablespoons
heavy cream**
**½ cup plus 3 table-
spoons sugar**
**½ vanilla bean, split
lengthwise in half and
seeds scraped out,
bean and seeds
reserved**
3 large egg yolks
**3½ tablespoons
cornstarch**

Pastry Cream

1. Combine 2 cups of the cream, ½ cup plus 1 tablespoon of the sugar, and the vanilla bean and seeds in a medium saucepan and bring to a gentle boil over medium heat, whisking to dissolve the sugar. Remove from the heat.

2. Combine the remaining 2 tablespoons heavy cream, the remaining 2 tablespoons sugar, the egg yolks, and cornstarch in a medium bowl and whisk until pale yellow. Slowly add ½ cup of the hot cream to the egg yolk mixture, whisking constantly until smooth. Add the egg yolk mixture to the hot cream, and whisk well to combine. Return to medium heat, and cook, stirring constantly with a heavy wooden spoon, until the mixture thickens enough to coat the back of a spoon, about 5 minutes. Remove from the heat and strain through a fine-mesh strainer into a clean container.

3. Cover with plastic wrap, pressing it directly against the surface of the pastry cream to prevent a skin from forming. Refrigerate until well chilled, about 4 hours. Whisk until smooth before using.

2 cups heavy cream
**1¼ pounds semisweet
chocolate, chopped
(about 3¼ cups)**

Chocolate Ganache

1. Scald the cream in a small saucepan over medium heat. Remove from the heat.

2. Place the chocolate in a heatproof bowl. Add the hot cream and let sit for 2 minutes, then whisk until smooth. Let cool slightly before pouring on the cake.

4 cups heavy cream

1½ cups whole milk

1½ cups plus 2 teaspoons
sugar

1 vanilla bean, split
lengthwise in half and
seeds scraped out, seeds
and bean reserved

2 large eggs

3 large egg yolks

½ cup cornstarch

1⅓ cups sweetened coconut
flakes, lightly toasted

1 recipe Sweet Pie Dough
(page 37)

1 recipe Meringue Topping

Coconut Cream Pie

Just as for the Banana Cream Pie (page 297), the pastry cream for this pie needs to be very stiff, so that the pie will not crumble or slide when sliced.

1. Combine 2 cups of the cream, the milk, ½ cup of the sugar, the vanilla bean, and the vanilla seeds in a large heavy saucepan and bring to a gentle boil over medium heat, whisking to dissolve the sugar. Remove from the heat.

2. Combine the eggs, egg yolks, cornstarch, and 1 cup of the sugar in a medium bowl and whisk until pale yellow. Slowly add 1 cup of the hot cream to the egg yolk mixture, whisking constantly until smooth. Gradually add the egg mixture to the hot cream. Bring to a simmer, stirring constantly with a heavy wooden spoon, and cook until the mixture thickens, about 5 minutes. (The pastry cream may separate slightly; if so, remove from the heat and beat with an electric mixer until thick and smooth.) Strain through a fine-mesh strainer into a clean bowl. Fold in 1 cup of the coconut flakes. Cover with plastic wrap, pressing it directly against the surface to prevent a skin from forming. Refrigerate until well chilled, about 4 hours.

3. In the meantime, on a lightly floured surface, roll out the dough to 12-inch circle, about ¼ inch thick. Transfer to a 9-inch pie pan, trim the edges to a ½-inch overhang, and fold over. Crimp the edges decoratively. Refrigerate for 20 to 30 minutes.

4. Preheat the oven to 400°F.

5. Line the pie shell with parchment paper and fill with pie weights or dried beans. Bake for 10 minutes. Remove the paper and weights and bake until golden brown, 10 to 15 minutes more. Let cool on a wire rack before filling. Increase the oven temperature to broil.

6. Pour the coconut cream into the piecrust and smooth with a rubber spatula. Spread the meringue over the filling, smoothing it out to the edges of the crust so the meringue won't shrink during baking. With a dull knife, make decorative peaks in the meringue.

7. Place under the broiler until the meringue is golden, 1 to 2 minutes, watching carefully to avoid burning. Remove from the oven and sprinkle with the remaining ⅓ cup toasted coconut. Refrigerate until completely cool, at least 2 hours.

8. Slice and serve.

Meringue Topping

4 large egg whites
¼ teaspoon cream of
*   tartar*
⅛ teaspoon salt
½ cup sugar

In a large bowl, beat the egg whites, cream of tartar, and salt with an electric mixer until soft peaks begin to form. Slowly beat in the sugar and continue to beat until stiff, glossy peaks form. (Be careful not to overbeat, as very stiff meringue is difficult to spread.) Use immediately.

Trevor Wisdom during cookbook recipe testing at Emeril's Homebase

White Chocolate Raspberry Mascarpone Cream Pie in a Pistachio Crust

MAKES ONE 9-INCH PIE;
8 TO 10 SERVINGS

1 teaspoon unsalted butter
1/3 cup finely ground
    pistachio nuts
1 cup all-purpose flour
2 tablespoons sugar
1/8 teaspoon salt
11 tablespoons cold
    unsalted butter, cut into
    small pieces
2 tablespoons sour cream
Ice water, as needed
1 recipe White Chocolate
    Mousse
1 recipe Raspberry Filling
1 cup heavy cream
1 tablespoon confectioners'
    sugar
3/4 cup shaved white
    chocolate
1 recipe Peach Purée

This pie isn't too difficult to prepare, despite its many steps. Be aware, though, that you'll need to start a day or two in advance in order for the filling to set up prior to serving.

1. Lightly grease a 9-inch deep-dish pie pan with the 1 teaspoon of butter, and set aside.

2. To make the crust, combine the pistachios, flour, sugar, salt, and cold butter in a bowl. With an electric mixer (use the paddle attachment if you have one), mix on medium speed until the mixture resembles coarse meal. Add the sour cream and mix until the dough forms a soft ball, adding ice water 1 teaspoon at a time as necessary if the dough is too dry. Shape the dough into a disk, wrap in plastic wrap, and refrigerate for 20 to 30 minutes.

3. In the meantime, on a lightly floured surface, roll out the dough to an 11-inch circle, about 1/4 inch thick. Fit it into the prepared pan, trim the edges to a 1/2-inch overhang, and fold over. Crimp the edges decoratively and prick the bottom all over with a fork. Place in the freezer for 20 minutes.

4. Preheat the oven to 400°F.

5. Line the pie shell with parchment paper or foil and fill with pie weights or dried beans. Place in the oven and immediately reduce the temperature to 350°F. Bake for 25 minutes. Remove the paper and weights and continue baking until golden brown, 12 to 14 minutes. Let cool on a wire rack.

6. Pour the mousse into the cooled pie shell. Refrigerate for at least 4 hours, or up to 24 hours, to allow the mousse to set firmly.

7. Remove the pie from the refrigerator and pour the raspberry filling on top of the white chocolate mousse. Smooth with a spatula, mounding it slightly in the center. Cover with plastic wrap and refrigerate for at least 3 hours, or overnight.

8. In a bowl, beat the cream until soft peaks form. Add the confectioners' sugar and beat until slightly stiff.

9. To serve, top the pie with the whipped cream and white chocolate shavings, and drizzle with peach purée.

MAKES ABOUT 1 CUP

2½ ounces good-quality
    white chocolate
2 tablespoons unsalted
    butter
1 large egg, separated
1 teaspoon Grand
    Marnier liqueur
1½ tablespoons sugar
⅓ cup heavy cream

White Chocolate Mousse

1. Melt the chocolate in the top of a double boiler or in a stainless steel bowl set over a pot of simmering water, stirring occasionally until smooth. Remove from the heat and whisk in the butter. Add the egg yolk and whisk until smooth (the mixture may separate, but continue whisking, and it will come back together). Whisk in the Grand Marnier.

2. In a large bowl, beat the egg white until frothy. Add the sugar and beat until stiff peaks form. In a medium bowl, whip the cream until stiff. Fold the cream into the egg white.

3. Fold one-third of the egg white mixture into the chocolate mixture. Fold the chocolate mixture into the remaining egg white mixture, being careful not to overwork it and deflate the egg whites. Refrigerate until ready to use.

Raspberry Filling

MAKES ABOUT 4 CUPS

1 recipe Raspberry Purée
*1 teaspoon unflavored
    gelatin*
4 large egg yolks
½ cup sugar
*10 ounces mascarpone
    cheese*
⅔ cup heavy cream

1. Put the raspberry purée in a small bowl, sprinkle with the gelatin, and stir to blend. Let stand until the gelatin softens, about 5 minutes.

2. In medium heatproof bowl, beat the egg yolks and sugar with an electric mixer until thick and yellow. Add the gelatin-raspberry mixture and mix well. Place the bowl over a pot of simmering water and whisk until the mixture is hot and slightly thickened. Remove from the heat and beat on medium speed until it cools and increases slightly in volume.

3. When the mixture is cool, add the mascarpone and beat until smooth. Transfer to a large bowl.

4. In a separate bowl, whip the cream until stiff peaks form. Fold into the mascarpone mixture. Use the filling immediately.

Raspberry Purée

MAKES ⅔ CUP

¼ cup sugar
¼ cup water
*2 cups fresh raspberries,
    rinsed and picked over*

1. Combine the sugar and water in a medium heavy saucepan and bring to a boil over high heat. Reduce the heat to medium-low and simmer until the sugar dissolves, about 2 minutes. Add the raspberries and cook, stirring occasionally, until the syrup thickens, about 5 minutes.

2. Transfer to a blender or food processor, and purée. Strain through a fine-mesh strainer, pressing down with a rubber spatula to extract as much purée as possible. If it seems too thick, add water 1 teaspoon at a time to reach the desired consistency. (The purée can be stored in an airtight container in the refrigerator for up to 3 days.)

Peach Purée

¼ **cup sugar**

¼ **cup water**

1⅔ **cups frozen peaches (not packed in syrup), thawed**

1 **tablespoon Grand Marnier liqueur**

1 **teaspoon fresh lemon juice**

1. Combine the sugar and water in a medium heavy saucepan and bring to a boil over high heat. Reduce the heat to medium-low and simmer until the sugar dissolves, about 2 minutes. Add the peaches, Grand Marnier, and lemon juice, and cook, stirring occasionally, until the peaches are softened and the syrup is thickened, about 5 minutes.

2. Transfer to a blender or food processor, and purée. Strain through a fine-mesh strainer, pressing down with a rubber spatula to extract as much purée as possible. If it seems too thick, add water 1 teaspoon at a time to reach the desired consistency. (The purée can be stored in an airtight container in the refrigerator for up to 3 days.)

Crème brûlée being prepared in Emeril's New Orleans Fish House kitchen

DESSERTS

Old-Fashioned Green Tomato Pie with Molasses Ice Cream

MAKES ONE 9-INCH PIE;
6 TO 8 SERVINGS

One recipe Sweet Pie Dough (page 37)
¾ cup packed light brown sugar
½ cup plus ½ teaspoon granulated sugar
¼ cup plus 2 tablespoons all-purpose flour
1 teaspoon ground cinnamon
⅛ teaspoon salt
⅛ teaspoon freshly ground white pepper
4 cups finely chopped green tomatoes
1 tablespoon fresh lemon juice
2 tablespoons unsalted butter, cut into pieces
2 teaspoons heavy cream
1 recipe Molasses Ice Cream

This sounds odd, but trust me, the slightly tart green tomatoes are very similar to apples, so this tastes very much like an apple pie.

1. Preheat the oven to 425°F.

2. Divide the dough in half and return one half to the refrigerator. On a lightly floured surface, roll out the other piece of dough to an 11-inch circle, about ⅛ inch thick. Transfer to a 9-inch pie pan. Trim the edges with scissors or a sharp knife to a ½-inch overhang.

3. In a large bowl, mix together the brown sugar, granulated sugar, flour, cinnamon, salt, and pepper. Sprinkle 2 tablespoons of the mixture across the bottom of the pie shell. Add the tomatoes and lemon juice to the bowl with the remaining mixture and toss to coat. Spoon the tomatoes into the pie shell, and dot with the butter.

4. Roll out the remaining dough to a 10-inch circle. Place on top of the tomato filling and tuck the overlapping crusts into the pan, forming a thick edge. Crimp the edges to seal. Cut small ½-inch-long steam vents in a decorative pattern in the top crust. With a pastry brush, brush the crust with the cream, and sprinkle with the remaining ½ teaspoon sugar.

5. Bake for 15 minutes, then reduce the oven temperature to 375°F. Bake until the crust is golden brown and the filling is bubbly, 35 to 40 minutes longer. Let cool on a wire rack for at least 1 hour before serving.

6. Serve warm or at room temperature with the ice cream.

Molasses Ice Cream

2 cups heavy cream
1 cup whole milk
1 cup sugar
2 large egg yolks
2 tablespoons molasses

This recipe calls for fewer egg yolks than are found in most ice creams, but the texture and flavor are just perfect!

1. Combine the cream, milk, and sugar in a medium heavy saucepan and bring to a gentle boil over medium heat. Remove from the heat.

2. Beat the egg yolks in a medium bowl until frothy and lemon colored, about 2 minutes. Whisk 1 cup of the hot cream in a slow, steady stream into the egg yolks. Gradually add the egg mixture to the hot cream, whisking constantly. Cook over medium-low heat, stirring occasionally, until the mixture thickens enough to coat the back of a spoon, about 5 minutes.

3. Remove from the heat and add the molasses, then strain through a fine-mesh strainer into a clean bowl. Cover with plastic wrap, pressing it directly against the surface to keep a skin from forming. Refrigerate until well chilled, about 2 hours.

4. Pour the mixture into an ice cream maker and freeze according to the manufacturer's instructions. Transfer to an airtight container and freeze until ready to serve.

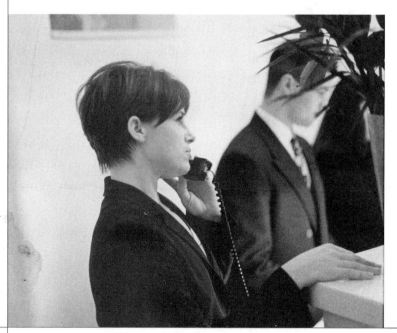

At the podium of Delmonico Steakhouse

DESSERTS

Emeril's NEW ORLEANS

5 large eggs

2 cups heavy cream

¼ cup plus 1½ tablespoons granulated sugar

¼ cup packed light brown sugar

¾ cup Steen's 100% Pure Cane Syrup (see Source Guide, page 333)

½ teaspoon pure vanilla extract

1 cup pecans, lightly toasted and chopped

1 tablespoon plus 1 teaspoon minced orange zest

⅓ cup fresh orange juice

2 tablespoons brandy

1 teaspoon grated ginger

½ teaspoon ground cinnamon

⅛ teaspoon grated nutmeg

5 cups ½-inch cubes day-old white bread (crusts removed)

1 tablespoon unsalted butter

1 recipe Espresso Crème Anglaise

Cane Syrup–Pecan Bread Pudding with Espresso Crème Anglaise

Bread pudding has long been a staple dessert in South Louisiana. One reason is because the cooks there are frugal and never waste anything; the other is that it's delicious! The pudding was traditionally made with day-old bread, milk, butter, and eggs, but we've been experimenting and found that the addition of cane syrup and pecans, both local ingredients, is fantastic. The rich, silky-smooth crème anglaise kicked up with espresso is a perfect topping for the pudding! If you don't have day-old bread, use fresh bread, but don't soak it as long.

1. Whisk together the eggs, cream, ¼ cup of the granulated sugar, the brown sugar, syrup, and vanilla in a large bowl. Add the pecans, orange zest, juice, brandy, ginger, cinnamon, and nutmeg and mix well. Add the bread cubes and let soak for at least 1 hour, or refrigerate in an airtight container for up to 8 hours.

2. Preheat the oven to 350°F. Grease a 9-inch square baking dish with the butter and dust with the remaining 1½ tablespoons granulated sugar.

3. Pour the pudding mixture into the prepared dish. Bake until set in the center and golden, about 1 hour. Remove from the oven and let cool for 10 minutes.

4. To serve, cut into equal portions and top with the crème anglaise.

Espresso Crème Anglaise

2 cups heavy cream
4 large egg yolks
½ cup sugar
1 tablespoon instant espresso powder
⅛ teaspoon ground cinnamon
2 tablespoons brandy
1 teaspoon pure vanilla extract

1. Bring the cream to a simmer in a medium saucepan over medium heat. Remove from the heat.

2. In a medium bowl, whisk together the egg yolks and sugar until frothy and lemon colored, about 2 minutes. Whisk ½ cup of the hot cream in a slow, steady stream into the egg yolks. Whisk in the espresso powder and cinnamon. Gradually add the egg mixture to the hot cream, whisking constantly. Cook over medium-low heat, stirring occasionally, until the mixture thickens enough to coat the back of a spoon, about 5 minutes.

3. Remove from the heat and strain through a fine-mesh strainer into a clean bowl, pressing against the strainer with a rubber spatula. Add the brandy and vanilla and stir to blend. Serve immediately. (If not serving immediately, press plastic wrap directly against the surface of the sauce to prevent a skin from forming. Refrigerate for up to 2 days. Reheat gently before serving.)

Preparing for dinner service at Emeril's New Orleans Fish House

DESSERTS

Emeril's HOMEBASE

Dessert Pizzas with Strawberries, Armagnac-Scented Goat Cheese, and Mint

MAKES TWO 10-INCH
PIZZAS; 4 TO 8 SERVINGS

This pizza is a departure from the usual rich dinner party fare, but no less delicious or impressive. While not complicated or overly sweet, the fresh strawberries with Grand Marnier pack just the right note.

One ¼-ounce envelope
   (2¼ teaspoons) active dry
   yeast
¾ cup warm water (110°F)
2 cups all-purpose flour
½ teaspoon salt
2½ tablespoons vege-
   table oil
1 tablespoon heavy cream
1 pound fresh strawberries,
   rinsed, patted dry, hulled,
   and thinly sliced
¼ cup Grand Marnier liqueur
2 tablespoons sugar
8 ounces goat cheese, at
   room temperature
3 tablespoons plus
   2 teaspoons honey
1 tablespoon Armagnac or
   brandy
⅛ teaspoon freshly ground
   black pepper
8 fresh mint leaves, torn
   into pieces

1. Combine the yeast, water, and 1 tablespoon of the flour in a large bowl and whisk well to blend. Let sit until the mixture becomes slightly foamy, about 5 minutes.

2. Add the remaining flour, the salt, 2 tablespoons of the oil, and the cream, stirring well with a wooden spoon until the dough begins to come together and pulls away from the sides of the bowl. Turn out onto a lightly floured work surface and knead into a smooth but slightly sticky dough, 4 to 5 minutes.

3. Oil a large bowl with 1 teaspoon of the oil and turn the dough in the bowl to lightly coat. Cover the bowl with plastic wrap or a kitchen towel and allow the dough to rise in a warm, draft-free place until doubled in size, about 40 minutes.

4. Lightly grease a baking sheet with the remaining ½ tea-spoon oil. Divide the dough into 2 equal pieces and form each one into a ball. Place on the greased sheet, cover with plastic wrap, and refrigerate until doubled in volume, about 2 hours.

5. Place a pizza stone in the oven and preheat to 500°F.

6. Combine the strawberries with the Grand Marnier and sugar in a medium bowl, tossing to coat.

7. Combine the goat cheese and 3 tablespoons of the honey in a bowl and mash with a fork until smooth. Add the Armagnac and mix well.

8. Remove the dough from the refrigerator. Roll one piece of dough out on a lightly floured pizza paddle or large chopping board into a 10-inch round. Make "dimples" with your fingertips in the dough. Spread half of the goat cheese mixture over the pizza, using a rubber spatula. Spread half of the berries over the pizza, leaving the liquid in the bowl. Repeat with the remaining dough, goat cheese, and strawberries.

9. One at a time, transfer the pizzas to the pizza stone (or bake both pizzas at the same time on two heavy baking sheets) and bake until golden brown, about 12 minutes. Remove from the oven and transfer to serving plates.

10. Sprinkle a pinch of the pepper and half of the mint leaves over each pizza and drizzle each with 1 teaspoon of the remaining honey. Serve.

General manager Fred Sutherland (standing) with NOLA guests

White Chocolate Crème Brûlées

4 cups heavy cream

8 ounces good-quality white chocolate, finely chopped, or 1½ cups white chocolate pieces

8 large egg yolks

⅓ cup plus 4 teaspoons sugar

Brûlé is the French word for "burned." Caramelizing the sugar on the surface of the chocolate crèmes adds a rich flavor to these wonderful little puddings.

1. Position a rack in the center of the oven and preheat the oven to 300°F. Arrange eight ¾-cup ramekins or custard cups in a large roasting pan.

2. Bring the cream to a simmer in a medium saucepan over medium heat. Remove from the heat. Place the chocolate in a heatproof bowl. Add the hot cream and let sit for 2 minutes, then whisk until smooth.

3. Whisk the egg yolks and ⅓ cup of the sugar in a large bowl until frothy and lemon colored, about 2 minutes. Gradually add the white chocolate mixture, whisking constantly. Divide the custard among the ramekins. Add enough hot water to the roasting pan to come halfway up the sides of the ramekins. Bake until the custards are firm yet jiggle slightly when shaken, about 45 minutes. Remove from the water bath and let cool. Cover with plastic wrap and refrigerate until well chilled, at least 4 hours, or overnight.

4. Sprinkle each custard with ½ teaspoon of the remaining sugar. Using a kitchen blowtorch, caramelize the sugar. (Alternatively, preheat the broiler. Place the ramekins on a baking sheet and broil until the sugar melts and caramelizes, watching closely to avoid burning, and rotating the cups as necessary, 1 to 2 minutes.) Place on small dessert plates and serve.

NOLA

1½ cups heavy cream
1¼ cups whole milk
½ cup plus 1 tablespoon
   sugar
¼ cup instant chicory
   coffee or 2 table-
   spoons instant
   espresso powder
½ teaspoon freshly
   ground black pepper
7 large egg yolks
1 recipe Brown Sugar
   Shortbread Cookies

Chicory Coffee Crème Brûlées with Brown Sugar Shortbread Cookies

Crème brûlée, literally "burned cream," is a popular New Orleans dessert, and it's easy to see why—it's simple to make and it can be flavored with just about anything your taste buds dictate. Here we've used the intensely flavored chicory coffee that is favored by New Orleanians and serve these with simple shortbread cookies.

1. Position a rack in the center of the oven and preheat the oven to 300°F. Arrange six ¾-cup ramekins or custard cups in a large roasting pan.

2. Combine the cream, milk, ½ cup of the sugar, the coffee, and pepper in a medium saucepan. Bring to a bare simmer over medium-high heat, stirring to dissolve the sugar and coffee. Remove from the heat.

3. In a medium bowl, whisk the egg yolks until frothy and lemon colored, about 2 minutes. Slowly add the hot milk mixture to the eggs, whisking constantly. Strain through a fine-mesh strainer into a bowl or pitcher.

4. Divide the custard among the ramekins. Add enough hot water to the roasting pan to come halfway up the sides of the ramekins. Bake for 30 minutes. Rotate the roasting pan and bake until the custards are firm yet jiggle slightly when shaken, 30 to 40 minutes more. Remove from the water bath and let cool. Cover with plastic wrap and refrigerate until well chilled, at least 4 hours, or overnight.

5. Sprinkle each custard with ½ teaspoon of the remaining sugar. Using a kitchen blowtorch, caramelize the sugar. (Alternatively, preheat the broiler. Place the custards on a baking sheet and broil until the sugar melts and caramelizes, watching closely to avoid burning and rotating the cups as necessary, 1 to 2 minutes.) Place on small dessert plates and serve with the shortbread cookies.

DESSERTS

½ *pound (2 sticks) plus*
   1 teaspoon unsalted
   butter, at room
   temperature
1 *cup packed light brown*
   sugar
2 *cups all-purpose flour*
⅛ *teaspoon salt*
1 *tablespoon granulated*
   sugar
¼ *teaspoon ground*
   cinnamon

Brown Sugar Shortbread Cookies

1. Preheat the oven to 325°F. Lightly grease a 9-inch springform pan with 1 teaspoon of the butter, and set aside.

2. In a large bowl, using an electric mixer, cream the remaining 2 sticks butter. Add the brown sugar and beat until light and fluffy. Add the flour and salt and mix just until blended, being careful not to overmix.

3. Press the dough into the bottom of the prepared pan. Pierce the dough all over with the tines of a fork, and press the edges decoratively with the back of the tines. Combine the granulated sugar and cinnamon in a small bowl and sprinkle lightly over the dough.

4. Bake until set and light golden brown, 30 to 40 minutes. Remove from the oven and release the sides of the pan. Cut into 12 wedges while warm.

5. Let cool. (The cookies can be stored in an airtight container for up to 3 days.)

ORLANDO

Vegetable cooking spray
¼ cup plus 1 tablespoon packed light brown sugar
¼ cup all-purpose flour
2 tablespoons granulated sugar
¼ teaspoon baking soda
Pinch of salt
1 large egg
6 tablespoons unsalted butter, softened
½ cup chopped pecan pieces

Pecan Lace Cookies

These delicate cookies accompany a flan at Emeril's Orlando, but you'll find they make a delicious lunch box treat or light afternoon snack.

1. Preheat the oven to 350°F. Line 2 baking sheets with parchment paper or aluminum foil and spray with vegetable cooking spray. Set aside.

2. Mix together the brown sugar, flour, sugar, baking soda, and salt in a large bowl.

3. In a small bowl, beat the egg. Add 2 tablespoons of the egg to the dry ingredients and discard the rest. Add the butter to the dry ingredients and beat with an electric mixer until smooth. Fold in the nuts.

4. Drop the batter by ½ teaspoonfuls onto the prepared sheets, leaving 3 inches between each. Bake until golden brown and spread on the sheet, 5 to 5½ minutes. Remove from the oven and transfer the cookies on the parchment paper to a wire rack to cool and firm up, about 20 minutes. Peel the paper away from the cookies and let finish firming on the wire rack.

5. Serve immediately, or keep in an airtight container at room temperature for up to 3 days.

DESSERTS

Bananas Foster

4 ripe bananas, peeled
4 tablespoons unsalted
    butter
1 cup packed light brown
    sugar
¾ teaspoon ground
    cinnamon
¼ cup banana liqueur
½ cup dark rum
2 cups Vanilla Ice Cream

Here's an indulgent treat that's long been a New Orleans favorite. The recipe can be easily cut in half, or doubled. And if you leave out the liqueur and rum, it's a perfect dessert or breakfast treat for the kids!

1. Cut the bananas in half crosswise and then lengthwise.

2. Melt the butter in a large skillet over medium heat. Add the brown sugar and cinnamon and cook, stirring, until the sugar dissolves, about 2 minutes. Add the bananas and cook, turning occasionally, until the bananas start to soften and brown, about 3 minutes. Add the banana liqueur and stir to blend into the caramel sauce. Carefully add the rum and shake the pan back and forth to warm the rum and flame it. (Or, off the heat, carefully ignite the pan with a match, then return to the heat.) Shake the pan back and forth, basting the bananas, until the flames die down.

3. Divide the ice cream among four dessert plates. Gently lift the bananas from the pan and place 4 pieces on each portion of ice cream. Spoon the sauce over the ice cream and bananas, and serve immediately.

2 cups heavy cream
2 cups whole milk
¾ cup sugar
1 vanilla bean, split
   lengthwise in half and
   seeds scraped out,
   seeds and bean
   reserved
6 large egg yolks

Vanilla Ice Cream

Vanilla ice cream is a big favorite all around. We use it for the Strawberries Romanoff (page 327), as well as for Bananas Foster, and the fresh vanilla bean taste makes it wonderful just on its own.

1. Combine the cream, milk, sugar, and vanilla seeds and bean in a medium heavy saucepan and bring to a gentle boil over medium heat. Remove from the heat.

2. Beat the egg yolks in a medium bowl until frothy and lemon colored, about 2 minutes. Whisk 1 cup of the hot cream into the egg yolks in a slow, steady stream. Gradually add the egg mixture to the hot cream, whisking constantly. Cook over medium-low heat, stirring occasionally, until the mixture thickens enough to coat the back of a spoon, about 5 minutes.

3. Remove from the heat and strain through a fine-mesh strainer into a clean bowl. Cover with plastic wrap, pressing it directly against the surface of the mixture to keep a skin from forming. Refrigerate until well chilled, about 2 hours.

4. Pour the mixture into an ice cream maker and freeze according to the manufacturer's instructions. Transfer to an airtight container and freeze until ready to serve.

1 sheet frozen puff pastry
(half of a 17¼-ounce
package), thawed
1 large egg white, beaten
3 tablespoons plus 1
teaspoon granulated
sugar
¼ teaspoon ground
cinnamon
½ cup balsamic vinegar
½ cup ruby Port
½ vanilla bean, split
lengthwise in half and
seeds scraped out,
seeds and bean reserved
2 cups Black Mission figs,
stems removed and cut
vertically in half
1 cup heavy cream
1 teaspoon pure vanilla
extract
1 tablespoon plus 1 tea-
spoon confectioners'
sugar

Fig-and-Balsamic Syrup Mille-Feuille

Mille-feuille *means a thousand leaves, or layers, in French, a reflection of the layers of the puff pastry used in this classic dessert. If you can't find Mission figs, by all means use Celeste figs or whatever figs are available in your area.*

1. Cover the puff pastry with a slightly damp kitchen cloth and bring to room temperature. Preheat the oven to 400°F. Line a baking sheet with parchment paper and set aside.

2. On a lightly floured work surface, roll out the pastry to an ⅛-inch thickness. Using a 3-inch round cutter dipped in flour, cut out 8 circles. Place on the prepared baking sheet. Brush the pastry with the egg white. Combine 1 teaspoon of the granulated sugar with the cinnamon and sprinkle evenly over the pastry. Cover with a sheet of parchment paper and top with a second baking sheet.

3. Bake until lightly browned and cooked through, about 30 minutes. Transfer to a wire rack to cool completely.

4. Combine the vinegar, Port, 1 tablespoon of the granulated sugar, and the vanilla bean and seeds in a small saucepan. Bring to a boil. Reduce the heat to medium-low and cook until the mixture is thick and syrupy, 12 to 15 minutes.

5. Add the figs, turning to coat evenly, and cook for 1 minute. Remove from the heat and let cool slightly. Discard the vanilla bean pods.

6. Beat the cream in a medium bowl until soft peaks form. Add the remaining 2 tablespoons granulated sugar and the vanilla extract and beat until stiff peaks form.

7. To assemble, place a small dollop of whipped cream in the center of each of four plates. Top with one pastry round and a dollop of whipped cream. Divide the figs evenly among the rounds, reserving 4 halves for garnish. Top with the remaining pastry rounds and whipped cream, and garnish with the fig halves. Dust with confectioners' sugar and serve.

Mascarpone Brioche Sandwiches with Chocolate Soup

MAKES 4 SERVINGS

1 cup heavy cream
1 cup whole milk
1 cup milk chocolate
    chips
¼ cup Kahlúa or other
    coffee-flavored
    liqueur
3 tablespoons cream
    cheese, at room
    temperature
1 tablespoon honey
3 tablespoons
    mascarpone cheese,
    at room temperature
Eight ⅓-inch-thick slices
    Brioche (page 34) or
    other egg bread or
    home-style white
    bread
4 tablespoons unsalted
    butter, at room
    temperature

The chocolate soup is really a delicious grown-up hot chocolate. If you're going to share this with the kids, be sure to leave out the liqueur!

1. Combine the cream and milk in a medium heavy saucepan and bring to a simmer over medium heat. Lower the heat, add the chocolate and cook, whisking constantly, until smooth, about 4 minutes. Remove from the heat and add the Kahlúa. Cover to keep warm.

2. Combine the cream cheese and honey in a small bowl and mix until well blended. Fold in the mascarpone. Spread the mixture on 4 slices of the bread and top with the remaining bread. Spread 1½ teaspoons of the butter on each side of each sandwich.

3. Heat a medium skillet over medium-high heat. Add the sandwiches one at a time and cook until golden brown, 1½ to 2 minutes per side. Cut each sandwich into 4 triangles.

4. To serve, ladle the soup into four shallow soup bowls and top each with a quartered sandwich. Serve immediately.

Crêpes Suzette

1 recipe Citrus Butter
½ cup Satsuma Marmalade
1 cup sugar
½ cup Triple Sec
¼ cup Grand Marnier liqueur
1 recipe Crêpes (page 324)
8 scoops Chocolate-Swirl Ice
   Cream

Some people like to make their crêpe batter a day in advance. If you choose to do so, do not add the orange juice until you are ready to cook the crêpes. (The acid in the juice will change the texture of the batter and cause the crêpes to fall apart while cooking.) This recipe can easily be cut in half if you want to serve fewer people. For more tips on cooking crêpes, see the headnote on page 133.

At Delmonico, we make a homemade satsuma marmalade for these dessert crêpes. What's a satsuma, you ask? It's a citrus hybrid grown in nearby Plaquemines Parish, Louisiana. If it is unavailable in your area, substitute tangerines or tangelos.

1. Heat 2 tablespoons of the citrus butter, 1 tablespoon of the marmalade, and 2 tablespoons of the sugar in each of two large skillets over medium-high heat, swirling the pans, until the sugar just starts to caramelize, about 2 minutes. Add ¼ cup of the Triple Sec and 2 tablespoons of the Grand Marnier to each pan, and carefully tilt the pans to ignite. (Alternatively, remove the pans from the heat and carefully light with a match. Return to the heat.) Add 4 crêpes to each pan, one at a time, folding them into quarters as you go. Stir to coat evenly with the sauce. Remove the pans from the heat. Place 1 scoop of ice cream in each of eight shallow bowls. Arrange the crêpes over the ice cream and spoon the sauce over the top.

2. Repeat with the remaining ingredients.

3. Serve hot.

Citrus Butter

½ pound (2 sticks)
    unsalted butter, at
    room temperature
¼ cup fresh orange juice
2 tablespoons fresh
    lemon juice
1 tablespoon grated
    orange zest
1½ teaspoons grated
    lemon zest
¼ teaspoon salt

1. Combine all the ingredients in a bowl and cream together with a wooden spoon or rubber spatula.

2. Spoon the butter mixture into the center of a large sheet of plastic wrap or wax paper, forming a log about 1 inch in diameter. Fold the wrap over the butter and gently push in and under to form a smooth cylinder. Twist the ends to seal. Refrigerate until firm, about 1 hour. (Refrigerate for up to 1 week or freeze for up to 1 month.)

MAKES 1½ TO 2 CUPS

Satsuma Marmalade

6 satsumas or tangerines
    or tangelos
1 cup sugar
1½ cups fresh orange
    juice

1. Cut the rinds from the satsumas. Remove as much white pith as possible from the rind and discard. Using a sharp knife, cut across the rinds to remove any remaining white pith and cut into thin strips. Discard or reserve the satsuma flesh for another use.

2. Combine the sugar and 1 cup of the orange juice in a medium pot and bring to a boil. Cook, stirring, until the sugar dissolves. Add the rind, reduce the heat to medium, and simmer gently, uncovered, until the rind is tender and the syrup is thick and reaches the jelly stage (220°F on a candy thermometer), 25 to 30 minutes.

3. Remove from the heat and let cool slightly. Stir in ¼ cup orange juice to thin slightly. (If the marmalade thickens too much as it cools, stir in the remaining ¼ cup orange juice, 1 tablespoon at a time, to thin it. (The marmalade will keep refrigerated for 1 week.)

DESSERTS

Crêpes

2/3 cup all-purpose flour
3 large eggs
2 tablespoons sugar
*1/4 cup unsalted butter,
melted*
*1 cup plus 2 tablespoons
whole milk*
*1 tablespoon grated orange
zest*
*2 tablespoons fresh orange
juice*
*2 teaspoons Grand Marnier
or other orange-flavored
liqueur, such as Triple Sec*

1. In a large bowl, whisk together all the ingredients, except 2 tablespoons of the butter, to form a smooth, thin batter. Cover and refrigerate for 1 hour.

2. Heat a 6-inch crêpe pan or a heavy small skillet over medium-high heat. When hot, brush lightly with some of the remaining 2 tablespoons melted butter. Ladle about 3 tablespoons of the batter into the pan, tilting it to coat evenly with batter. Cook until the crêpe is golden brown on the bottom and the top is beginning to dry, 1 to 2 minutes. Using a rubber spatula, carefully turn the crêpe, and cook just until the bottom colors slightly, about 30 seconds. Transfer to a plate. Repeat with the remaining batter, adding a small amount of butter to the pan for each crêpe. Stack the crêpes between sheets of wax paper and set aside until ready to use.

Chocolate-Swirl Ice Cream

2 cups heavy cream
2 cups whole milk
3/4 cup sugar
*2 tablespoons chopped
orange zest*
*1 vanilla bean, split
lengthwise in half and
seeds scraped out, seeds
and bean reserved*
6 large egg yolks
*6 ounces semisweet
chocolate, chopped
(about 1 cup)*
2 tablespoons vegetable oil

1. Combine the cream, milk, sugar, orange zest, and vanilla seeds and bean in a medium heavy saucepan, and bring to a gentle boil over medium heat. Remove from the heat.

2. Beat the egg yolks in a medium bowl until frothy and lemon colored, about 2 minutes. Whisk 1 cup of the hot cream in a slow, steady stream into the egg yolks. Gradually add the egg mixture to the hot cream, whisking constantly. Cook over medium-low heat, stirring occasionally, until the mixture thickens enough to coat the back of a spoon, about 5 minutes.

3. Remove from the heat and strain through a fine-mesh strainer into a clean bowl. Cover with plastic wrap, pressing it directly against the surface of the mixture to keep a skin from forming. Refrigerate until well chilled, about 2 hours.

4. Combine the chocolate and oil in a small saucepan and heat over medium heat, stirring occasionally, until melted and smooth. Remove from the heat and let cool slightly.

5. Pour the cooled custard mixture into an ice cream maker and freeze according to the manufacturer's instructions.

6. Transfer to a bowl and stir in the cooled chocolate. Place in an airtight container and freeze until ready to serve.

Homemade Graham Crackers with Brûléed Marshmallows and Lavender Honey

MAKES 4 SERVINGS

*1 recipe Homemade
   Graham Crackers*
1 recipe Marshmallows
1 cup lavender honey

If you're a graham cracker lover, you are going to love this recipe. I think you'll be amazed at how simple it is to make your own. The "burnt" marshmallows and the lavender-flavored honey make these something like grown-up "s'mores."

1. Place 1 graham cracker on each of four dessert plates and top with a marshmallow. Using a kitchen blowtorch, brown the top of the marshmallow. Continue stacking to create 3 more layers, browning the marshmallows, and end with a graham cracker on top. (Alternatively, preheat the oven to 400°F. Place the cookie and marshmallow stacks on a baking sheet. Watching carefully, bake until the marshmallows just start to get gooey, 2 to 3 minutes, being careful not to overcook. Transfer to plates.)

2. Drizzle each serving with the honey, and serve immediately.

*Chef Neal Swidler in
Emeril's Delmonico kitchen*

DESSERTS

2¾ cups bread flour
⅓ cup whole wheat flour
¼ cup packed light brown
    sugar
1 teaspoon baking soda
1 teaspoon salt
7 tablespoons unsalted
    butter, at room
    temperature
¼ cup honey
1 teaspoon pure vanilla
    extract
¼ cup plus 3 to 4 teaspoons
    water

Graham Crackers

1. Preheat the oven to 300°F.

2. Combine the bread flour, whole wheat flour, brown sugar, baking soda, and salt in a large bowl. Add butter, honey, vanilla, and ¼ cup of the water. Work the mixture until a stiff dough forms, adding more water as necessary 1 teaspoon at a time.

3. On a lightly floured work surface, roll out the dough to a ⅛-inch thickness. Transfer to a large ungreased baking sheet. With the tines of a fork, prick the dough every ½ inch. Score into 3½ × 4-inch rectangles with a sharp knife (you should have at least 16 crackers).

4. Bake until golden brown, 25 minutes. Transfer the sheet of graham crackers to a wire rack to cool.

5. Cut into separate cookies. (The cookies will keep in an airtight container at room temperature for 1 week.)

1 teaspoon vegetable oil
2 cups granulated sugar
1¼ cups cool water
1 cup light corn syrup
One ¼-ounce envelope
    (1 tablespoon) unflavored
    gelatin
1 teaspoon pure vanilla
    extract
½ cup confectioners' sugar

Marshmallows

1. Lightly grease a small baking sheet with the oil and set aside.

2. Combine the granulated sugar, ¾ cup of the water, and ½ cup of the corn syrup in a medium heavy saucepan and bring to a simmer over low heat. Cook, stirring occasionally, until the sugar is dissolved. Continue cooking, without stirring, until the syrup reaches the soft-ball stage (240°F on a candy thermometer). Transfer to a large bowl.

3. Place the remaining ½ cup water in a small bowl, sprinkle with the gelatin, and stir to blend. Let stand until the gelatin softens, about 5 minutes. Add to the syrup and stir to dissolve the gelatin. Add the remaining ½ cup corn syrup and the vanilla. Beat with an electric mixer on high speed until cooled and fluffy, 10 to 12 minutes. Spread on the prepared baking sheet and sift the confectioners' sugar evenly over the top. Cover with plastic wrap and refrigerate until firm, at least 2 hours, or overnight.

4. Cut into 12 individual marshmallows slightly smaller than the graham crackers.

Strawberries Romanoff with Mint Syrup

Named after the Russian royal family, this classic dessert is taken a step higher by serving the strawberries in homemade graham cracker tartlet shells, with the mint syrup adding a refreshing note.

½ *recipe Graham Cracker dough (page 326)*
1½ *pints fresh strawberries, rinsed, patted dry, hulled, and quartered*
2 *tablespoons Grand Marnier liqueur or other orange-flavored liqueur, such as Triple Sec*
1 *tablespoon granulated sugar*
½ *cup Vanilla Ice Cream (page 319) or good-quality store-bought ice cream*
¼ *cup sour cream*
1 *tablespoon fresh orange juice*
1 *tablespoon Cognac*
1 *tablespoon light brown sugar*
1½ *teaspoons grated orange zest*
¼ *teaspoon pure vanilla extract*
⅛ *teaspoon ground cinnamon*
1 *recipe Mint Syrup*
6 *sprigs fresh mint*

1. Preheat the oven to 300°F.

2. On a lightly floured surface, roll out the dough to a ⅛-inch thickness. Using a plate as a guide, cut out six 5-inch circles. Fit the dough into six 3¾-inch tartlet pans and trim the edges with a sharp knife. Prick the bottoms of the tarts with a fork.

3. Place on a baking sheet and bake the tartlet shells until golden brown, 18 to 20 minutes. Remove from the oven and transfer the tartlet pans to a wire rack to cool. When cool, invert and remove the crusts from the pans.

4. Combine the strawberries, Grand Marnier, and sugar in a medium bowl, tossing to coat. Let stand for 20 minutes.

5. Let the ice cream melt in another medium bowl. Add the sour cream, orange juice, Cognac, brown sugar, orange zest, vanilla, and cinnamon and mix well. Add the strawberries and mix well.

6. Place 1 tartlet shell on each of six dessert plates and fill with about ½ cup of the strawberry mixture. Drizzle with the mint syrup and garnish with the mint sprigs. Serve immediately.

Mint Syrup

½ cup sugar
½ cup water
15 fresh mint leaves

1. Combine the sugar and water in a small saucepan and bring to a boil over high heat. Reduce the heat to medium-low and simmer, stirring occasionally, until the sugar dissolves, about 5 minutes. Pour the syrup into a container and refrigerate until completely cold, about 1 hour.

2. Bring a small pot of water to a boil. Add the mint leaves and blanch for just 2 seconds. Remove with a slotted spoon and cool in a bowl of ice water. Pat dry.

3. Place the cooled syrup and mint leaves in a blender or food processor, and purée. Strain through a fine-mesh strainer and set aside until ready to use. (The syrup can be stored in an air-tight container in the refrigerator for up to 1 week.)

NOLA pies

Emeril's ORLANDO

Chilled Hazelnut Glacées with Apricot Sauce and Chocolate Drizzles

MAKES 6 SERVINGS

Vegetable cooking spray
2 tablespoons confectioners' sugar
1 tablespoon dark corn syrup
2 tablespoons warm water
5 ounces hazelnuts, lightly toasted (1¼ cups)
¼ cup granulated sugar
1 cup heavy cream
3 large egg yolks
2 tablespoons sweet Marsala wine
2 tablespoons Frangelico liqueur
¼ teaspoon pure vanilla extract
1 recipe Apricot Sauce (page 280)
1 recipe Chocolate Sauce

Glacées are frozen desserts usually made in one large mold, but we make these in individual ramekins. The apricot and chocolate wonderfully complement the hazelnut ice cream. These are terrific just about any time, but especially so during warm weather.

1. Spray six ½-cup ramekins or a muffin tin with six ½-cup wells with vegetable spray and dust with the confectioners' sugar. Set aside.

2. Combine the corn syrup and water in a small bowl and whisk until smooth.

3. Blend the hazelnuts and 2 tablespoons of the granulated sugar to a paste in a food processor or blender. Set aside.

4. Beat the cream with the remaining 2 tablespoons granulated sugar in a bowl until soft peaks form. Set aside.

5. Combine the corn syrup mixture, egg yolks, Marsala, and Frangelico in a metal bowl or in the top of a double boiler. Place over boiling water and beat with an electric mixer until the mixture is very thick and forms a ribbon when the beaters are lifted. Remove from the heat and continue to beat until cool. Fold in the vanilla, then fold in the whipped cream until just blended. Fold in the hazelnut paste.

6. Divide the mixture among the prepared ramekins. Cover with plastic wrap, and freeze for at least 3 hours, or overnight.

7. To serve, transfer the glacées from the freezer to the refrigerator to soften for 30 minutes.

8. Drizzle about ⅓ cup of the apricot sauce over each of six dessert plates. Carefully unmold the glacées, drizzle with the chocolate sauce, and serve.

DESSERTS

Chocolate Sauce

¾ *cup heavy cream*
½ *cup sugar*
4 *tablespoons unsalted*
  butter
4 *ounces unsweetened*
  chocolate, finely chopped
3 *tablespoons dark corn*
  syrup
¾ *teaspoon pure vanilla*
  extract

1. Combine the cream, sugar, and butter in a small heavy saucepan and bring to a simmer over medium heat. Remove from the heat.

2. Place the chocolate in a medium heatproof bowl. Add the hot cream mixture and let sit for 2 minutes, then whisk until smooth. Add the corn syrup and vanilla and whisk until smooth. Cover to keep warm until ready to serve. (The sauce can be refrigerated in an airtight container for up to 3 days. Rewarm gently before serving.)

Lemon Grass Basil Sorbet

MAKES 1 QUART

2½ cups water

2 cups sugar

1 cup chopped lemon grass

1 tablespoon grated lemon zest

2 tablespoons fresh lemon juice

6 fresh basil leaves

6 fresh mint leaves

Lemon verbena is an aromatic herb with a very strong lemon flavor, which Chef Dave says reminds him of his childhood. For this reason, he devised a sorbet combining the more readily available lemon grass, lemon zest, basil, and mint to achieve the bright citrus notes he so well remembers. This sorbet would make a refreshing palate cleanser between courses at a multicourse dinner, or a light dessert on a hot summer's evening. For an extra kick, drizzle the sorbet with icy cold citron-flavored vodka before serving.

1. Combine the water, sugar, lemon grass, lemon zest, and juice in a medium heavy saucepan and bring to a boil. Reduce the heat to medium-low, add the basil and mint, and simmer for 5 minutes, stirring occasionally to dissolve the sugar.

2. Remove from the heat and strain through a fine-mesh strainer into a clean bowl. Let cool, then refrigerate until well chilled, about 2 hours.

3. Pour the mixture into an ice cream maker and freeze according to the manufacturer's instructions. Transfer to an airtight container and freeze until the sorbet firms up, about 2 hours, before serving.

Entrance at Emeril's Delmonico

SOURCE GUIDE

Emeril's Homebase
829 St. Charles Avenue
New Orleans, LA 70130
Tel: 800–980–8474; 504–558–3940
www.emerils.com
Emerilware and cutlery, cookbooks,
specialty food products, chefwear,
and more

Michael's Provision Company
317 Lindsey Street
Fall River, MA 02720
Tel: 508–672–0982; 508–672–1307
Portuguese food items, such as dried
salt cod, dried fava beans, and
chouriço and linguiça sausages,
patties, and franks

Steen's Syrup
119 North Main Street
Abbeville, LA 70510
Tel: 800–725–1654
Fax: 337–893–2478
www.steensyrup.com
100% Pure Cane Syrup, dark and
light molasses

Hudson Valley Foie Gras
80 Brooks Road
Ferndale, NY 12734
Tel: 845–292–2500
Fax: 845–292–3009
www.hudsonvalleyfoiegras.com
Duck products, including foie gras,
fat, confit, mousse, magret, legs, and
thighs

D'Artagnan
280 Wilson Avenue
Newark, NJ 07105
Tel: 800–327–8246
Fax: 973–465–1870
www.dartagnan.com
Goose and duck foie gras, pâtés,
sausages, smoked meats, and
organic game and poultry (including
venison, rabbit, quail, squab, and
pheasant)

New Orleans Fish House
821 South Dupre Street
New Orleans, LA 70125
Tel: 800–839–3474; 504–821–9700
www.nofh.com
Full line of fresh and smoked
seafood, including shrimp, crabmeat,
crawfish, and fish and other products

Conrad Rice Mill
307 Ann Street
New Iberia, LA 70560
Tel: 800–551–3245
Fax: 337–365–5806
www.konriko.com
Medium- and long-grain white rice,
wild pecan rice

Zatarain's
82 First Street
New Orleans, LA 70053
Tel: 504–367–2950
Fax: 504–362–2004
www.zatarain.com
Spices, crab and shrimp boil mixes,
and Creole mustard (also available at
supermarkets nationwide)

The Hawaii Store
3725 Noriega Street
San Francisco, CA 94122
Tel: 877–446–9948
Fax: 415–566–0508
www.dahawaiistore.com
Ogo and limu seaweed and other
Hawaiian foods and delicacies,
including Kona coffees, Hawaiian salt,
taro chips and pancake mix, Malolo
flavored syrups, and fresh and frozen
poi

Niman Ranch
1025 East 12th Street
Oakland, CA 94606
Tel: 510–808–0340
www.nimanranch.com
Dry-aged beef, including New York
steaks, rib-eyes, and prime rib roast;
non-aged beef cuts including
Châteaubriand and beef short ribs;
pork chops, pork tenderloins,
applewood smoked bacon, slab
bacon; lamb loin chops and lamb
shanks, and other meats

WEBSITES

Chef Emeril Lagasse

www.emerils.com
Official website for everything Emeril.
You will find listings for all his
restaurants, shows, merchandise and
in-depth background into Emeril's
culinary world, as well as a monthly
on-line magazine and recipes. Bam!

Fetzer Vineyards

www.fetzer.com
An environmentally and socially
conscious grower, Fetzer Vineyards
produces Emeril's Classics Wines for
the home chef.

Waterford/Wedgwood

www.wcdesigns.com
The world's leading luxury lifestyle
group produces Emeril At Home,
ageless additions to the home kitchen.

All-Clad Cookware

www.emerilware.com
The cookware that Chef Emeril
believes in. Here you will find the
entire range of Emerilware by
All-Clad, from skillets to sauté pans.

B&G Foods

www.bgfoods.com
If you want to kick up your kitchen a
notch, look for Emeril's original spice
blends, salad dressings, marinades,
hot sauces, and pasta sauces
distributed by B&G Foods and
available at supermarkets
nationwide.

Good Morning America

http://abcnews.go.com
Wake up to Chef Emeril on Friday
mornings on ABC, when he shares
his culinary creations with America.

Food Network

www.foodtv.com
Log onto the Food Network's site for
recipes and scheduling information
for *Emeril Live* and *The Essence of
Emeril* shows, and ticket information
for *Emeril Live*.

HarperCollins Publishers

www.harpercollins.com
This informative site offers
background on and chapter excerpts
from all of Chef Emeril's best-selling
cookbooks.

Wüsthof Knives

www.wusthof.com
Emerilware Knives gift and block
sets, made to Emeril's
specifications by one of the world's
leading manufacturers of quality
cutlery.

EMERIL'S RESTAURANTS

Emeril's New Orleans
800 Tchoupitoulas Street
New Orleans, LA 70130
504–528–9393

NOLA
534 Rue St. Louis
New Orleans, LA 70130
504–522–6652

Emeril's Delmonico
1300 St. Charles Avenue
New Orleans, LA 70130
504–525–4937

Emeril's New Orleans Fish House
at the MGM Grand Hotel and
Casino
3799 Las Vegas Boulevard South
Las Vegas, NV 89109
702–891–7374

Delmonico Steakhouse
at the Venetian Resort and
Casino
3355 Las Vegas Boulevard South
Las Vegas, NV 89109
702–414–3737

Emeril's Orlando
6000 Universal Boulevard
at Universal Studios City Walk
Orlando, FL 32819
407–224–2424

Emeril's Tchoup Chop
at Universal Orlando's
Royal Pacific Resort
6300 Hollywood Way
Orlando, FL 32819
407-503-2467

Emeril's Atlanta
One Alliance Center
3500 Lenox Road
Atlanta, GA 30326
404-564-5600

Emeril's Miami Beach
at Loews Miami Beach Hotel
1601 Collins Avenue
Miami Beach, FL 33139

INDEX

INDEX

341

INDEX